W9-AYI-643

PRAISE FOR *THE CASE FOR JESUS*

"I've lost count of how many times I've heard critics say the Gospels are late, anonymous, and untrustworthy sources that don't prove Jesus was divine. At last there is a book that meticulously refutes these claims with an engaging discussion of the real Jesus that will benefit both scholars and laymen who read it."

—Trent Horn, author of *Answering Atheism*

"Thanks to Dr. Pitre's magnificent book, you will now be equipped to make the case for Jesus and the truth of the Gospels to even the most ardent skeptics."

—Jennifer Fulwiler, author of *Something Other Than God*

"In *The Case for Jesus*, Pitre breaks his down research, in typically accessible prose, to bring us a readable and fascinating account of how questioning one accepted academic idea put him on a path of discovery that served to strengthen, not sever, his faith. Readers who loved *Jesus and the Jewish Roots of the Eucharist* will come away from this book with a similar sense of gratitude for such a faith-affirming presentation, and also a bit of awestruck wonder at how faith and reason can complement each other so well when allowed to. I loved this book!"

—Elizabeth Scalia, author of *Strange Gods: Unmasking the Idols in Everyday Life* and *Little Sins Mean a Lot*

"Brant Pitre does a stellar job setting forth a robust and rock-solid case for Jesus. The sensationalistic claims of superskeptics are exposed as a sham as Pitre provides a meticulous presentation of the evidence about the reliability of the Gospels, who Jesus thought he was, and what Jesus means today."

—Michael F. Bird, Ridley College, Melbourne, Australia

"*The Case for Jesus* topples the naive skepticism that too often dominates the study of the Gospels, by showing that the evidence for the truth of the Gospels is far stronger than is often assumed. Pitre has a unique talent for putting scholarly work of the highest caliber into an accessible and engaging form. This book should be on the shelf of every homilist, catechist, and Bible study leader."

—Mary Healy, Sacred Heart Major Seminary

"Brant Pitre, who has already demonstrated his brilliant scholarship in earlier works, explains here in remarkably easy to understand ways why we can trust the Gospels. Behind his effective communication, however, is wide-ranging research and careful rethinking. In fact, this book has given me a number of important new matters to consider myself."

—Craig S. Keener, Asbury Theological Seminary

"In this important book, one of America's most brilliant young scholars wrestles with issues of profound importance concerning Jesus and his identity. Pitre, in a lively and direct manner informed by up-to-date scholarship, presents a case for Jesus as the divine Son of God, fully human and fully God. Along the way he bursts some scholarly bubbles and sets a much needed cat among the proverbial pigeons. A delight to read!"

—Chris Tilling, King's College, London

"Like a room full of stale air, the popular-level conversation about Christian origins could use an open window or two. Thankfully, we now have one in Brant Pitre's *The Case for Jesus*. Personable, accessible, engaging—all supported by top-notch scholarship. Read it."

—Nicholas Perrin, dean of Wheaton College Graduate School

the reasons he converted from atheism to Christianity. In that book, Lewis gives a classic argument against the common idea that Jesus was just a great moral teacher or a prophet. In Lewis's own words:

> I am trying here to prevent anyone saying the really foolish thing that people often say about Him: "I'm ready to accept Jesus as a great moral teacher, but I don't accept his claim to be God." That is the one thing we must not say. *A man who was merely a man and said the sort of things Jesus said would not be a great moral teacher. He would either be a lunatic*—on the level with the man who says he is a poached egg—*or else he would be the Devil of Hell. You must make your choice. Either this man was, and is, the Son of God, or else a madman or something worse.* You can shut him up for a fool, you can spit at him and kill him as a demon or you can fall at his feet and call him Lord and God, but let us not come with any patronising nonsense about his being a great human teacher. He has not left that open to us. He did not intend to. . . . Now it seems to me obvious that He was neither a lunatic nor a fiend: and consequently, however strange or terrifying or unlikely it may seem, I have to accept the view that He was and is God.[4]

When I first read these words, I found them to be compelling. After all, if Jesus went around claiming to be God, then he really did leave us with only three options:

1. **Liar:** Jesus knew he wasn't God, but he said he was;
2. **Lunatic:** Jesus thought he was God, but he actually wasn't;
3. **Lord:** Jesus was who he said he was—God come in the flesh.

At the time, this logical "trilemma" made sense to me, and I considered it, among other things, a good reason for continuing to believe that Jesus was divine.

However, as I continued to study the quest for Jesus, it slowly dawned on me that for many people, there was a *fourth option:* namely, that the stories about Jesus in the Gospels in which he claims to be God are "legends." In other words, they are not historically true. Consider, for example, the words of Bart Ehrman. This is how he responds to C. S. Lewis's argument:

> Jesus probably never called himself God. . . . This means that he doesn't have to be either a liar, a lunatic, or the Lord. He could be a first-century Palestinian Jew who had a message to proclaim other than his own divinity.[5]

Now, I suspect that some readers may be thinking: What is Ehrman talking about? Of course Jesus claimed to be God! What about when Jesus says, "I and the Father are one" (John 10:30)? Or when he says "He who has seen me has seen the Father" (John 14:9)? Here it is necessary to make two very important points.

On the one hand, most scholars admit that Jesus does claim to be divine in the Gospel of John.[6] Think here of the two occasions on which Jesus is almost stoned to death because of who he claims to be:

> The Jews said to him, ". . . Are you greater than our father Abraham, who died? . . . Who do you claim to be?" . . . Jesus said to them, *"Truly, truly, I say to you, before Abraham was, I am."* So they took up stones to throw at him. (John 8:52, 53, 58-59)

> [Jesus said:] *"I and the Father are one."* The Jews took up stones again to stone him. Jesus answered them, "I have shown you many good works from the Father; for which of these do you stone me?" The Jews answered him, "We stone you for no good work but for *blasphemy;* because *you, being a man, make yourself God."* (John 10:30-33)[7]

Notice here that Jesus refers to himself as "I am" (Greek *egō eimi*) (John 8:58). In ancient Jewish Scripture, "I am" was the name of God—the God who had appeared to Moses in the burning bush on Mount Sinai (see Exodus 3:14). In a first-century Jewish context, for Jesus to take the name "I am" as his own is tantamount to claiming to *be God*. Should there be any doubt about this, notice that some of the people in Jesus's Jewish audience get the point. That's why they respond by accusing him of "blasphemy" for making himself "God" (Greek *theos*). They even take up stones to kill him.

On the other hand, as I came to learn, many contemporary scholars, such as Bart Ehrman, do not consider the Gospel of John to be historically true when it depicts Jesus saying these things about himself.[8] One of the most common arguments for this position is that Jesus does not make these kind of divine claims in the three earlier Gospels of Matthew, Mark, and Luke (known as the Synoptic Gospels). According to some scholars, we have three Gospels in which Jesus doesn't claim to be God (Matthew, Mark, and Luke), and only one Gospel in which Jesus does (John). Now, if this were correct—and as we will see later on in the book, it isn't—then it would raise serious doubts about whether Jesus ever actually claimed to be God. If the score is really 3–1, then the divine Jesus in the Gospel of John loses.

More than anything else, it was this idea—the idea that Jesus never actually claimed to be God—that led me personally to begin having serious doubts about who Jesus was. It slowly dawned on me that C. S. Lewis's Liar, Lunatic, or Lord argument had assumed that all four Gospels (including John) tell us what Jesus actually did and said. Take that assumption off the table and everything changes.

(Almost) Losing My Religion

To make a long story very short: by the end of my studies at Vanderbilt, my grip on the Christian faith of my youth was starting to slip. By the time I was about to graduate, I didn't know what I believed anymore. Little by little, what had started as a quest to find Jesus ended up with me on a path to losing my belief in him.

Then came a major turning point in my life. One evening, not long before I graduated, I was driving around the hills of Nashville by myself, and a thought suddenly dawned on me: *Do I really even believe in Jesus anymore?* By this point, I had pretty much accepted the idea that we didn't know who wrote the Gospels and that Jesus may not have actually claimed to be God. Moreover, I didn't know what to make of passages in the Synoptic Gospels where Jesus almost seems to deny that he is God, such as when he says to the rich young man: "Why do you call me good? No one is good but God alone" (Mark 10:18). (I promise we'll look at this passage later.) This led me to start questioning: If Jesus didn't really claim to be God, then *was* he? Or was he just a man? How could I believe in the divinity of Jesus if Jesus himself didn't teach it?

At that moment, I made a decision. The only way I could really know was to try to say *out loud* that I no longer believed that Jesus was God. So, alone in the car, I tried. But I couldn't do it. I couldn't say it. Not because I was afraid to. After years of study, I had learned to follow the evidence wherever it led me. No. I couldn't say it because *something in me wasn't yet fully convinced that Jesus wasn't divine*. Perhaps it was what I was learning about first-century Judaism, which was already helping me to understand Jesus and his words from an ancient Jewish perspective. Or perhaps it was just the last embers of my faith, still burning low. Whatever the case, I couldn't honestly say the words. A part of me still believed that Jesus *was* God, even though I wasn't sure how to reconcile this with some of the theories I had been learning. My faith and my reason had never seemed further apart, and the former was dangling over an abyss of doubt by a thread. But there was still a thread. So that's what I hung on to.

In the end, I finished my master's degree, graduated with honors, and did what any Christian on the brink of almost losing his faith would do: I entered a doctoral program in theology in order to earn my PhD in New Testament studies. And that's when things slowly began to change.

What I Later Discovered

During the years I spent as a PhD student at the University of Notre Dame, I threw myself headlong into my studies. I went beyond just reading the writings of modern scholars and dove into the original sources themselves: the Hebrew Bible, the Greek New Testament, ancient Jewish writings outside the Bible, and the works of the ancient Christian writers known as the church fathers. I took courses in advanced Greek, Hebrew, and Aramaic. I even learned Coptic, a form of ancient Egyptian, just so that I could read the "lost" Gospel of Thomas in its original language and see what it had to say. During these intense but unforgettable years, I made three important discoveries.

First and foremost, given my interest in the quest for Jesus, I began looking for the "anonymous" copies of the Gospels that I had learned about during my undergraduate years. Surely, I thought, there must be some anonymous manuscripts, since every textbook I had read started with the assertion that the four Gospels were originally anonymous and that we don't know who actually wrote them. But I wanted to see for myself.

Guess what? *I couldn't find any anonymous copies.* I even asked one of my professors: "Where are all the anonymous manuscripts of Matthew, Mark, Luke, and John?"

"That's a good question," he said. "You should do some research."

And I did. What I quickly discovered is that *there are no anonymous manuscripts of the four Gospels. They don't exist.* In fact, as we will see in chapter 2, the only way to defend the theory that the Gospels were originally anonymous is to ignore virtually all of the evidence from the earliest Greek manuscripts and the most ancient Christian writers. Moreover, when you compare what the earliest church fathers tell us about the origins of the four Gospels with what those same church fathers say about the origins of the lost gospels, the differences are striking. As we will see, there are compelling reasons for concluding that the four Gospels are first-century biographies of Jesus, written within the lifetime of the apostles, and based directly on eyewitness testimony.

Second, and equally important, the more I studied first-century Judaism, the more I began to see clearly that *Jesus did claim to be God—but in a very Jewish way.* And he does so in *all four* first-century Gospels: Matthew, Mark, Luke, and John. But in order to see this clearly, you have to take one very important step. You have to go back and read the Synoptic Gospels from an ancient Jewish perspective. Otherwise, it's easy to miss what Jesus is really saying about himself.

To be sure, Jesus doesn't go around shouting, "I am God!" But this doesn't mean that he didn't claim to be divine. As we will see, Jesus reveals the secret of his identity by using *riddles* and *questions* that would have made sense to a first-century Jewish audience. In fact, it was precisely because his audiences understood that Jesus was claiming to be God that some of the Jewish authorities charged him with "blasphemy" and handed him over to the Romans to be crucified. And by the way, in a first-century Jewish context, it wasn't blasphemy to claim to be the Messiah. *But it was blasphemy to claim to be God.*

Third and finally, and most important of all, I gradually realized that confusion about who Jesus claimed to be is everywhere, and it's spreading. Despite the arguments of writers like C. S. Lewis, the old notion that Jesus was just a prophet or a great moral teacher is still alive and well. It's in the universities and college classrooms, where many students arrive as Christians and leave as agnostics or atheists. It's in the television documentaries that air right around Christmas and Easter that seem specially designed to raise doubts about the truth of Christianity and are often full of everything except actual history. It's in the dozens of books that are published every year claiming to reveal that Jesus was really a Zealot, or that he was really married to Mary Magdalene, or whatever the latest theory is. In fact, the idea that Jesus never claimed to be God may be more widespread today than ever before in history.[9]

That's why I finally decided to write this book. In it I want to lay out the case for Jesus as I see it. I should emphasize from the start that it's not a complete case. That would need a much longer book. It's also not written for scholars, though I cite lots of them in the endnotes. It's written for anyone—anyone who has ever had questions about exactly who Jesus of Nazareth claimed to be. And in my experience as a professor, that's a lot more people than you might think. It includes both Christians and non-Christians, practicing and nonpracticing, believers and doubters, and those who are a little bit of both. In fact, many people who do believe that Jesus is God often can't explain *why* they believe it, and many people who think that Jesus was only a good teacher or prophet often haven't looked carefully at exactly *who* the

Gospels say he claimed to be. In both cases, people are often not able to see Jesus through ancient Jewish eyes. As a result, it's easy to miss *the Jewish roots of Jesus's divinity.*

So if you've ever wondered: Did Jesus really claim to be God? And how do we know?—then I invite you to come along with me on this quest. Whether you are Christian, Jewish, Muslim, agnostic, or atheist—whatever your religious outlook—if you've ever wanted to judge for yourself the biblical and historical evidence for Jesus, then this book is for you.

We will begin where my professor began, all those years ago: with the origins of the Gospels. Were the four Gospels originally anonymous?

Were the Gospels Anonymous?

Imagine for a moment that you're browsing the shelves of your local bookstore, and you come across two biographies of Pope Francis. One of them is written by a longtime friend and contemporary of the pope. The other biography is anonymous. *Which one would you buy?* Most people, I would venture to guess, would go for the one written by someone who had actually spent time with him, someone who was a friend of Jorge Bergoglio, the man who later became pope.[1] At the same time, I think most people would also view the anonymous biography with some level of suspicion. Who wrote this? Where did they get their information? Why should I trust that they know what they're talking about? And if they want to be believed, why didn't they put their name on the book?

When it comes to the biography of Jesus of Nazareth—or any historical figure, for that matter—we find ourselves in a similar situation. The first question we have to answer is *How do we know what we know about Jesus?* How is it possible for twenty-first-century people to know with any reasonable certainty what he did and said in the first century? Obviously, none of us was there when Jesus walked the earth. So how do we gain access to him as a historical person?

For many people, the answer to this question is simple: open up your Bible and read the Gospels of Matthew, Mark, Luke, and John; *they* tell us what Jesus did and said. Indeed, for almost nineteen centuries, most Christians—and virtually everyone else, for that matter—believed that the Gospels of Matthew and John were written by eyewitnesses and disciples of Jesus and that the Gospels of Mark and Luke were written by companions of the apostles Peter and Paul.

Yet, as I mentioned in the first chapter, in the last century or so, a new theory came onto the scene. According to this theory, the traditional Christian ideas about who wrote the Gospels are not in fact true. Instead, scholars began to propose that the four Gospels were originally anonymous. In particular, this theory was formulated in the early twentieth century by scholars known as "form critics," who believed that the Gospels were not biography but folklore.[2] In the words of New Testament scholar Richard Bauckham:

> The assumption that Jesus traditions circulated anonymously in the early church and therefore the Gospels in which they were gathered and recorded were also originally anonymous was very widespread in twentieth-century Gospels scholarship. It was propagated by the form critics as a corollary to their use of the model of folklore, which is passed down anonymously by communities. The Gospels, they thought, were folk literature, similarly anonymous. This use of the model of folklore has been discredited . . . partly because there is a great difference between folk traditions passed down over centuries and the short span of time—less than a lifetime—that elapsed before Gospels were written. But it is remarkable how tenacious has been the idea that not only the traditions but the Gospels themselves were *originally anonymous.*[3]

"Tenacious" is just the right word. By the end of the twentieth century, when I was a student, the assumption that the four Gospels in the New Testament were *not* originally attributed to anyone was so widespread that it was rarely ever discussed, much less questioned. As a result, many scholars today believe that we do not know who wrote the four

Gospels, which are our primary historical sources for what Jesus did and said.

What are we to make of this theory? What evidence is there that the Gospels were in fact originally anonymous? In this chapter, we will take a closer look at the theory and see why there are some good reasons to doubt it.

The Theory of the Anonymous Gospels

In his recent book *How Jesus Became God*, Bart Ehrman provides a concise summary of the theory of the anonymous Gospels. It can be broken down into four basic claims.

First, according to this theory, all four Gospels were originally published without any titles or headings identifying the authors.[4] This means no "Gospel according to Matthew," no "Gospel according to Mark," no "Gospel according to Luke," and no "Gospel according to John." Not for any one of the four. Just blanks. According to this theory, in contrast to many other ancient biographies published under the name of an actual author, the original authors of the Gospels deliberately chose to keep their identities hidden.[5]

Second, all four Gospels supposedly circulated without any titles for almost a century before anyone attributed them to Matthew, Mark, Luke, or John.[6] Recall that in the ancient world, all books were handmade copies known as manuscripts. Thus, according to this hypothesis, every time one of the Gospels was hand-copied for decade after decade, no one added any titles.

Third, it was only much later—sometime after the disciples of Jesus were dead and buried—that the titles were finally added to the manuscripts. According to the theory, the reason the titles were added was to give the four Gospels "much needed authority."[7] In other words, the inclusion of titles was a deliberate attempt to deceive readers into falsely believing that the Gospels were written by apostles and their disciples. As Bart Ehrman writes elsewhere, the titles of the four Gospels are a "not at all innocent" form of ancient false attribution or forgery—a practice widely condemned by both pagans and Christians.[8]

Fourth and finally, and perhaps most significant of all, according to this theory, because the Gospels were originally anonymous, it is reasonable to conclude that none of them was actually written by an eyewitness.[9] For example, for Ehrman, the four Gospels are the last links in a long chain of writings by anonymous storytellers who were not themselves eyewitnesses to Jesus and who may never have even met an eyewitness.

This, in a nutshell, is the theory of the anonymous Gospels.[10] The theory is remarkably widespread among scholars and non-scholars alike. It is especially emphasized by those who wish to cast doubts on the historical reliability of the portrait of Jesus in the four Gospels.[11] The only problem is that the theory is almost completely baseless. It has no foundation in the earliest manuscripts of the Gospels, it fails to take seriously how ancient books were copied and circulated, and it suffers from an overall lack of historical plausibility. Let's take a careful look at each of these weaknesses.

No Anonymous Copies Exist

The first and perhaps biggest problem for the theory of the anonymous Gospels is this: *no anonymous copies of Matthew, Mark, Luke, or John have ever been found.* They do not exist. As far as we know, they never have.

Instead, as New Testament scholar Simon Gathercole has demonstrated, the ancient manuscripts are unanimous in attributing these books to the apostles and their companions. Consider, for example, the following chart of the titles in the earliest Greek manuscripts of each of the Gospels.[12]

THE MANUSCRIPT EVIDENCE: NO ANONYMOUS GOSPELS

Gospel Title	Earliest Greek Manuscript	Date[13]
Gospel according to Matthew	Papyrus 4	2nd century
Gospel according to Matthew	Papyrus 62	2nd century
According to Matthew	Codex Sinaiticus	4th century
According to Matthew	Codex Vaticanus	4th century
[Go]spel according to Mat[th]e[w]	Codex Washingtonianus	4th–5th century
Gospel according to Matthew	Codex Alexandrinus	5th century
Gospel according to Matthew	Codex Ephraemi	5th century
Gospel according to Matthew [End]	Codex Bezae	5th century
According to Mark	Codex Sinaiticus	4th century
According to Mark	Codex Vaticanus	4th century
Gospel according to Mark	Codex Washingtonianus	4th–5th century
[Gosp]el according to Mark	Codex Alexandrinus	5th century
Gospel according to Mar[k] [End]	Codex Ephraemi	5th century
Gospel according to Mark	Codex Bezae	5th century
Gospel according to Luke	Papyrus 75	2nd–3rd century
According to Luke	Codex Sinaiticus	4th century
According to Luke	Codex Vaticanus	4th century
Gospel according to Luke	Codex Washingtonianus	4th–5th century
Gospel according to Luke	Codex Alexandrinus	5th century
Gospel according to Luke	Codex Bezae	5th century
Gospel according to [J]ohn	Papyrus 66	late 2nd century
Gospel according to John	Papyrus 75	2nd–3rd century
According to John	Codex Sinaiticus	4th century
According to John	Codex Vaticanus	4th century
According to John [End]	Codex Washingtonianus	4th–5th century
Gospel according to John [End]	Codex Alexandrinus	5th century
Gospel according to John	Codex Bezae	5th century

Notice three things about this evidence.

First, there is a striking absence of any anonymous Gospel manuscripts. That is because *they don't exist.* Not even one. The reason this is
so significant is that one of the most basic rules in the study of New Testament manuscripts (a practice known as textual criticism) is that you go
back to the earliest and best Greek copies to see what they actually say.
Not what you *wish* they said, but what they actually say. When it comes to
the titles of the Gospels, not only the earliest and best manuscripts, but
all of the ancient manuscripts—without exception, in every language—
attribute the four Gospels to Matthew, Mark, Luke, and John.[14]

Second, notice that there is some variation in the form of the titles
(for example, some of the later manuscripts omit the word "Gospel").
However, as New Testament scholar Michael Bird notes, there is "absolute uniformity" in the *authors* to whom each of the books is attributed.[15] One reason this is so important is because some scholars will
claim that the Greek manuscripts support the idea that the titles of the
Gospels were added later. For example, Bart Ehrman writes:

> Because our surviving Greek manuscripts provide such a wide variety
> of (different) titles for the Gospels, textual scholars have long realized
> that their familiar names (e.g., "The Gospel according to Matthew")
> do not go back to a single "original" title, but were added later by
> scribes.[16]

Look back at the chart showing the titles of the earliest Greek manuscripts. Where is the "wide variety" of titles that he is talking about? The
only significant difference is that in some later copies, the word "Gospel" is missing, probably because the title was abbreviated.[17] In fact, it
is precisely the familiar names of Matthew, Mark, Luke, and John that
are found in every single manuscript we possess! According to the basic
rules of textual criticism, then, if anything is original in the titles, it is
the names of the authors.[18] They are at least as original as any other part
of the Gospels for which we have unanimous manuscript evidence.

Third—and this is important—notice also that the titles are present in *the most ancient copies* of each Gospel we possess, including

the earliest fragments, known as papyri (from the papyrus leaves of which they were made). For example, the earliest Greek manuscript of the Gospel of Matthew contains the title "The Gospel according to Matthew" (Greek *euangelion kata Matthaion*) (Papyrus 4). Likewise, the oldest Greek copy of the beginning of the Gospel of Mark starts with the title "The Gospel according to Mark" (Greek *euangelion kata Markon*). This famous manuscript—which is known as Codex Sinaiticus because it was discovered on Mount Sinai—is widely regarded as one of the most reliable ancient copies of the New Testament ever found. Along similar lines, the oldest known copy of the Gospel of Luke begins with the words "The Gospel according to Luke" (Greek *euangelion kata Loukan*) (Papyrus 75). Finally, the earliest manuscript of the Gospel of John that exists is only a tiny fragment of the Gospel. Fortunately, however, the first page is preserved, and it reads: "The Gospel according to John" (Greek *euangelion kata Iōannēn*) (Papyrus 66).

In short, the earliest and best copies of the four Gospels are unanimously attributed to Matthew, Mark, Luke, and John. There is absolutely no manuscript evidence—and thus no actual historical evidence—to support the claim that "originally" the Gospels had no titles. In light of this complete lack of anonymous copies, New Testament scholar Martin Hengel writes:

> Let those who deny the great age and therefore the basic originality of the Gospel superscriptions in order to preserve their "good" critical conscience give a better explanation of the completely unanimous and relatively early attestation of these titles, their origin and the names of the authors associated with them. Such an explanation has yet to be given, and it never will be.[19]

The Anonymous Scenario Is Incredible

The second major problem with the theory of the anonymous Gospels is the utter implausibility that a book circulating around the Roman

Empire without a title for almost a hundred years could somehow at some point be attributed to exactly the same author by scribes throughout the world and yet leave no trace of disagreement in any manuscripts.[20] And, by the way, this is supposed to have happened not just once, but with each one of the four Gospels.

Think about it for a minute. According to the theory of the anonymous Gospels, the Gospel of Matthew was "originally" the Gospel according to nobody. This anonymous book was copied by hand, and recopied, and recopied, and circulated throughout the Roman Empire for decades. Likewise, the Gospel of Mark, which was also "originally" the Gospel according to nobody, was copied and recopied and circulated and recopied for decades. And so on for the third anonymous Gospel, and then the fourth anonymous Gospel. Then, sometime in the early second century AD, *the exact same titles* were supposedly added to not one, not two, not three, but all four of these very different, anonymous books. Moreover, this attribution of authorship supposedly took place even though by the second century the four Gospels had already been spread *throughout the Roman Empire:* in Galilee, Jerusalem, Syria, Africa, Egypt, Rome, France, and so on, wherever copies were to be found.

This scenario is completely incredible. Even if *one* anonymous Gospel could have been written and circulated and then somehow miraculously attributed to the same person by Christians living in Rome, Africa, Italy, and Syria, am I really supposed to believe that the same thing happened not once, not twice, but with four different books, over and over again, throughout the world? How did these unknown scribes who added the titles know whom to ascribe the books to? How did they communicate with one another so that all the copies ended up with the same titles?

Moreover, the idea that it would have taken almost a hundred years for the titles to be added completely fails to take into account the fact that from the moment there was even more than one Gospel in circulation, readers would have needed some way to distinguish them from one another. In the words of Graham Stanton:

[A]s soon as Christian communities regularly used more than one written account of the actions and teaching of Jesus, it would have been necessary to distinguish them by some form of title, especially in the context of readings at worship.[21]

Now, we know from the Gospel of Luke that "many" accounts of the life of Jesus were already in circulation by the time he wrote (see Luke 1:1-4). So to suggest that no titles whatsoever were added to the Gospels until the late second century AD completely fails to take into account the fact that multiple Gospels were already circulating before Luke ever set pen to papyrus, and that there would be a practical need to identify these books.

Finally, if things happened the way the anonymous theory proposes, then why aren't *some* copies attributed to Matthew, Mark, Luke, or John, but *other* copies attributed to someone else—for instance, Andrew, or Peter, or Jude? If the Gospels really got their titles from scribes falsely adding them to manuscripts up to a century later, we would expect to find both (1) anonymous copies—which, as we've already seen, don't exist—as well as (2) contradictory titles, with some scribes attributing one copy of a Gospel to Matthew and another attributing the same Gospel to Peter or Jesus or whomever.

Should there be any doubt about this, it's important to compare the manuscript evidence for the four Gospels with the manuscript evidence for the New Testament letter to the Hebrews. Unlike the four Gospels, the letter to the Hebrews is *actually anonymous*. It never explicitly identifies its author, not even in the title.[22] So guess what happens when you have a real anonymous book? It ends up either remaining anonymous or being attributed to different authors, as is shown in the following chart.

THE LETTER TO THE HEBREWS:
ACTUAL ANONYMOUS MANUSCRIPTS

Title/Subscript	Greek Manuscript	Date[23]
To the Hebrews	Papyrus 64	2nd century
To the Hebrews	Codex Sinaiticus	4th century
To the Hebrews	Codex Vaticanus	4th century
To the Hebrews, written from Rome	Codex Alexandrinus	5th century
To the Hebrews, written from Italy	Codex Porphyrianus	9th century
To the Hebrews, written from Italy *by Timothy*	Minuscule 1739	10th century
To the Hebrews, written from Rome *by Paul* to those in Jerusalem	Minuscule 81	11th century
To the Hebrews, written in Hebrew from Italy *anonymously* *by Timothy*	Minuscule 104	11th century

Notice the variety of suggested authors: some manuscripts remain anonymous, some say Hebrews was written "by Timothy," others by "Paul." The title of one manuscript even explicitly states that it was written "anonymously" (Greek *anonymōs*)! The same thing is true among ancient Christian writers: some early Church writers say Paul wrote Hebrews but didn't identify himself; others say Luke translated Paul's letter from Hebrew into Greek; others say Hebrews was written by Barnabas, the companion of Paul; and still others say it was written by Clement, the bishop of Rome.[24] In the late second century AD, Origen of Alexandria simply threw up his hands and declared: "As to who wrote the epistle [to the Hebrews]," only "God knows" (Eusebius, *Church History*, 6.25.14).

That's what you get with a truly anonymous book of the New Testament: actual anonymous manuscripts, and actual ancient debates over who wrote it. But that's precisely what you *don't* find when it comes to the Gospels of Matthew, Mark, Luke, and John. No anonymous copies, and—as we'll see in chapter 3—no debate among ancient Christians over who wrote the Gospels. Scholars who continue to claim that the Gospels were originally anonymous cannot explain why we don't find the same variety of suggested authors as we do with the letter to the Hebrews. Once again, in the words of Martin Hengel:

> [I]f [the Gospels] had first circulated anonymously and had been given their titles only at a secondary stage and independently of one another in the different communities, because a title was needed for announcing reading in worship, this must necessarily have resulted in a diversity of titles, as can be illustrated by many examples from antiquity. . . . *There is no trace of such anonymity.*[25]

In short, the theory of the anonymous Gospels suffers not only from a lack of manuscript evidence but also from a lack of logic. It simply does not pass muster when it comes to basic criteria of historical plausibility.

Why Attribute Mark and Luke to Non-Eyewitnesses?

The third major problem with the theory of the anonymous Gospels has to do with the claim that the false attributions were added a century later to give the Gospels "much needed authority."[26] If this were true, then why are two of the four Gospels attributed to *non-eyewitnesses*? Why, of all people, would ancient scribes pick Mark and Luke, who (as we will see in chapter 3) never even knew Jesus?

Once again, put yourself in the place of the ancient scribes who supposedly knowingly added the false titles to the Gospels. If *you* wanted to give authority to your anonymous book, would you pick Luke, who was neither an eyewitness himself nor a follower of an eyewitness, but a companion of Paul, who never met Jesus during his earthly life? And if *you* wanted to give authority to your anonymous life of Jesus, would you pick Mark, who was not himself a disciple of Jesus? If authority is what you were after, why not attribute your anonymous Gospel directly to Peter, the chief of the apostles? Or to Andrew, his brother? For that matter, why not go straight to the top and attribute your Gospel to Jesus himself?

As we will see in chapter 5, such attributions to the apostles and other eyewitnesses is exactly what we find when we look at the so-called "lost gospels"—also known as the apocryphal gospels (from the Greek word *apocryphon*, meaning "hidden book"). Virtually all scholars agree that the apocryphal gospels—such as the *Gospel of Peter*, the *Gospel of Thomas*, and the *Gospel of Judas*—are forgeries that were falsely attributed to disciples of Jesus long after the apostles were all dead.[27] Note that none of the later apocryphal gospels are attributed to non-eyewitnesses like Mark and Luke.[28] The later false gospels are attributed to people with firsthand access to Jesus: people like Peter, or the apostle Thomas, or Mary Magdalene, or Judas, or even Jesus himself. They are never attributed to mere followers or companions of the apostles. Why? Because it is the authors of the *apocryphal* gospels who wanted to give much-needed authority to their writings by falsely ascribing them to people with the closest possible connections to Jesus.

In short, the theory of the anonymous Gospels fails to explain not only the lack of manuscript evidence but also why the Gospels of Mark and Luke aren't attributed to eyewitnesses and companions of Jesus. Indeed, when subjected to critical scrutiny, the overall implausibility of the theory is remarkable. Of course, the weakness of this theory alone doesn't answer the question of who actually wrote the Gospels. In order to answer that question, we need to take a closer look at the names contained in the earliest Gospel manuscripts. If the four Gospels were not anonymous, then who are the people to whom they are attributed? Who exactly were Matthew, Mark, Luke, and John?

The Titles of the Gospels

Before beginning our exploration of who wrote the four Gospels, it will be helpful to take a moment to think about how we determine the authorship of any book, ancient or modern. To take a contemporary example: How do we know that Pope Benedict XVI wrote the three-volume work *Jesus of Nazareth*? There are basically two ways to find out.

First, you can look inside the books for information about the author. In each volume, you will find a title page, which attributes the work to "Joseph Ratzinger (Pope Benedict XVI)." You might also read the beginning (foreword or preface) or the end (afterword) to see if there is any autobiographical information indicating how the book came to be. All of this is called *internal evidence*—evidence from within the book about who wrote it and, sometimes, when it was written and why it was written.

Nevertheless, it sometimes happens that there are reasons to doubt the internal evidence. After all, books can be forged. This was true in ancient times as well as in our own day. So if you have some reason to be skeptical about the internal evidence, there is a second way to find out who wrote a work. You can also go outside the book for information. In the case of Pope Benedict, you could consult his contemporaries—people who know him personally or who have had access to people who know him—and see what they have to say. Do the pope's living contemporaries (or in the case of deceased authors, people who lived shortly thereafter) say he wrote a book about Jesus? Do they think *Jesus of Nazareth* is correctly attributed to him? Was it published during his lifetime or shortly thereafter? Did he authorize its publication? Do any of his contemporaries claim that it was a forgery? In this way, you would be using what scholars call *external evidence*.

If you did this, you would discover that the internal evidence and the external evidence corroborate each other: both point to the conclusion that Joseph Ratzinger (Pope Benedict) was the author of *Jesus of Nazareth*. Notice here that saying the pope is the author does not mean that he personally wrote down every word in every version of his book. No. For one thing, the book *Jesus of Nazareth* was immediately translated into several different languages. Nevertheless, the pope's identity as author applies when the work is published in various *translations* of the original German, even when he himself played no role whatsoever in the translation.

These very same principles work when you are investigating the authorship of the four Gospels—and any other ancient book, for that matter. You should always consult, whenever possible, both internal and external evidence. In this chapter, we will follow the same basic rules for exploring the authorship of the four Gospels. First, we will look at clues from inside the Gospel manuscripts (internal evidence). Then, in the next chapter, we will look at clues from ancient Christian writers living closest to the time of Jesus himself (external evidence). The goal is to answer the question: If the Gospels were not originally anonymous, then to whom does the internal and external evidence point? We begin with the most explicit internal evidence of all: the titles themselves.

THE CASE FOR JESUS

Matthew the Tax Collector and Apostle

As we saw in the last chapter, every ancient manuscript we possess of the book of Matthew, the first book of the New Testament, bears the title "The Gospel according to Matthew" (Greek *euangelion kata Matthaion*).[1] This title is referred to by scholars as the "superscription," because it is ordinarily "written above" (Latin *superscriptio*) the first lines of the book.

But who is this "Matthew"? The Gospel contains some further evidence that helps us to identify the person to whom the book is attributed. First, it tells us about how Jesus calls Matthew to leave behind his life as a tax collector and become one of his followers:

> As Jesus passed on from there, he saw *a man called Matthew* sitting at the tax office; and he said to him, "Follow me." And he rose and followed him. (Matthew 9:9)

Second, the Gospel also tells us that Matthew was later chosen by Jesus to be one of the inner circle of the twelve disciples:

> *And he called to him his twelve disciples and gave them authority* over unclean spirits, to cast them out, and to heal every disease and every infirmity. The names of *the twelve apostles* are these: first, Simon, who is called Peter, and Andrew his brother; James the son of Zebedee, and John his brother; Philip and Bartholomew; Thomas and *Matthew the tax collector;* James the son of Alphaeus, and Thaddaeus; Simon the Cananaean, and Judas Iscariot, who betrayed him. (Matthew 10:1-4)

In terms of internal evidence, this is pretty much all we get. When combined with the evidence of the title, we can conclude that the Gospel is being attributed to Matthew, the former tax collector who, at some point during Jesus's public ministry, became one of the twelve apostles.

Notice something very intriguing about this internal evidence: the first Gospel is attributed to the only one of Jesus's apostles who would likely have been literate: that is, able to both read and write.[2] The reason this is significant is that some scholars claim that the Gospels couldn't have been written by any of Jesus's disciples, because the disciples were fishermen and, therefore, were probably illiterate. Consider the words of Bart Ehrman:

> [F]or the most part, Christians came from the ranks of the illiterate. *This is certainly true of the very earliest Christians, who would have been the apostles of Jesus.* In the Gospel accounts, we find that most of Jesus' disciples are simple peasants from Galilee—uneducated fishermen, for example. Two of them, Peter and John, are explicitly said to be "illiterate" in the book of Acts (4:13).[3]

On the basis of their illiteracy, this same scholar goes on to claim that "even if the original apostles had been forward looking . . . they would not have been able to write a Gospel."[4]

Now, on the one hand, it is true that most of Jesus's disciples were fishermen and were not from the elite classes of Jewish society. And it is also true that Peter and John are described as "uneducated" or "illiterate" (Greek *agrammatoi*) (Acts 4:13). However, as Bart Ehrman strangely fails to mention, *at least one of Jesus's disciples almost certainly was literate:* Matthew the tax collector![5] In fact, Ehrman himself admits that being a tax collector in the ancient world involved some reading and writing:

> Throughout most of antiquity, since most people could not write, there were local "readers" and "writers" who hired out their services to people who needed to conduct *business that required written texts: tax receipts,* legal contracts, licenses, personal letters, and the like.[6]

If this is true, then in all likelihood a tax collector in "Galilee of the Gentiles" would have been literate, and would probably even have had to know how to write in Greek, the primary language of commerce at the time.[7] And it is precisely "Matthew the tax collector" (Matthew 10:3) who happens to have a Gospel attributed to him.

Think about it for a minute: If you were one of the twelve apostles, listening to Jesus's teaching day in and day out, do you think it might have occurred to someone to take notes at some point? We know other ancient students did.[8] And if it did occur to the disciples, whom might they have selected? Let's see . . . fisherman, fisherman, fisherman, fisherman, *tax collector*. As New Testament scholar Richard Bauckham writes:

> The old suggestion that, among the Twelve, it would be Matthew the tax-collector who would most likely, owing to his profession, be able to write might after all be a sound guess and a clue to the perplexing question of the role he might have played somewhere among the sources of the Gospel of Matthew.[9]

Along similar lines, another expert on the Gospel of Matthew concludes: "[T]he little we know about the individuals who made up the original apostolic group indicates that Matthew was better equipped than most by his previous profession for the role of gospel-writer."[10]

With that said, I should probably point out that the most common objection to Matthew's having written the Gospel attributed to him is based on the widespread scholarly belief that the Gospel of Matthew uses the Gospel of Mark as a source. We will get into the question of the order in which the Gospels were written and who copied from whom later on (see chapter 6). For now, it is important to note that many people who take the view that the Gospel of Mark was written first find it unbelievable that an eyewitness such as the apostle Matthew would rely on or copy from a Gospel written by a non-eyewitness such as Mark.[11] But this just isn't true. For one thing, as we will see in the next chapter, there are good reasons to conclude that the Gospel of Mark is directly based on the testimony of the apostle Peter, who was both the leader of the twelve disciples and an eyewitness to much more of Jesus's ministry than the apostle Matthew (see Matthew

16:13-18). If Mark's Gospel is based on the testimony of Peter, there's nothing remotely implausible about Matthew using it as a source. Even more important, history gives us other examples of eyewitnesses who relied on other people's testimony when composing biographies of their own teachers. For example, when writing his account of the death of Socrates, the ancient Greek writer Xenophon (who was a disciple of Socrates) used the "reports" (Greek *exēngeile*) of another disciple named Hermogenes (see Xenophon, *Apology*, 1.2, 10).[12] The reason was that Xenophon was not present at the trial and death of Socrates, whereas Hermogenes was.[13] In the same way, it is entirely possible that the apostle Matthew could have relied on the Gospel of Mark's record of Peter's testimony, especially for any events at which Matthew himself was not present—such as the early days of Jesus's ministry (see Matthew 3–8) or the events of Jesus's passion and death, which Matthew did not witness because he had fled the scene (see Matthew 26–28). It's not as if all of the apostles were witnesses to everything that happened in the life of Jesus.

In short, the evidence of the title points us to the Gospel having been composed by Matthew the tax collector, who may have been one of the few disciples who could both read and write.

Mark, the Companion of Paul and Disciple of Peter

When we turn to the Gospel of Mark, the first piece of explicit internal evidence for who authored the Gospel is, once again, the title: "The Gospel according to Mark" (Greek *euangelion kata Markon*).[14] In this case, the body of the Gospel contains no further explicit internal evidence to help us identify who this "Mark" might be.

The reason is probably that Mark was a very well known figure in the first-century Church, both in Jerusalem and in Rome. Indeed, other writings in the New Testament provide us with a remarkable amount of information about Mark.[15] For example, the letters of Paul identify Mark as a "man of the circumcision" (meaning he was Jewish) and a cousin of Barnabas, Paul's fellow missionary (Colossians 4:10-11). These letters also tell us that Mark stayed with Paul during one of his periods of imprisonment, probably in Rome (Philemon 23-24; 2 Timothy 4:11). Along similar lines, the Acts of the Apostles tells us that Mark's full name was "John Mark"; that his mother, Mary, lived in Jerusalem; and that he traveled with Barnabas and Paul (see Acts 12:12-14, 25). Perhaps the most interesting story about Mark is the account of a falling-out between him and the apostle Paul:

> And after some days Paul said to Barnabas, "Come, let us return and visit the brethren in every city where we proclaimed the word of the Lord, and see how they are." *And Barnabas wanted to take with them John called Mark.* But Paul thought best not to take with them one who had withdrawn from them in Pamphylia, and had not gone with them to the work. *And there arose a sharp contention, so that they separated from each other; Barnabas took Mark with him and sailed away to Cyprus,* but Paul chose Silas and departed, being commended by the brethren to the grace of the Lord. (Acts 15:36-40)

Apparently, even apostles can get into a scuffle or two every now and then! As this story clearly shows, John Mark was a real person, well known in the early Church, both among Jewish Christians in Jerusalem and among some of the churches associated with Paul.

Finally, and perhaps most significant, there is evidence that not only did Mark travel with Paul and Barnabas, but he was also with the apostle Peter during Peter's time in the city of Rome. This evidence comes from the first letter of Peter, which ends by referring to the pagan city of Rome in early Christian code as "Babylon":

> By Silvanus, a faithful brother as I regard him, I have written briefly to you, exhorting and declaring that this is the true grace of God; stand fast in it. She who is at Babylon, who is likewise chosen, sends you greetings; *and so does my son Mark.* (1 Peter 5:12-13)[16]

Notice here that Peter appears to be using a scribe named Silvanus to write his letter—this fits well with the evidence that Peter was "unlettered" or "illiterate" (Acts 4:13). Notice also that Peter describes Mark as his spiritual "son" or disciple.[17] As we will see in the next chapter, this last piece of information about Mark's relationship with Peter will prove very important when we look at the external evidence for who wrote this Gospel.

For now, the main point is this: John Mark was a well-known and well-connected man in the early Church, a companion and follower of both Peter and Paul, the two great apostles of the Church, and he is mentioned on more than one occasion in connection with the city of Rome.

Luke the Physician, Companion of Paul, and Author of Acts

When we turn to the Gospel of Luke, the first piece of explicit internal evidence for who authored the Gospel comes once again from the title: "The Gospel according to Luke" (Greek *euangelion kata Loukan*).[18]

But who is this Luke? As with the Gospel of Mark, since Luke is never mentioned in the Gospel, we have to look at other first-century writings to deduce his identity.[19] And as with Mark, the letters of Paul[20] refer to Luke on several occasions:

> Epaphras, my fellow prisoner in Christ Jesus, sends greetings to you, and so do Mark, Aristarchus, Demas, *and Luke, my fellow workers.* (Philemon 23-24)

> Aristarchus my fellow prisoner greets you, and Mark the cousin of Barnabas, . . . and Jesus who is called Justus. These are the only men of the circumcision among my fellow workers for the kingdom of God, and they have been a comfort to me. . . . *Luke the beloved physician* and Demas greet you. (Colossians 4:10-11, 14)

> *Luke alone is with me*. Get Mark and bring him with you; for he is very useful in serving me. (2 Timothy 4:11)

Notice four key points here. First, Luke is identified as a "physician" by trade. Second, he is also apparently a Gentile, since Paul does not list him among his Jewish companions (the "men of the circumcision"). Third, Luke is consistently described as staying with Paul while he was a prisoner. (This will prove important later, when we turn to the dating of the Gospels.) This may be in part why Paul describes him as "beloved." Fourth, and finally, notice that all three references to Luke also contain references to Mark! This implies that Mark and Luke would have known each other and had contact by way of their relationship with Paul. Thus, according to the New Testament evidence, Luke was a Gentile doctor turned Christian missionary who traveled with Paul, stayed with him while he was a prisoner, and was known to other prominent early Christians like Mark.

However, we can't stop there. For the Gospel of Luke also contains an important literary prologue, in which Luke tells us why and for whom he is writing. As we will see, this prologue will prove extremely important in our investigation, so it needs to be read very carefully.[21] This is how the Gospel according to Luke begins:

Inasmuch as *many* have undertaken to compile a narrative of the things which have been accomplished among us, *just as they were delivered to us by those who from the beginning were eyewitnesses* and ministers of the word, *it seemed good to me also, having followed all things closely for some time past, to write carefully in order for you, most excellent Theophilus,* that you may know the facts concerning the things of which you have been informed. (Luke 1:1-4)[22]

Several key pieces of information need to be highlighted here.

First, Luke's Gospel was not the first one to be written. By the time he set pen to papyrus, "many" other people had already composed narratives about Jesus. Second, Luke is very up front about the fact that he himself was not an eyewitness to Jesus. Yet he emphasizes that his account is *based on* the testimony of "those who were eyewitnesses

(Greek *autoptai*) from the beginning" (Luke 1:1). Third and finally, the Gospel according to Luke—which is dedicated to the mysterious figure of "Theophilus" (Luke 1:3)—is written by the same person who authored the Acts of the Apostles. We know this because the book of Acts is also dedicated to "Theophilus" and contains multiple passages in which the author speaks in the first person about traveling with the apostle Paul:

> In the first book, O Theophilus, I have dealt with all that Jesus began to do and teach, until the day when he was taken up. (Acts of the Apostles 1:1-2)

> And a vision appeared to Paul in the night: a man of Macedonia was standing beseeching him and saying, "Come over to Macedonia and help us." And when he had seen the vision immediately *we sought to go on into Macedonia, concluding that God had called us* to preach the gospel to them. (Acts of the Apostles 16:9-10)

On the basis of these and several other passages, known as the "We Passages" (Acts 16:11-17; 20:5-15; 21:1-18; 27:1-28:16), there are good reasons to identify the author of the Gospel according to Luke as the author of the Acts of the Apostles and a traveling companion of the apostle Paul.[23]

Indeed, in light of the prologue, the case for the originality of the title of the Gospel of Luke is particularly strong. For, unlike the other three Gospels, Luke explicitly names the individual for whom his Gospel is written. In the words of Richard Bauckham: "The clearest case [for an original title] is Luke because of the dedication of the work to Theophilus (1:3), probably a patron. *It is inconceivable that a work with a named dedicatee should have been anonymous.*"[24] In other words, if the Gospel of Luke was dedicated to a known individual, it was probably written by a known individual! That, at least, is where the internal evidence of the title points: to Luke, the physician and traveling companion of Paul.

John the Fisherman and Beloved Disciple

By this point, you won't be surprised to discover that for the Gospel of
John, the first internal clue to who wrote the book is yet again the title:
"The Gospel according to John" (Greek *euangelion kata Iōannēn*).[25]
Who is this John? In this case, the name "John" is never used of any
disciple in the book. Therefore, in order to answer the question, we
have to bring together several key pieces of evidence.

The first piece of internal evidence from the body of the Gospel is
that it was written by one of Jesus's disciples, the one who lay on his
breast at the Last Supper:

> Peter turned and saw following them *the disciple whom Jesus loved,*
> who had lain close to his breast at the supper and had said, "Lord,
> who is it that is going to betray you?" . . . *This is the disciple who is
> bearing witness to these things, and who has written these things;
> and we know that his testimony is true.* But there are also many other
> things which Jesus did; were every one of them to be written, I sup-
> pose that the world itself could not contain the books that would be
> written. (John 21:20, 24-25)[26]

Now, some scholars do attempt to evade the explicit assertion that
"the disciple whom Jesus loved" is the one "who has written" (Greek
grapsas) the book. Nevertheless, the text is quite clear.[27] In the words
of Richard Bauckham: "John 21:24 means that the Beloved Disciple
composed the Gospel, whether or not he wielded the pen."[28] Likewise, Pope Benedict XVI states: "[T]he disciple whom Jesus loved . . .
is once again named as the author of the Gospel in John 21:24."[29] To
be sure, the combined use of "I" (first person singular) with "we" (first
person plural) and "his testimony" (third person) can be a bit confus-
ing. However, even a quick look at other passages in the Gospel show
Jesus doing the same thing: he speaks about himself in the third
person ("the Son of Man") and shifts from "I" to "we" when giving a
solemn pronouncement (see John 3:10-15; 6:52-58).[30] That is what the

Beloved Disciple is doing here: he is solemnly pronouncing himself the author of the Gospel and affirming the truth of its testimony.[31]

Second, the account of the Last Supper clearly identifies the Beloved Disciple (to whom the Gospel is attributed) as part of the innermost circle of Jesus's disciples:

> When Jesus had thus spoken, he was troubled in spirit, and testified, "Truly, truly, I say to you, one of you will betray me." The disciples looked at one another, uncertain of whom he spoke. *One of his disciples, whom Jesus loved, was lying close to the breast of Jesus;* so Simon Peter beckoned to him and said, "Tell us who it is of whom he speaks." So lying thus, close to the breast of Jesus, he said to him, "Lord, who is it?" Jesus answered, "It is he to whom I shall give this morsel when I have dipped it." (John 13:21-26)

Notice here that the Beloved Disciple is not just present at the Last Supper; he is seated closer to Jesus than Peter! That is why Peter has to ask the Beloved Disciple, who is lying closest to Jesus, to get more information from Jesus about who it is that will betray him.

Third, when the Beloved Disciple's position at the Last Supper is combined with other evidence about John the apostle, the most plausible explanation is that they are one and the same person.[32] For example, according to the other Gospels, John the son of Zebedee was one of the twelve disciples (Matthew 10:1-4; Mark 3:16-19; Luke 6:14-16) and present at the Last Supper (Mark 14:17-25; Luke 22:14-30). Moreover, John was part of the innermost circle, one of the three disciples closest to Jesus—Peter, James, and John—who were specially chosen to accompany him at "private" events, such as the raising of Jairus's daughter, the Transfiguration, and Jesus's agony in Gethsemane (Mark 5:37; 9:2; 14:33). Finally, the close relationship between Peter and the Beloved Disciple in the Gospel of John (John 20:1-9) mirrors the relationship between Peter and John the son of Zebedee, who are sent into Jerusalem together to prepare the Last Supper (Luke 22:8) and evangelize side by side after Pentecost (Acts 3:1; 8:14).

In short, if we follow both internal evidence from the Gospel of John (including the title) and external evidence from other writings, there is every reason to conclude that the Gospel is being attributed to John, the son of Zebedee, an eyewitness to Jesus of Nazareth and a beloved disciple.[33] In the words of Raymond Brown:

> When all is said and done, the combination of external and internal evidence associating the Fourth Gospel with John son of Zebedee makes this the strongest hypothesis, if one is prepared to give credence to the Gospel's claim of an eyewitness source.[34]

If John the son of Zebedee is the author, why then does he refer throughout the Gospel to himself in such a mysterious way? The answer may lie in the contribution of a scribe or secretary (see below); or it may lie in John's distinctive style. In keeping with his practice of occasionally preferring to use symbolic rather than ordinary names—such as "Woman" instead of "Mary" (John 2:4; 19:26)—he may refer to himself in the third person as "the disciple whom Jesus loved" (John 13:23; 21:7, 20), in order invite readers of the Gospel to see themselves in him.

As soon as we say this, however, a potential objection arises: How could the apostle John, the son of Zebedee, have written a Gospel if he was just a fisherman from Galilee? As we saw earlier, some scholars claim that it is impossible for the Gospels to have been written by the disciples of Jesus since they were "illiterate" (Acts 4:13).[35] But several points need to be kept in mind.

For one thing, nobody is actually claiming that a fisherman wrote the Gospel. What the title is claiming is that the Gospel was authored by an *ex-fisherman* who first became a student of arguably the most influential Jewish rabbi in history and later became an apostle and evangelist. Indeed, if the Gospel of John was written toward the end of his life (which, as we will see, is what most ancient Christians believed), then he would have had some five or six *decades* of practice preaching and teaching about Jesus in Judea and the Greek diaspora before ever setting down a single word.

Moreover, according to the evidence, John's father, Zebedee, was wealthy enough to pay "hired servants" (Greek *misthōton*) to help with the fishing business:

> And going on a little farther, [Jesus] saw James the son of Zebedee and John his brother, who were in their boat mending the nets. And immediately he called them; and *they left their father Zebedee in the boat with the hired servants*, and followed him. (Mark 1:19-20)

At the very least, this description suggests that John's family was relatively well-off, what one scholar describes as "middle class status."[36] In the words of Pope Benedict XVI: "the Gospel makes clear that Zebedee was no simple fisherman."[37]

Moreover, although the apostle John is certainly described as "uneducated" (Acts 4:13), this may not mean that he was completely unable to read and write. In context, the description of Peter and John is presented in contrast to the figures of the Jewish leaders and the "scribes" (Greek *grammateis*):

> On the morrow *their rulers and elders and scribes* were gathered together in Jerusalem, with Annas the high priest and Caiaphas and John and Alexander, and all who were of the high-priestly family. . . . *Now when they saw the boldness of Peter and John, and perceived that they were uneducated, common men*, they wondered; and they recognized that they had been with Jesus. (Acts 4:5-6, 13)

In light of this context, some scholars suggest that the Greek word usually translated as "illiterate" (*agrammatos*) is being used here in a broader sense to indicate Peter and John's "lack of formal education."[38] Should there be any doubt about this, it is crucial to note that the first-century Greek writer Epictetus actually speaks about a man "writing in an illiterate way" (Greek *graphein agrammatōs*) (*Discourses*, 2.9.10)![39] In other words, the description of Peter and John may simply refer to their lack of formal scribal literacy of the kind possessed by the Jewish leaders in Jerusalem.

Third and finally, even if Acts is describing John as unable to read and write, he still could have authored the Gospel attributed to him by using the common first-century (and twenty-first-century) custom of *dictating to a secretary.* For example, even the apostle Paul, who was certainly literate, dictated the letter to the Romans to the scribe Tertius (Romans 16:22). Many other examples could be given showing the use of both secretaries (1 Corinthians 16:21; Galatians 6:11-18) and co-authors (1 Corinthians 1:1-2; 2 Corinthians 1:1; Philippians 1:1; 1 Thessalonians 1:1; Philemon 1:1). As Richard Bauckham points out, the description of the Beloved Disciple as having "written" the Gospel (John 21:24) could refer to "the dictation of a text to a scribe,"[40] In fact, as we will see in the next chapter, that's exactly what some ancient Christians believed: that John's Gospel had been dictated.

Of course, in theory, all of this internal evidence could be fabricated. As we will see in chapter 5, there were plenty of other Gospels falsely attributed to eyewitnesses and apostles of Jesus. Because of the existence of such writings, we can't stop our investigation with the internal evidence from the titles of the Gospels of Matthew, Mark, Luke, and John. We also have to look at the *external evidence* to see what other ancient Christian writers have to say about the origins of the four Gospels. Did any of the early church fathers think the four Gospels were originally anonymous or falsely attributed?

The Early Church Fathers

I will never forget when I first started reading the ancient Christian writings outside the Bible. For most of my life, I never knew there *were* early Christian writings besides those in the New Testament. These were written by ancient Christian leaders who lived (for the most part) after the lifetime of the apostles, and who came to be known as the early "church fathers."[1] The church fathers provide us a fascinating window into the Christian world of the first several centuries AD. My goal at the time was to learn what they had to say about the origins and authorship of the four Gospels. Having heard and believed for years that "we do not know who wrote the Gospels," I naturally assumed that the early church fathers would either not have much to say about the matter or that they would be as vague and agnostic as the modern scholars I was reading at the time.

I was completely unprepared for what I discovered. As I quickly learned, the earliest Christian writings outside of the New Testament are *completely unambiguous* and *totally unanimous* about who wrote the four Gospels. Even more, some of these writings come from authors who either knew the apostles themselves, or who were only one generation removed from the apostles. The church fathers not only confirm the evidence from the manuscripts and titles discussed in the last chapter, they also add to the mix important insights into the authors and origins of the four Gospels. Again, this is what scholars refer to as *external evidence*. As you will see, there is a very good reason that people who claim the Gospels were originally anonymous also consistently ignore this external evidence—almost as if it didn't exist.[2]

In this chapter, we'll look briefly at the external evidence for the origins of the four Gospels. Unfortunately, we cannot examine all of it—we just don't have enough space.[3] Instead, I'll focus on the earliest and most geographically widespread evidence. Following is a list of writings from the period immediately following the New Testament (second to third centuries AD). These sources are important because they are the earliest examples we possess of what Christians only one or two generations removed from the New Testament period have to say about who wrote the Gospels. (You may want to bookmark this chart for future reference.)

EXTERNAL EVIDENCE FROM THE EARLY CHURCH FATHERS

Ancient Witness	Location	Significance	Time of Writing
1. Papias	Asia Minor (Hierapolis)	Disciple of apostle John	around AD 130
2. Justin Martyr	Palestine (Nablus)	Former philosopher turned Christian apologist	around AD 140–165
3. Irenaeus	France (Lyons)	Disciple of Polycarp, disciple of apostle John	around AD 180
4. Muratorian Canon	Italy (Rome)	Fragment of authoritative list of Scriptures	around AD 180
5. Clement	Egypt (Alexandria)	Disciple of elders who knew the apostles	around AD 200
6. Tertullian	North Africa (Carthage)	Latin Christian apologist	around AD 200–225

Some of these Fathers either knew the apostles personally (like Papias) or knew people who knew the apostles (like Irenaeus and Clement of Alexandria). To use a modern analogy: Papias, for example, was as closely related to the apostles as the children of Holocaust survivors living in the twenty-first century are to those who personally experienced World War II. Notice also that the evidence comes from all over the Roman Empire: Asia Minor (modern-day Turkey), Italy, France, North Africa, and Egypt. When ancient witnesses from such geographically diverse regions agree with one another, their testimony needs to be taken very seriously.

With that said, let's turn now to the earliest external evidence we possess regarding the origins of the four Gospels.

The Early Fathers and the Origin of Matthew's Gospel

What do the earliest church fathers have to say about the origin of the Gospel of Matthew? Did any of them think that this Gospel was originally anonymous? Consider the following evidence, taken from second-century Christians writing in Asia Minor, the Holy Land, France, and Egypt:

Matthew composed the sayings in the Hebrew dialect and each person interpreted them as best he could. (Papias of Hierapolis)[4]

For in the Memoirs [=Gospels] of the apostles and their successors it is written . . . (Justin Martyr)[5]

Now Matthew published among the Hebrews a written gospel also in their own tongue while Peter and Paul were preaching in Rome and founding the church. (Irenaeus of Lyons)[6]

Of all those who had been with the Lord only Matthew and John left us their recollections, and tradition says they took to writing perforce. Matthew had first preached to the Hebrews, and when he was on the point of going to others he transmitted in writing in his native language the Gospel according to himself, and thus supplied by writing the lack of his own presence to those from whom he was sent. (Clement of Alexandria)[7]

What we find in this evidence are answers to some basic historical questions you can ask about any book: Who wrote it? When was it written? Why was it written? How was it written?[8]

Who wrote this Gospel? The church fathers agree: Matthew, one of Jesus's "apostles" who had "been with the Lord," is the author of the Gospel attributed to him. Notice that there is not the slightest trace of an idea that the Gospel of Matthew was ever anonymous. The church fathers are in complete unanimity in believing that an eyewitness and apostle wrote the book of Matthew.

When was the Gospel of Matthew written? The Fathers do not give us exact dates. They claim that the Gospel was written while the apostle Matthew was still alive and "preaching": so it would have been sometime after the resurrection of Jesus (ca. AD 33) and before the apostle Matthew's death. Irenaeus gives us some extra information, claiming that the Gospel of Matthew was written "while Peter and Paul were preaching in Rome" (Irenaeus, *Against Heresies*, 3.1). As we'll see in chapter 7, scholars have debated exactly which decade this refers to. Since Peter and Paul were executed by Caesar Nero in the mid-60s, at the very least, the earliest external evidence we possess indicates that the Gospel of Matthew was written *while Peter and Paul were still alive* (so, before ca. AD 66). Significantly, this information comes from Irenaeus, who was a disciple of Polycarp, who was a disciple of the apostle John.

How was the Gospel of Matthew written? The Fathers who say something about how the Gospel was composed agree that Matthew originally wrote in his "native language" (Greek *patriō glōttē*) or "the Hebrew dialect" (Greek *Hebraidi dialektō*). The book was then "interpreted" or "translated" (Greek *hērmēneuse*), presumably into Greek.[9] Notice that the Fathers do not tell us *who* translated Matthew's Gospel into Greek. Papias just says "each person" did so "as he was able." Later on, in the fourth century, Saint Jerome wrote that Matthew "first composed his Gospel of Christ in Hebrew letters" and that a copy was preserved in Jerome's day "in the library of Caesarea." Jerome also admitted that "who it was that later translated it into Greek is not certain" (Jerome, *Lives of Illustrious Men*, 3).[10]

Why was the Gospel of Matthew written? According to the early church fathers, it was composed to provide Jewish Christians ("the Hebrews") with a written record of Matthew's oral teachings about Jesus before the apostle departed from them to preach the good news to others.

This, in a nutshell, is the external evidence for who wrote the Gospel of Matthew. For our purposes here, the most important point is that *there is not the slightest trace of an idea that the Gospel was ever anonymous.* Nor is there the slightest suggestion that the Gospel was written by anyone other than Matthew, the eyewitness to Jesus's life and one of the twelve apostles. The popular modern assertion that "we have no idea who wrote the Gospel of Matthew" is not one that ever seemed to cross the minds of the ancient Christians who were closest to the apostles. Notice also that their affirmation of the apostolic authorship of Matthew was in no way jeopardized by the fact that some of them believed the Greek Gospel of Matthew was translated by someone other than the apostle himself.

The Early Fathers and the Origin of Mark's Gospel

So much for the Gospel of Matthew. What do the earliest church fathers claim about the Gospel of Mark?

Despite the fact that Matthew's Gospel was the most frequently cited Gospel in the early Church, we actually have more information about the origin of Mark's Gospel. This evidence goes all the way back to Papias, who was taught by the apostle John himself. Here's what the earliest church fathers have to say:

And the elder [John] used to say this: "Mark, having become Peter's interpreter, wrote down accurately everything he remembered, though not in order, of the things either said or done by Christ. For

THE CASE FOR JESUS

he neither heard the Lord nor followed him, but afterward, as I said, followed Peter, who adapted his teachings as needed but had no intention of giving an ordered account of the Lord's sayings. Consequently Mark did nothing wrong in writing down some things as he remembered them, for he made it his one concern not to omit anything that he heard or make any false statement in them." (Papias of Hierapolis)[11]

After their [Peter and Paul's] departure, Mark also, the disciple and interpreter of Peter, himself handed down to us in writing the things which were preached by Peter. (Irenaeus of Lyons)[12]

But a great light of godliness shone upon the minds of Peter's listeners that they were not satisfied with a single hearing or with the oral teaching of the divine proclamation. So, with all kinds of exhortations, they begged Mark (whose gospel is extant), since he was Peter's follower, to leave behind a written record of the teaching given to them verbally, and did not quit until they had persuaded the man, and thus they became the immediate cause of the scripture called "The Gospel according to Mark." And they say that the apostle, aware of what had occurred because the Spirit had revealed it to him, was pleased with their zeal and sanctioned the writing for study in the churches. (Clement of Alexandria)[13]

There's a lot to discuss here, but first let's sum up the Fathers' answers to our basic questions:

Who wrote the Gospel of Mark? According to the church fathers, the author was Mark, who was both the "disciple" or "follower" and the "interpreter" or "translator" (Greek *hermēneutēs*) of the apostle Peter. Notice that Papias admits that Mark was *not* an eyewitness to Jesus: "he neither heard the Lord nor followed him."[14]

How was the Gospel written? The earliest Christian writers agree that the Gospel of Mark was based on the "teachings" or "preaching" of the apostle Peter. Significantly, Papias states that while Mark did not necessarily write down what Jesus said "in order," Mark's "one concern" was to accurately represent Peter's oral teaching.[15] In other words, according to ancient Christian belief, Mark acted as a kind of secretary or scribe who wrote on Peter's behalf and made it his goal to faithfully record what Peter said Jesus did and taught.

When was the Gospel of Mark written? With this, we hit our first potential disagreement about the origin of this Gospel. On the one hand, Irenaeus seems to suggest that the Gospel of Mark was published or "handed down" in writing *after* the "departure" (Greek *exodon*) of Peter and Paul—presumably a reference to their death by martyrdom (usually dated around AD 66).[16] This would place the origin of Mark's Gospel sometime in the late 60s of the first century AD. On the other hand, Clement of Alexandria claims that Mark was written *while Peter was still alive* and that the apostle himself "sanctioned" the reading of Mark's text in his churches.[17] This would place the origin of Mark's Gospel *before* the death of Peter, and thus sometime before AD 66. We will take up the question of dating the Gospels again in chapter 7. For now, we can say that the church fathers agree that the Gospel was written within the lifetime of Mark, Peter's disciple and interpreter.

Once again, notice that *there is not the slightest trace of an idea that the Gospel of Mark was ever originally anonymous.* Although the church fathers disagree about exactly when the Gospel was written— some say before Peter's death, some say after—there is complete unanimity on who wrote the Gospel and how it was written. Mark wrote down the oral teaching of the apostle Peter. Significantly, Papias claims that this account of Mark's origins goes back to "John the elder," whom Papias elsewhere identifies as one of "the Lord's disciples" (Eusebius, *Church History*, 3.39.4).

The Early Fathers and the Origin of Luke's Gospel

The evidence for the origin of the Gospel of Luke is not quite as ancient as that for Matthew and Mark. However, it comes from just as broad an area in the ancient world, including writers in France, Rome, North Africa, and Egypt:

> Luke also, who was a follower of Paul, put down in a book the gospel which was preached by him. (Irenaeus of Lyons)[18]

> The third book of the Gospel is that according to Luke. Luke, the well-known physician, after the ascension of Christ, when Paul had taken him with him as one zealous for the law, composed it in his own name, according to [the general] belief. Yet he himself had not seen the Lord in the flesh; and therefore, as he was able to ascertain events, so indeed he begins to tell the story from the birth of John. (Muratorian Fragment, Rome)[19]

> Luke, however, was not an apostle, but only an apostolic man . . . not a master, but a disciple, and so inferior to a master—at least as far subsequent to him as the apostle [Paul] whom he followed . . . was subsequent to the others. . . . Even Luke's form of the Gospel men usually ascribe to Paul. (Tertullian of Carthage)[20]

> And thirdly, that according to Luke, who wrote, for those who from the Gentiles [came to believe] the Gospel that was praised by Paul. (Origen of Alexandria)[21]

If we follow our basic line of questions, an interesting profile of the origin of Luke's Gospel emerges.

Who wrote the Gospel attributed to Luke? All of the earliest witnesses agree that it was Luke, the "follower" (Greek *akolouthos*) of the apostle Paul. This Luke is identified as the "well-known physician," which suggests he was no stranger to the early Church. From a historical perspective, it's interesting that none of the Fathers tries to hide the fact that Luke was neither an apostle nor an eyewitness to Jesus. They are very open about Luke's status as a second-generation Christian.

How was the Gospel of Luke written? On the one hand, like Mark, Luke is described as writing down "in a book" the "gospel" (Greek *euangelion*) that was preached orally by the apostle Paul.[22] This description seems to imply that Paul's oral preaching contained more information about the life of Jesus than we find in Paul's letters, in which he rarely quotes Jesus (e.g., 1 Corinthians 11:23-25). On the other hand, unlike with Mark, there is no hint that Luke was acting as a translator for Paul, presumably since Paul was speaking in Greek.

Why was the Gospel of Luke written? According to the early church fathers, the Gospel was composed by Luke for the "Gentiles"—that is, non-Jewish Christians. This makes sense, insofar as Luke was a companion of Paul, the self-described "apostle to the Gentiles" (Romans 11:13).

When was the Gospel of Luke written? According to Origen of Alexandria, Luke's Gospel was written "third"—that is, after the Gospels of Matthew and Mark. Even more intriguing, Origen asserts that the Gospel of Luke was written *while Paul was still alive.* When Origen says that "Luke wrote . . . the Gospel (Greek *euangelion*) that was praised by Paul,"[23] he is referring to a line from 2 Corinthians, in which Paul speaks about a companion of his who is famous in all the churches:

> With him [Titus] we are sending *the brother who is famous in the Gospel among all the churches;* and not only that, but he has been appointed by the churches to travel with us in this gracious work which we are carrying on, for the glory of the Lord and to show our good will. (2 Corinthians 8:18-19)[24]

Although many English Bibles translate this line as "famous among all the churches for his *preaching of* the gospel," the original Greek is actually a noun: "famous in the gospel" (Greek *en tō euangeliō*) (2 Corinthians 8:16). Origen, a native Greek speaker, interpreted these words of Paul as a reference to the *written Gospel* that made Luke famous in all the churches in which his book had circulated (Eusebius,

Church History 6.25.3, 6). For what it's worth, in the late fourth century AD, Saint Jerome interpreted Paul's words in the same way:

> Luke, a physician from Antioch, indicated in his writings that he knew Greek and that he was a follower of the apostle Paul and the companion of all his journeying; *he wrote a gospel about which the same Paul says*, "We have sent with him a brother whose praise is in the gospel throughout all the churches" (2 Corinthians 8:18). (Jerome, *Lives of Illustrious Men*, 7)[25]

We'll come back to questions about the dates of the Gospels later in our study. For now, it is simply interesting to note that according to Origen and Jerome, the Gospel of Luke was written before Paul finished writing all of his letters, not after.

The Early Fathers and the Origin of John's Gospel

Finally there is the Gospel according to John. The church fathers provide more detail about the composition of this Gospel than they do about any other. The following quotations give us some fascinating insights into what ancient Christians believed about the origin of John's Gospel:

> In the memoirs [=Gospels], which I say have been composed by the apostles and those who followed them . . . (Justin Martyr)[26]

> Then [after the publication of the Gospels of Matthew, Mark, and Luke] John, the disciple of the Lord, who had even rested on his breast, himself also gave forth the Gospel, while he was living at Ephesus in Asia. (Irenaeus of Lyons)[27]

> The fourth of the Gospels is that of John, [one] of the disciples. To his fellow disciples and bishops, who had been urging him [to write], he said, "Fast with me today for three days, and what will be revealed to each one let us tell it to one another." In the same night it was revealed

to Andrew, [one] of the apostles, that John should write down all things in his own name while all of them should review it. (Muratorian Canon of Rome, nos. 9–16)[28]

Of all those who had been with the Lord only Matthew and John left us their recollections (*hypomnēmata*), and tradition says that they took to writing perforce. . . . John, it is said, used all the time a message which was not written down, and at last took to writing for the following cause. The three gospels which had been written down before were distributed to all including himself; it is said he welcomed them and testified to their truth but said that there was only lacking to the narrative the account of what was done by Christ at first and at the beginning of the preaching. . . . They say accordingly that John was asked to relate in his own gospel the period passed over in silence by the former evangelists. (Clement of Alexandria)[29]

We lay it down as our first position, that the evangelical Testament has apostles for its authors. . . . Of the apostles, therefore, John and Matthew first instill faith into us; whilst of apostolic men, Luke and Mark renew it afterwards. (Tertullian of Carthage)[30]

Let's walk carefully through our four questions again.

Who wrote the Gospel according to John? Taken together, the external evidence presented here is unanimous: the apostle John, an eyewitness to and disciple of Jesus himself. The most important early witness is Irenaeus, who was a disciple of Polycarp, himself a disciple of John. Irenaeus not only identifies the author of the Gospel as the "disciple" who lay on Jesus's breast at the Last Supper; he elsewhere explicitly states that the author is "John . . . the apostle." (See Irenaeus, *Against Heresies*, 1.9.2).[31] Along similar lines, Justin Martyr, Clement of Alexandria, and Tertullian all agree that the Gospel was written by one of the "apostles" of Jesus.

One reason it is necessary to highlight this evidence is because in recent years, some scholars have proposed a new theory about who wrote the Gospel. According to this view, the Gospel was not written by John *the apostle* but by another disciple named "John": the so-called "John the Elder."[32] Now, it is true that the letters we know as 2 and 3 John are attributed to "the elder" (2 John 1; 3 John 1), and that they sound a lot like the Gospel of John. And it is also true that some fourth-century church fathers such as Eusebius of Caesarea believed that the book of Revelation was not written by John the apostle, but by another man named "John the Elder."[33] Yet *none of the early church fathers—including Irenaeus—ever claims that this "other John" wrote the Fourth Gospel.*[34] Even Eusebius makes it quite clear that the Gospel of John was written by one of the "the apostles" (Eusebius, *Church History*, 3.39.5). In other words, although there was some debate among the church fathers about who wrote 2 and 3 John and the book of Revelation, there was *no debate* about the apostolic authorship of the Gospel of John.[35]

When was the Gospel written? Once again, when it comes to the question of date, there is some disagreement. On the one hand, the earliest witnesses—Irenaeus, the Muratorian Canon, and Clement—claim that the Gospel of John was published *after* the Gospels of Matthew, Mark, and Luke. On the other, Tertullian claims that the Gospels of Matthew and John were "prior" to Luke and Mark (see Tertullian, *Against Marcion*, 4.5). In either case, the Fathers agree that the Gospel was written while the apostle John was still alive.

Why was the Gospel of John written? According to the earliest Fathers, there were two main reasons. First, according to several Fathers, the Gospel of John was written to supplement the information about Jesus contained in the Gospels of Matthew, Mark, and Luke.[36] Second, and perhaps even more important, the Gospel of John was written *to defend the divinity of Jesus* against the teachings of a man named Cerinthus and a group known as the Ebionites, both of whom denied that Jesus was divine.[37] In the words of Irenaeus:

> John, the disciple of the Lord, preaches this faith, and seeks, by the proclamation of the Gospel, to remove that error which by Cerinthus had been disseminated among men. . . . According to the opinion of no one of the heretics was the Word of God made flesh. . . . Therefore

the Lord's disciple, pointing them all out as false witnesses, says, "And the Word was made flesh, and dwelt among us" [John 1:14]. (Irenaeus, *Against Heresies*, 3.11.1–2)[38]

Irenaeus isn't the only church father who recognized the Gospel of John's distinctive emphasis on the divinity of Jesus.[39] Nevertheless, this emphasis did not lead ancient Christians to reject the Gospel of John as unhistorical. Instead, the Fathers explained John's emphasis on Jesus's divinity by pointing out that the Gospel had been written against early Christian heretics who were denying that Jesus was God.

Finally, how was the Gospel of John written? In this regard, it is fascinating to note that some church fathers, such as Clement of Alexandria, describe the apostle John as "simple . . . in speech" and having "neither the knowledge nor the desire to represent the teachings of the Master in persuasive or artistic language" (see Eusebius, *Church History*, 3.24.1–7). This dovetails with what we saw in the last chapter about Peter and John being described as "uneducated" or "illiterate" (Acts 4:13). On the other hand, John's apparent simplicity does not mean he wasn't the author of the Gospel. In fact, one ancient Christian text claims that the Gospel was *dictated* by John to a secretary:

> This Gospel therefore, written after the Apocalypse, was also given to the churches in Asia by John while still living in the flesh, as the bishop of Hierapolis, Papias by name, a dear disciple of John, has related in his "exoteric," that is, in [his] last five books, who wrote out this Gospel, John dictating it to him. (Anti-Marcionite Prologue to the Gospel of John, Recension 2)[40]

Scholars debate whether or not this text comes from the second century AD. Nevertheless, it is still intriguing that ancient Christians were open to the possibility that the Gospel of John may have been "dictated" (Latin *dictante*) to one of his disciples. Not only would this allow for some editorial work on the part of a scribe, it would also go a long way toward explaining the distinctive "voice" of the Gospel of John, in which Jesus, John the Baptist, and the narrator all sound very much alike (compare the three "voices" in John 3:1-35). In any case, however it was written, the early church fathers are unanimous in attributing the book to the apostle John.

What About Early Heretics and Pagan Critics?

Before ending this chapter, it's important to highlight that it wasn't only the early church fathers who believed that the four Gospels went back to the apostles and apostolic men. In the first three centuries after Christ, even those identified as heretics and enemies of the Church seem to have accepted that the four Gospels were actually written by Matthew, Mark, Luke, and John.

For example, in the second century AD, Irenaeus points out that early Christian heretics appealed to the Gospels in order to make the case for their various teachings:

> So firm is the ground upon which these Gospels rest, that the very her-
> etics themselves bear witness to them, and, starting from these [docu-
> ments], each one of them endeavors to establish his own peculiar
> doctrine. . . . Since, then, our opponents do bear testimony to us, and
> make use of these [documents], our proof derived from them is firm
> and true. (Irenaeus, Against Heresies, 3.11.7) [41]

Now, Irenaeus tells us that the various sects tended to pick one of the four Gospels: for example, the Ebionites used only the Gospel of Matthew; the Marcionites used only a shorter version of the Gospel of Luke; others (who appear to be Gnostics) used only the Gospel of Mark; and the Valentinians used only the Gospel of John. But all of the early heretical groups seem to *take for granted* the apostolic authorship of the four Gospels. For the first three centuries of the Church, the authorship of the Gospels was apparently not a topic of debate.[42]

Remarkably, this is even true of the pagan writer Celsus, who lived in the late second century AD. Celsus was one of the fiercest enemies and critics of Christianity in the early Church, and he devoted a substantial portion of his time to attacking it. This is what he has to say about the authorship of the Gospels:

> The disciples of Jesus, having no undoubted fact on which to rely, devised the fiction that he foreknew everything before it happened. . . . *The disciples of Jesus wrote such accounts regarding him,* by way of extenuating the charges that told against him. (Celsus, *Against the Christians*)[43]

Notice here that Celsus definitely thinks that the Gospels are *fiction*. However, he never questions that they were actually written by "disciples of Jesus." This is extremely significant, since Celsus could have easily strengthened his case against Christianity by arguing that none of the Gospels were written by eyewitnesses and apostles. But he makes no such claim. Instead, this pagan critic *takes the apostolic authorship of the Gospels for granted* and argues against them on other grounds. Origen points out that pagan critics like Celsus will not go so far as to deny the fact that "Jesus's own pupils and hearers" left behind "their reminiscences of Jesus in writing" (Origen, *Against Celsus*, 2.13).[44]

To sum up what we've learned so far: when the earliest Christian writings outside the New Testament are taken into account, there is not the slightest trace of external evidence to support the now popular claim that the four Gospels were originally anonymous. As far as we know, for almost four hundred years after the lifetime of Jesus, no one—orthodox or heretic, pagan or Christian—seems to have raised any serious doubts about who wrote the Gospels of Matthew, Mark, Luke, and John.[45] As we have seen previously, there was some debate among the church fathers about the exact order and dating of the Gospels, but there was no debate about their authorship. In other words, the theory of the anonymous Gospels not only fails to do justice to the internal evidence from the most ancient manuscripts; it also fails to do justice to the *external* evidence from the earliest Christian writings outside the New Testament.

As soon as I say this, I can imagine someone objecting: "Well, maybe ancient Christians *did* agree that the four Gospels were authored by Matthew, Mark, Luke, and John. And maybe there is no evidence that the four Gospels were ever anonymous. But what about all the other gospels that didn't make it into the New Testament? What about all these lost gospels that I've heard about? Haven't scholars recently discovered gospels that have titles attributing them to Peter or Judas or Thomas? How do we know these *other* gospels weren't also written by apostles?"

These are good questions. In order to answer them, we need to turn now to the next chapter and look carefully at these so-called "lost gospels."

The Lost Gospels

If you've ever watched one of those television documentaries on the Bible, or if you've paid attention to the media for the last several years, you've definitely heard of the so-called "lost gospels." These books are also known as the *apocryphal* gospels, from the Greek word *apokry-phon*, meaning "hidden book." These are writings about Jesus that claim to have been written by eyewitnesses such as Peter, Judas, or Thomas. However, these gospels tell a story about the words and deeds of Jesus that is very different from the one most Christians are used to hearing in the writings of the New Testament. The differences can be so striking that they are often shocking, and so members of the media (who love shock value) like to talk about these gospels, usually right around Christmas and Easter, when Christians are celebrating the life, death, and resurrection of Jesus.

The annual Easter hullabaloo about the apocryphal gospels can be annoying. It's often the same old story: "Scholars unearth the 'hidden' truth about Jesus and Judas!" "Did the Church suppress the real story of Jesus and Mary Magdalene?" And so on. On the other hand, the existence of these other gospels is a fact. And all the talk about them actually helps raise an extremely important historical question that every thoughtful Christian needs to answer: *Is* there a difference between the four Gospels and the apocryphal gospels? *Why* should I accept the claim that the Gospels of Matthew, Mark, Luke, and John go back to the apostles and their disciples but not the gospels of Thomas, Peter, or Judas? Don't the apocryphal gospels also have titles attributing them to apostles? Are there good historical reasons for accepting the apostolic origins of the four Gospels while rejecting the apocryphal gospels?

These are important questions. In order to answer them, we will have to look carefully at the relevant internal and external evidence on the lost gospels. As we will see, the lost gospels certainly include titles attributing them to eyewitnesses. But when it comes to *external evidence*, the contrast between what the early church fathers say about the origins of the four Gospels versus what they say about the origins of the apocryphal gospels couldn't be more striking. Unlike the four Gospels, the "lost gospels" were almost immediately rejected as fakes and forgeries. Far from being the recent discoveries they are so frequently touted to be, the existence of these books has been known for a very, very long time.

Four Apocryphal Gospels

As with all of the topics we've looked at so far, a whole book could be easily written about the apocryphal gospels.[1] For our purposes here, we will focus on a few examples of the earliest apocryphal gospels in order to point up the difference between what ancient Christians said about who wrote the four New Testament Gospels as opposed to what they believed about the origins of the lost gospels.

For the sake of space, then, I've chosen what are widely regarded by scholars to be four of the earliest apocryphal gospels, all likely dating back to the second century AD. (We'll come back to the issue of dating in a later chapter. For now, we're just looking at the question of authorship.) The four apocryphal gospels I've selected are the following:

FOUR APOCRYPHAL GOSPELS

Title of Gospel	*Contents*
1. *Infancy Gospel of Thomas*	Stories about the childhood of Jesus
2. *Gospel of Thomas*	Collection of 114 sayings attributed to Jesus
3. *Gospel of Judas*	Dialogues between Jesus and Judas
4. *Gospel of Peter*	Accounts of the passion, death, and resurrection of Christ

In this section, I will briefly introduce each of these gospels. Since many people have heard of these gospels but never actually read them, I will present some sample passages so that you can see exactly who these gospels claim to be written by and so that you can get a feel for what these writings are like.

Written in Greek, the *Infancy Gospel of Thomas* claims to be an account of the childhood of Jesus written by the apostle Thomas. In keeping with our attention to internal evidence and titles, this is how the book begins:

> The account of Thomas the Israelite philosopher concerning the childhood of the Lord:
>
> I, Thomas the Israelite, tell and make known to you all, brethren from among the Gentiles, all the works of the childhood of our Lord Jesus Christ and his mighty deeds, which he did when he was born in our land. (*Infancy Gospel of Thomas* 1)[2]

Notice that the title and the opening line attribute the book to "Thomas the Israelite." One Greek manuscript makes explicit that this attribution refers to "the holy apostle Thomas."[3] The book then goes on to narrate a number of remarkable stories about Jesus during his childhood. Perhaps the most memorable of them are the following:

When this boy Jesus was five years old he was playing at the ford of a brook, and he gathered together into pools the water that flowed by, and made it at once clean. . . . But the son of Annas the scribe was standing there with Joseph; and he took a branch of willow and dispersed the water which Jesus had gathered together. When Jesus saw what he had done he was enraged and said to him: "You insolent, godless dunderhead, what harm did the pools and the water do to you? See, now you shall also wither like a tree and shall bear neither leaves nor root nor fruit." And immediately the lad withered up completely. . . . After this, [Jesus] again went through the village, and a lad ran and knocked against his shoulder. Jesus was exasperated and said to him: "You shall not go further on your way," and the child immediately fell down and died. (*Infancy Gospel of Thomas* 2.1, 3.1-3, 4.1)[4]

Well, so much for Jesus "meek and mild"! According to the Infancy Gospel of Thomas, the boy Jesus was a murderer who killed other children if they so much as aggravated him—but only after calling them "godless dunderheads"! It should go without saying that what we are dealing with in this apocryphal gospel stands in stark contrast with the comparatively sober stories of Jesus's childhood found in the Gospels of Matthew and Luke. For our purposes here, the point is simply that, according to the internal evidence, these stories about the boy Jesus are being attributed to the apostle Thomas (compare Matthew 10:3).

The second apocryphal gospel that merits our attention is also attributed to the apostle Thomas, but is referred to by scholars simply as the *Gospel of Thomas*. This book, which seems to have been originally written in Greek but which is only fully preserved in Coptic (an ancient Egyptian language), is not a narrative of Jesus's life and death. It is a collection of 114 distinct sayings supposedly given to the apostle Thomas in secret by Jesus. This is how the book begins and ends:

These are the hidden sayings that the living Jesus spoke and Judas Thomas the Twin recorded. (*Gospel of Thomas*, Prologue)

The Gospel according to Thomas (*Gospel of Thomas*, Subscript)[5]

Notice that the opening lines and the subscript attribute the book to "Thomas" (Coptic *Tōmas*), whom the prologue identifies as "the Twin" (Coptic *Didymos*). This is a clear reference to the apostle Thomas, who is identified in the Gospel of John as "Thomas, one of the Twelve, called the Twin (Greek *Didymos*)" (John 20:24). Notice also the emphasis on the hidden nature of the sayings of this book, which the text claims were given directly by Jesus and that Thomas wrote down. Although much could be said about the many interesting sayings contained in this gospel, perhaps the most famous of them is the final saying in the book:

> Simon Peter said to them, "Mary should leave us, for females are not worthy of life." Jesus said, "Look, I shall guide her to make her male, so that she too may become a living spirit resembling you males. *For every female who makes herself male will enter heaven's kingdom.* (*Gospel of Thomas* 114)[6]

That's how this apocryphal gospel ends: with Jesus claiming that he will make Mary Magdalene male so that she can enter the kingdom of heaven, just as any woman who "makes herself male" will be equally rewarded!

The third and perhaps most famous of the apocryphal gospels is the *Gospel of Judas*, which is also written in Coptic. It has the unique status of being the most recently discovered of all the apocryphal gospels. According to reports, it was found by peasants in a burial cave in Egypt in 1978. It created something of a media frenzy when it was finally translated into English and published—you guessed it, around Easter—in the year 2006.[7] It consists of several dialogues (some of them private) between Jesus and his disciples, especially Judas. And it begins as follows:

> The Gospel of Judas
> The secret word of revelation that Jesus spoke with Judas Iscariot in the course of eight days, three days before he celebrated Passover. (*Gospel of Judas* 33)[8]

Notice once again the emphasis on the secret nature of the contents of the gospel, as something between Jesus and Judas alone. This secretive atmosphere continues throughout the gospel. For example, in one exchange, Jesus tells Judas that he will give him a special teaching that he gives to no one else:

> And they [the apostles] all said, "We are strong." Yet the spirits could not dare to stand before him, except Judas Iscariot. He was able to stand before him, yet he could not look him in the eye, but rather turned his face away. Judas said to him, "I know who you are and where you have come from. You have come from the immortal aeon of Barbelo, and from the one that has sent you, whose name I am not worthy to utter." But Jesus, knowing that he was thinking of something lofty, said to him, *"Separate from them, and I will tell you the mysteries of the kingdom."* (Gospel of Judas 35)[9]

Much of the rest of the *Gospel of Judas* is like this: lots of esoteric exchanges between Jesus and Judas about "immortal aeons" with strange names like "Barbelo." Because the book is so fragmentary, scholars continue to debate whether Judas is the "hero" of the book, or whether he is described as being ultimately condemned.[10] For our purposes here, it doesn't matter. What matters is that the gospel is attributed to an eyewitness and an apostle: Judas Iscariot.

The fourth and final apocryphal gospel we will examine is the so-called *Gospel of Peter*. This book, which is preserved in Greek, is a fragmentary account of the passion, death, and resurrection of Jesus. Although the title of the gospel is not preserved, the book ends with Peter writing about what the disciples did after the resurrection in the first person ("I"):

> It was the final day of the Feast of Unleavened Bread. . . . But we, the twelve disciples of the Lord, wept and grieved; and each one returned to his home, grieving for what had happened. *But I, Simon Peter, and my brother Andrew,* took our nets and went off to the sea. And with us was Levi, the son of Alphaeus. (Gospel of Peter 58)[11]

As this and other passages make clear, the narrator of this gospel claims to be the apostle Peter (see also *Gospel of Peter* 26). It is striking how different this account of Jesus's death sometimes is from the passion narratives in the four Gospels. Consider, for example, its description of Jesus's last words:

> Now it was midday and a darkness had covered all Judea. . . . And many went about with lamps, since they supposed that it was night, and they stumbled. And the Lord called out and cried, *"My power, O power, thou hast forsaken me!"* And having said this, *he was taken up.* (*Gospel of Peter* 15, 18-19)[12]

Notice that according to this gospel, Jesus does not quote the first line of Psalm 22—"My God, my God, why have you forsaken me?"—as he does in the other Gospels (see Matthew 27:46; Mark 15:34). Instead, he cries out to his "Power" (Greek *dynamis*), which most scholars interpret as a reference to his divinity "leaving" him.[13] Moreover, unlike the Gospel of Luke, in which Jesus ascends into heaven after his resurrection (Luke 24:51), in the *Gospel of Peter* Jesus is somehow taken up immediately *before* his death.

To sum up what we've seen so far: when we look carefully at four examples from the apocryphal gospels—the *Infancy Gospel of Thomas*, the sayings in the *Gospel of Thomas*, the *Gospel of Judas*, and the *Gospel of Peter*—in every case, we have internal evidence from the gospel itself (whether title or text or both) claiming that these books contain the testimony of the apostles Thomas, Judas, and Peter. At first glance—and this is what the media loves to highlight for an unsuspecting and uninformed audience—these apocryphal gospels seem to have an *equal claim* to having been written by apostles as, say, the Gospels according to Matthew and John. So what do we make of this internal evidence?

At this point, we could dive headfirst into other internal features of these books that suggest to scholars that they were not in fact written by eyewitnesses and apostles: features such as their emphasis on secret knowledge and special angel names that correspond remarkably well to what we know about the second-century Christian groups known as "gnostics" (from Greek *gnōsis*, meaning "knowledge").[14] We could also examine their seeming lack of familiarity with Jewish Scripture and first-century Jewish practice and belief. However, for our purposes, we'll cut right to the chase and get to what may be the most historically significant difference between the Gospels of Matthew, Mark, Luke, and John and these four apocryphal gospels: namely, that the latter were almost immediately rejected by ancient church fathers as forgeries and fakes. In other words, as we shall see, the *external* evidence suggests that these so-called "gospels" are not authentic.

What Did the Early Fathers Say about the Lost Gospels?

As I mentioned earlier, every year, about twice a year, the popular media love to trot out the lost gospels and get a buzz going about them. Usually, the goal is to get people talking about whether or not Christians will have to fundamentally rethink basic teachings about Jesus in light of this newly discovered evidence. In other words, the existence of the lost gospels is presented as *news*. And, to be sure, the discoveries of complete copies of some of these texts—like the *Gospel of Thomas* in 1945 and the *Gospel of Judas* in 1978—were in fact groundbreaking developments in our knowledge of early Christianity. At the same time, the existence of these gospels is not news at all. Or if it is news, it's *very old* news. Almost nineteen hundred years old, to be more precise. For when we turn to the writings of the early church fathers, we discover that not only did they speak about the authorship and origins of the Gospels of Matthew, Mark, Luke, and John; they also spoke about the origins of some of the lost gospels that we have been discussing— the gospels that have only recently been rediscovered.

The reason that the church fathers' remarks are important to our investigation is that there is a contrast between what they say about the lost gospels and what they say about the four Gospels. In every case, ancient Christian writers in the churches dating back to the apostles rejected these books as forgeries. Let's take each one of them in turn.

We'll start with the *Infancy Gospel of Thomas*, which, as we have seen above, contains rather shocking stories of the boy Jesus killing his playmates. Already in the second century AD, Irenaeus of Lyons—who, remember, was a disciple of Polycarp, the disciple of John—knew about this book. And this is what Irenaeus had to say about how the book came to be:

> [T]hey adduce an unspeakable number of apocryphal and spurious writings, which they themselves have forged, to bewilder the minds of foolish men, and of such as are ignorant of the Scriptures of truth. Among other things, they bring forward that false and wicked story which relates that our Lord, when He was a boy learning His letters, on the teacher saying to him, as is usual, "Pronouce Alpha," replied "Alpha." (Irenaeus of Lyons, *Against Heresies*, 1.20.1)[15]

Although Irenaeus does not name the book he is referring to, a quick comparison shows that he is speaking about one of the stories contained in the *Infancy Gospel of Thomas*.[16] For our purposes, what matters is the striking contrast between what Irenaeus has to say about the *Infancy Gospel of Thomas* and what he has to say about the Gospels of Matthew, Mark, Luke, and John. While Irenaeus unhesitatingly attributes the four Gospels to the apostles and their followers, he emphatically describes the book containing this story about the child Jesus as a "spurious" forgery.

Along similar lines, another text by Irenaeus gives us our earliest reference to the recently discovered *Gospel of Judas*. Once again, this ancient church father has no doubts about exactly who wrote this so-called gospel:

> Others again declare that Cain derived his being from the Power above, and acknowledge that Esau, Korah, the Sodomites, and all such persons, are related to themselves. . . . They produce a *fictitious history* of this kind, *which they style the Gospel of Judas.* (Irenaeus of Lyons, *Against Heresies*, 1.31.1)[17]

It is fascinating to realize that through the writing of Irenaeus we have a window onto what ancient Christians believed about a Gospel that has been lost now for almost two thousand years. And what did apostolic Christians like Irenaeus believe? That the *Gospel of Judas* was "a fictitious history" attributed to Judas but actually written by a group of second-century gnostic heretics known as the "Cainites" (not to be confused with the Old Testament "Canaanites").

   Almost the exact same situation applies when we turn to the earliest references we possess to the so-called *Gospel of Peter*. The evidence, found in a story about a second-century Syrian bishop named Serapion, shows that Bishop Serapion did not immediately reject the *Gospel of Peter*. But once he had read it for himself, this is what he had to say to his congregation:

> For we, brethren, receive both Peter and the other apostles as Christ;
> but we reject intelligently the writings *falsely ascribed* to them, know-
> ing that such were not handed down to us. (Serapion, bishop of
> Antioch)[18]

Notice here that Serapion ultimately rejects the *Gospel of Peter* because it was "falsely ascribed" or, more literally, a "false writing" (Greek *pseudepigrapha*). Contrary to what some modern people claim, ancient Christians knew the difference between authentic writings and forgeries falsely named after the apostles, and they did not approve of the latter.[19]

   Finally, even the famous *Gospel of Thomas* was known to the early church fathers and rejected by them as a forgery. In this case, we have the testimony of both Eusebius of Caesarea (AD 325) and Cyril, bishop of the Church in Jerusalem (around AD 350), who agree:

> *[There are] writings which are put forward by heretics under the
> name of the apostles containing gospels such as those of Peter, and
> Thomas. . . .* To none of these has any who ever belonged to the eccle-
> siastical teachers ever thought it right to refer in his writings. More-
> over, the type of phraseology differs from apostolic style, and the

opinion and tendency of their contents is widely dissonant from true orthodoxy and clearly shows that *they are the forgeries of heretics*. (Eusebius, *Church History*, 3.25.6-7)[20]

Then of the New Testament there are the four Gospels only, for *the rest have false titles and are mischievous*. The Manicheans also wrote a Gospel according to Thomas, *which being tinctured with the fragrance of the Gospel title corrupts the souls of the simple* sort. (Cyril of Jerusalem, *Catechetical Lectures*, 4.36)[21]

What did the early church fathers have to say about the *Gospel of Thomas*? That it was a "false writing" (Greek *pseudepigrapha*), one of the "forgeries (Greek *anaplasmata*) of heretics." For the church fathers, the internal claim for apostolic authorship by Thomas was *not enough* to justify believing that the book was actually written by an apostle. They also wanted external evidence that these books actually went back to the disciples of Jesus and that the leaders of the churches founded by the apostles remembered these books as having been authored by the apostles. When this kind of external confirmation was lacking, and when that lack of proof was combined with the books' strange contents and heretical teachings, the church fathers did not hesitate to reject the so-called "lost gospels" as not being gospels at all but acts of deception.

Much more, of course, could be said. But for this book, what matters most is that the evidence from the early church fathers shows they were unanimous in believing that the Gospels of Matthew, Mark, Luke, and John were actually written by the apostles and their disciples. Likewise, they were unanimous in their judgment that the apocryphal gospels attributed to Thomas, Judas, and Peter were not written by the apostles or their disciples. This contrast is devastating for the theory that the four Gospels were originally anonymous and then later falsely ascribed to the apostles and their disciples. If this were true, then why don't we find a single ancient Christian saying as much? If the four Gospels were really forgeries like the later apocryphal gospels, then why didn't at least *some* of the early church fathers harbor doubts about whether Matthew really wrote Matthew, or John really wrote John?

Maybe, just maybe, it is because the four Gospels *never were anonymous*. And maybe, just maybe, it is because the four first-century Gospels—in contrast to the later apocryphal gospels—were actually authored by the apostles and their followers.

Are the Gospels Biographies?

At this point in our investigation, some readers might want to stop asking questions about the Gospels and move on to the words and deeds of Jesus. After all, if the four Gospels actually go back to the apostles and their followers, then what else is there to discuss? Surely these writings must give us reliable accounts of Jesus's words and actions, right?

Not necessarily. Although we've explored the historical *origins* of the Gospels, we still have to look at the literary *genre* of the Gospels. In a nutshell, when we're looking at "genre" we are asking the question: *What kind of book is this?* Is it history? Is it biography? Is it fictional, like a novel? Is it a myth? The reason genre is important is that if you get the genre wrong, then you will misinterpret the writing. Think about it: if you walk into a library looking for a history of World War II but accidentally pick up a misshelved novel from the fiction section, then you're going to seriously miss the author's point. The very reason libraries everywhere organize their collections according to the various kinds of books is because *genre matters*. That's also why the Bible is arranged according to genres: law, history, prophecy, wisdom literature, Gospels, Acts, letters, and so on.

Authors often provide clues to the genre of a work. The form, contents, length, tone, and so on all work together to help the reader to identify the kind of book it is. If a story begins with the words "Once upon a time . . ." then you know that what you are about to read is a fairy tale, not a history.

Getting the genre right when we are evaluating the four Gospels as historical sources of knowledge about Jesus is important because some scholars today claim that the Gospels are much more like folklore than biography or history. One recent scholar claims that the authors of the Gospels were often not even trying to give their readers "biographical information" about "what Jesus really said and did."[1] Is this true? Are the Gospels a form of folklore? Or are they ancient biographies? What literary clues do they contain that might help us determine their genre? In order to answer these questions, let's start by looking briefly at the modern theory that the Gospels are not biographies.

The Gospels as Folklore?

For the first eighteen hundred years or so of their existence, the four Gospels were read as if they were *biographies*—accounts of the "life" (Greek *bios*) of Jesus, telling us what he really did and what he really said. For example, in the second century AD, Justin Martyr refers to the Gospels as "the memoirs of [the] apostles" and interprets them as having "recorded" what Jesus actually said and did (see Justin Martyr, *1 Apology*, 66; *Dialogue with Trypho*, 100.4). By referring to the Gospels as "memoirs" (Greek *apomnēmoneumata*), Justin is using language from the biographical tradition in the Hellenistic world and thus giving us a clue as to how the Gospels were read by ancient readers.[2] Along similar lines, Augustine of Hippo described the four Gospels as "trustworthy testimonies," based on the "remembrance" of the disciples, of "the words heard from his lips, and the deeds wrought by him beneath their eyes" (Augustine, *Harmony of the Gospels*, 1.1). In light of such examples, New Testament scholar Graham Stanton concludes: "There

is little doubt . . . that early Christian readers of the gospels did read
them as biographies."[3]

Fast-forward almost fifteen hundred years, and a dramatic shift
takes place. In the late nineteenth and early twentieth centuries,
some scholars began insisting that the Gospels were *not* biographies.[4]
Perhaps the most influential proponent of this idea was the German
scholar Rudolf Bultmann, who wrote:

> [M]ust we look around for analogies to the explanation of the form
> of the Gospel? What analogies can be suggested? There are none in
> the Greek Tradition; for there is no point in considering either the
> Memoirs which Justin . . . might have been thinking with his refer-
> ence to *apomnēmoneumata*, or the Hellenistic biography. *There is
> no historical-biographical interest in the Gospels*, and that is why they
> have nothing to say about Jesus' human personality, his appearance
> and character, his origin, education, and development.[5]

Notice that Bultmann knows full well that Justin Martyr described
the Gospels as biographical "memoirs." Yet he simply brushes this
evidence aside and asserts that there is "no historical-biographical
interest" in the Gospels because they don't tell us what Jesus looked
like! He appears to be saying that because the Gospels are not like
modern biographies—which focus on exact details like appearance,
psychological development, and education—they are not biographies
at all. Instead, for Bultmann, the Gospels are more like "folktales" and
"fairy stories."[6]

This idea that the Gospels are like folklore is alive and well. For
example, in his best-selling introduction to the New Testament—
once again, the textbook I used when I was in school—Bart Ehrman
claims that ancient Christians weren't all that concerned about historical truth, since they believed that a story about Jesus could be true
"whether or not it happened."[7] As a modern analogy, Ehrman appeals
to the contemporary folktale of the young George Washington refusing
to lie about having chopped down his father's cherry tree! He writes:

Consider, for example, a story that every second-grader in the country has heard, the story of George Washington and the cherry tree. . . . [W]e tell the story, not because it really happened, but because in some sense we think it is true. The stories about Jesus in the early Church may have been similar.[8]

To be fair, Ehrman does admit that many of the episodes in the Gospels are accounts of events that really did happen. He even lays out some criteria for how to identify what is historical and what isn't.[9] Nevertheless, he still chooses a modern-day children's folktale widely regarded as being false to provide the primary analogy for the kinds of stories he thinks the Gospels contain. In so doing he creates the impression that the Gospels are the equivalent of ancient folklore, which has little or nothing to do with actual historical events.

The Gospels Are Ancient Biographies

When you actually take the time to compare the Gospels with other ancient writings, however, the closest literary parallels are in fact Greco-Roman biographies.[10] These biographies are known as "lives" (Greek *bioi*) because they focus on the life of a particular person, whether a philosopher, a teacher, a politician, an emperor, or whoever. Here are a few examples of some ancient biographies written shortly after the time period of the Gospels:

FOUR ANCIENT GRECO-ROMAN BIOGRAPHIES

Biography	Author	Time Period
1. *Life of Josephus*	Josephus—Jewish historian	ca. AD 99
2. *Parallel Lives*	Plutarch—Greek historian	ca. AD 90–100
3. *Lives of the Caesars*	Suetonius—Roman historian	ca. AD 120
4. *Life of Demonax*	Lucian—writer, student of Demonax	ca. AD 150–180

In this section, we will compare some of the key features in these Greco-Roman biographies with the life of Jesus as recorded in the four Gospels. For this discussion I am drawing on the critically acclaimed book by the New Testament scholar Richard Burridge, *What Are the Gospels? A Comparison with Graeco-Roman Biography* (2004).[11] This book highlights key parallels that have led many recent scholars to conclude that in terms of literary genre, the Gospels are closest to ancient Greco-Roman biographies.[12]

1. Ancient biographies focus on the life and death of a single individual.

The first parallel between ancient biographies and the four Gospels is that they both focus on the "life" (*bios*) of a single person—whether that person be the Jewish historian Josephus or Alexander the Great, Caesar Nero, the philosopher Demonax, or Jesus of Nazareth. The overall structure of an ancient biography can usually be broken down into three main parts—the birth, public life, and death of the person—with the bulk of the book being devoted to the subject's public career:

Greco-Roman Biographies	The Four Gospels
1. Birth and childhood (brief or missing)	1. Birth and childhood (Matthew 1–2, Luke 1–2, absent in Mark and John)
2. Public career (longest section of book)	2. Public career (Matthew 3–25; Mark 1–13; Luke 3–21; John 1–12)
3. Death (relatively brief)	3. Passion and death (Matthew 24–27; Mark 14–15; Luke 22–23; John 18–19)

Of course, not every ancient biography covers the childhood of its subject. For example, Plutarch's life of the Greek statesman Timoleon dives straight into the story of his public deeds (see *Timoleon* 1). Likewise, the Gospel of Mark does not begin with the birth of Jesus but with the ministry of John the Baptist (see Mark 1). Nevertheless, the general focus on the life and death of a single person marks out biography as different from other kinds of writing, such as history, which tend to focus on the events of an entire nation or people.

2. Ancient biographies often average between 10,000 and 20,000 words in length.

As anyone who has spent time in a bookstore knows, the size of a book can often be a very important clue to its genre. History books tend to be long and detailed; novels can be any length; children's books tend to be short. Long books with tons of footnotes immediately tell the reader: "For scholars only!" And so on. According to Richard Burridge, ancient Greco-Roman biographies often averaged somewhere between 10,000 and 20,000 words—"the amount on a typical scroll about 30–35 feet long."[13] (To give an idea of how many pages this would translate into in our own day, 10,000 to 20,000 words usually takes up 40 to 80 typewritten pages.) When we examine the length of the four Gospels, they fall within this ballpark.

Greco-Roman Biographies	The Four Gospels
Common Length	Matthew: about 18,000 words
10,000 to 20,000 words	Mark: about 11,000 words
	Luke: about 19,000 words
	John: about 15,000 words

To be sure, some biographies were much longer than the Gospels (such as Philostratus's *Life of Apollonius of Tyana*). In other cases they were quite short. For example, the Gospel according to Mark and Lucian's biography of Demonax can be read easily in a single sitting. Nevertheless, most biographies were usually of medium length. Then, as today, they tended to be longer than letters but shorter than histories.

3. Ancient biographies often begin with ancestry.

The beginning of a book is usually where the author clues you in to the genre. As I have mentioned previously, when a story begins with the words "Once upon a time . . . ," you know you're reading a fairy tale. Likewise, if a short piece of writing begins with the words "Paul . . . to all God's beloved in Rome," then you know you're reading a letter (Romans 1:1-7). Along these lines, ancient biographies would often begin with some kind of genealogy. For example, Josephus's autobiography and Lucian's biography of Demonax both begin by listing the subject's ancestry:

> My family is no ignoble one, tracing its descent far back to priestly ancestors. . . . Moreover, on my mother's side I am of royal blood. . . . My great-grandfather's grandfather was Simon surnamed Psellus. He was a contemporary of the high-priest Hyrcanus. . . . I cite [my pedigree] as I find it recorded in the public registers. (Josephus, *Life*, 1)

> He [Demonax] was a Cypriot by birth, and not of common stock as regards civic rank and property. . . . (Lucian, *Life of Demonax*, 3)

In the same way, two of the four Gospels provide detailed genealogies of Jesus, giving important insights into his family tree:

> The book of the genealogy of Jesus Christ, the son of David, the son of Abraham. Abraham was the father of Isaac, and Isaac the father of Jacob. . . . (Matthew 1:1-2)

> Jesus, when he began his ministry, was about thirty years of age, being the son (as was supposed) of Joseph, the son of Heli, the son of Matthat, the son of Levi, the son of Melchi. . . . (Luke 3:23-24)

Once again, not every ancient biography began with a genealogy, nor does every Gospel contain one (compare Mark 1:1-3; John 1:1-14).

That both Matthew and Luke contain genealogies at the beginning of their narratives is an important clue to the fact that they are intending to give readers biographical information about Jesus.

4. Ancient biographies don't have to be in chronological order.

Another significant parallel between Greco-Roman biographies and the four Gospels is that they are not necessarily strictly chronological accounts of a person's life. In fact, the text can also be arranged topically or thematically.[14] For example, the Roman biographer Suetonius writes the following in his life of Caesar Augustus:

> Having given as it were a summary of his life, I shall now take up its various phases one by one, *not in chronological order, but by categories,* to make the account clearer and more intelligible. (Suetonius, *Life of the Deified Augustus,* 9)[15]

This is strikingly similar to what Papias, the early church father, has to say about the Gospel of Mark:

> Mark, having become Peter's interpreter, wrote down accurately everything he remembered, *though not in order,* of the things either said or done by Christ. (Papias of Hierapolis)[16]

In other words—and this is important—ancient biographers were not as worried about *exactitude* as are modern biographers, who often want to provide the precise date, time, and place something happened. Sometimes ancient biographies give you this kind of information, but lots of times they don't. As a result, when it comes to ancient biographies, you can't assume that because one thing is recorded after another, the events necessarily happened exactly in that order. On the other hand, arranging a biography thematically rather than chronologically doesn't magically transform it into folklore or fiction. The same thing is true for the Gospels. Just because the authors of the Gospels did not follow the standards of modern biography does not mean that they did not intend to tell us what Jesus actually said and did.

5. Ancient biographies don't tell you everything about a person.

Ancient biographers—unlike some modern biographers, who often strive to give comprehensive portraits of their subjects—often did not even attempt to tell readers everything about the person whose life they were describing. Consider, for example, the words of Plutarch, the Greek historian, in his biography of Alexander the Great:

> It is the life of Alexander the king, and of Caesar, who overthrew Pompey, that I am writing in this book, and the multitude of deeds to be treated is so great that I shall make no other preface than to entreat my readers, in case I do not tell of all the famous actions of these men, nor even speak exhaustively at all in each particular case, but in epitome for the most part, not to complain. For it is not Histories I am writing, but Lives. (Plutarch, *Life of Alexander*, 1.1)[17]

Because Plutarch is not writing a "history" (Greek *historia*) of the Greek empire but a "life" (Greek *bios*) of Alexander the Great, by definition he is not going to speak exhaustively about all the deeds done by Alexander. This does not mean Plutarch's biography is "unhistorical"; it just means that it is incomplete.[18]

The same thing is true of the Gospels: they are not written to tell us *everything* Jesus did and said. Should there be any doubt about this, notice the striking similarity between the ending of Lucian's biography of his teacher Demonax and the ending of the Gospel of John:

> These are a very few things out of many which I might have mentioned, but they will suffice to give my readers a notion of the sort of man he [Demonax] was. (Lucian, *Life of Demonax*, 67)[19]

> But there are also many other things which Jesus did; were every one
> of them to be written, I suppose that the world itself could not contain
> the books that would be written. (John 21:25)

What an amazing parallel! Could it be any clearer that John is writing a kind of biography of Jesus? In light of such evidence, the idea that the Gospels are not biographies just because they are incomplete records of Jesus's life represents a complete failure to pay attention to literary clues in the books. The selective nature of the Gospels puts them on equal footing with ancient biographies, which also tended to be very selective.

In light of such parallels, twenty-first-century New Testament scholars have done almost a complete about-face on the question of whether or not the Gospels are biographies. In the words of Graham Stanton and James Dunn:

> I do not think it is now possible to deny that the Gospels are a subset of
> the broad literary genre of "lives," that is, biographies.[20]

> Since the 1970s . . . it has become much clearer that the Gospels are
> in fact very similar in type to *ancient* biographies (Greek *bioi;* Latin,
> *vitae*).[21]

Numerous other examples could be given, but let these two suffice to make the point. The old idea that the Gospels are not biographies but folklore and fairy stories completely fails to reckon with the literary evidence. It is long since time for it to be consigned to the trash bin of history. The Gospels are biographies.

Of course, this does not mean that there are *no* differences between the four Gospels and ancient Greco-Roman biographies. Perhaps the most obvious one is that these four books are entitled "Gospels" or "Good News" (Greek *euangelion*) and not "lives" (Greek *bios*). Why? For now, it's enough to point out that the language of "good news" comes straight from the book of Isaiah, which proclaims the "good news" of the coming of God:[22]

Get you up to a high mountain,
O Zion, herald of *good news;*
lift up your voice with strength,
O Jerusalem, herald of *good news,*
lift it up, fear not;
say to the cities of Judah,
"Behold your God!"
Behold, the Lord GOD comes with might. (Isaiah 40:9-10)[23]

All four Gospels explicitly quote this passage in their opening chapters
(see Matthew 3:1-3; Mark 1:1-3; Luke 3:1-6; John 1:23). As such, Isaiah's
prophecy may provide us with a clue to the real difference between
the Gospels and ancient Greco-Roman biographies. The Gospels are
not just about the life of the man Jesus of Nazareth; they are about the
coming of God in the person of Jesus. As we will see in later chapters,
the Gospels may be a unique kind of biography, because they are recording the life of a unique person.

The Gospels Are Historical *Biographies*

But we can't stop there. The four Gospels are not just *any* kind of ancient biography. They are *historical* biographies, two of which explicitly claim to tell us what Jesus actually did and said and to be based on
eyewitness testimony (Luke 1:1-4; John 21:20-24).

The reason the historical character of the Gospels is important is
that some scholars claim that the authors of the Gospels did not even
intend to give us the historical truth about the words and deeds of
Jesus. The only way to hold such a view, however, is to ignore the fact
that *ancient biographers often insist that they are recording the truth
about what someone did and said.* For example, in his biography of the
philosopher Demonax, Lucian makes sure to let the reader know that
he was an eyewitness and a disciple of Demonax himself:

I speak with reference to the Boeotian Sostratus . . . and to Demonax, the philosopher. *Both these men I saw myself,* and saw with

wonderment: and under one of them, Demonax, *I was long a student.* (Lucian, *Life of Demonax,* 1)[24]

One reason that Lucian may stress this point is that elsewhere in his writings, he insists on the ancient historian's obligation to tell the truth:

The historian's task is one: to tell it as it happened. . . . This is the one peculiar characteristic of history, and to truth alone must sacrifice be made. (Lucian, *How to Write History,* 39, 40)[25]

Along similar lines, the first-century Jewish writer Josephus insists on the historical truth of his autobiography:

Having reached this point in my narrative, I propose to address a few words to Justus, who has produced his own account of these affairs, and to others who, while professing to write history, care little for truth, and either from spite or partiality, have no scruples about false-hood. The procedure of such persons resembles indeed the forgers of contracts, but, having no corresponding penalty to fear, they can afford to disdain veracity. . . . [But] veracity is incumbent upon a his-torian. (Josephus, *Life,* 336–39)

Notice that there is no trace of the idea that accounts in a biogra-phy can be true "whether or not they happened." To the contrary, Josephus insists that the biography he is writing is a subset of "his-tory" (Greek *historia*). This means that an author ought to tell the "truth" (Greek *alētheia*) about what happened, rather than "false-hood" (Greek *pseudos*). Of course, scholars may dispute whether or not Josephus or any other biographer was successful in telling the truth. But they can't dispute that the genre of his writing is historical biography, and that he is purporting to tell what actually happened. As a result, any scholar who were to compare Josephus's autobiog-raphy to "folklore" or "fairy stories" would be considered ridiculous.

Nonetheless, this is exactly how scholars such as Rudolf Bultmann portray the Gospels.

If we look at what the four Gospels actually *say* about what kinds of books they are, we discover that two of them emphasize that they are recording what Jesus actually did and said. They also claim that they are based on eyewitness testimony. In other words, they insist that they are historical biographies. Consider, once again, the prologue to the Gospel of Luke:

> Inasmuch as many have undertaken to compile a *narrative* of the things which have been accomplished among us, just as they were delivered to us by *those who from the beginning were eyewitnesses* and ministers of the word, it seemed good to me also, having followed all things closely for some time past, to write carefully in order for you, most excellent Theophilus, *that you may know the facts* concerning the things of which you have been informed." (Luke 1:1-4)[26]

In order to understand the importance of Luke's prologue for our argument, four points need to be explained. First, as many scholars point out, Luke's prologue is strikingly similar to the prologues found in ancient Greco-Roman histories, by authors such as Herodotus, Thucydides, and Josephus.[27] Like the prologues of other ancient histories, Luke's prologue is intended to signal to the reader that the Gospel is historical in character. Second, Luke uses the word "narrative" (Greek *diēgēsis*) to describe his book. As Joseph Fitzmyer has shown, ancient Greco-Roman authors often use this word specifically for "the writing of history" (see Josephus, *Life*, 336; Lucian, *How to Write History*, 55).[28] Third, Luke insists that his historical narrative is based on the testimony of "eyewitnesses (Greek *autoptai*) from the beginning" of Jesus's public ministry. Now, why would Luke emphasize the eyewitness nature of his sources if he were just telling folktales? Clearly, Luke wants his readers to know that what he says about Jesus can be corroborated by those who knew him. Fourth and finally, Luke explicitly states that he is writing so that his audience might know "the facts" (Greek *asphaleian*). Although some English Bibles translate the Greek word *asphalēia* as "truth," elsewhere Luke consistently uses it to refer to secure and verifiable facts (see Acts 21:34; 22:30; 25:26).[29] In other words, *the Gospel of Luke begins by insisting that it is an accurate, factual account, based directly on eyewitness testimony of what Jesus did and said.* In support of this, in the book of Acts, Luke refers back to his own Gospel as an account of "all that Jesus began to do and teach" (Acts 1:1). So much for the idea that the writers of the Gospels did not intend to tell us "what Jesus really did and said"![30] According to Luke, that is *exactly* what he did in writing his Gospel.

And it's not just Luke. The same thing is true of the Gospel of John. In John's account of the death of Jesus on the cross and at the very end of the Gospel, the author insists that his Gospel is based on eyewitness testimony:

> *He who saw it has borne witness*—his testimony is true, and he knows that he tells *the truth*—that you also may believe. (John 19:35)

> *This is the disciple who is bearing witness to these things, and who has written these things; and we know that his testimony is true.* But there are also many other things which Jesus did; were every one of them to be written, I suppose that the world itself could not contain the books that would be written. (John 21:24-25)

Notice that the eyewitness "testimony" (Greek *martyria*) contained in the Gospel of John is not just any kind of truth. It is the truth about the things Jesus "did" (Greek *epoiēsen*). In this way, the author of the Gospel signals to his readers that he is writing a kind of historical biography in which he intends to record what Jesus actually did (see also John 20:30; 21:25).[31]

Are the Gospels Verbatim Transcripts?

Before I bring this chapter to a close, it's important to be clear about what it means to say the Gospels are historical biographies and what it does not mean. On the one hand—and I cannot overemphasize the point—it does *not* mean that the Gospels are verbatim transcripts of what Jesus said and did. One reason this needs to be stressed is because it's very easy for modern-day people in our age of audio and video recording to equate the historical truth of the Gospels with word-for-word accuracy. On the other hand, the historical character of the Gospels *does* mean that the authors intend to record *the substance* of what Jesus really said and did.

For example, the ancient Greek historian Thucydides makes clear that when he is recording the speeches that were given during the Peloponnesian War, he is not necessarily giving a verbatim account:

> With reference to the speeches in this history, some were delivered before the war began, others while it was going on; some I heard myself, others I got from various quarters; *it was in all cases difficult to carry them word for word in one's memory*; so my habit has been to make the speakers say what was in my opinion demanded of them by the various occasions, *of course adhering as closely as possible to the general sense of what they really said.* (Thucydides, *History of the Peloponnesian War* 1.22.1)[32]

Notice here that when it comes to the question of the content of historical speeches, "one size does not fit all." Some speeches are based on Thucydides's own memory, some on the testimony of others. Either way, he always attempts to stick as closely as possible to "the general sense" of what was really said. The same thing is probably true for the Gospels: some accounts of what Jesus said are firsthand testimony, based on the memory of the disciples, while others are secondhand and based on oral tradition (see Luke 1:1-4). In either case, the primary goal is not necessarily to give a word-for-word account, but to record the substance of what Jesus actually said.

For this reason, the primary focus of this book is not on the exact details of the Gospel accounts but rather—to use the words of Thucydides—the "general sense" of what Jesus "really said." Indeed, the Gospels show us that although the writers are interested in real history, they did not intend to create verbatim transcripts. For example, if you compare Jesus's words of institution at the Last Supper among the various New Testament accounts, you will quickly discover that they are not identical (see Matthew 26:26-29; Mark 14:22-25; Luke 22:19-20; 1 Corinthians 11:23-26). As New Testament scholar John Meier points out:

> [T]here is real reason to wonder whether the Gospel tradition and the evangelists were all that concerned about the precise wording of what Jesus said. . . . For example, we have four reports of what Jesus said over the bread and wine at the Last Supper, . . . and all four versions differ among themselves. . . . Obviously, Jesus was able to say these words only once before his life abruptly ended. . . . We have here a telling datum: the "eucharistic words" were clearly important to the early Church—witness their four formulations! Yet importance to the early Church guaranteed *agreement in substance, not in exact wording.* If this is true for these vital "words of institution" at the Last Supper, do we have any reason to think that other words of Jesus were preserved with greater zeal for word-for-word accuracy?[33]

Along similar lines, Joseph Ratzinger (Pope Benedict XVI) emphasizes that the four Gospels "make no claim to literary accuracy" in the manner of a "recorded transcript." However, they do claim to correctly render "the *substance* of the discourses" of Jesus.[34] They do so precisely because they *are* biographies.

To sum up what we've learned in this chapter: it should be clear by now that the contention that the Gospels are not biographies is just plain wrong. Moreover, the use of modern-day children's folktales like the story of George Washington and the cherry tree as analogies for the kind of stories the Gospels contain is historically indefensible and, quite frankly, academically irresponsible. Like the Telephone game, these kinds of comparisons utterly fail to do justice to the actual literary genre and historical character of the four Gospels. The Gospels are ancient biographies that intend to record the substance of what Jesus of Nazareth really did and said.

Of course, the fact that the Gospels are biographies doesn't settle the question of whether their authors *are* telling us the truth about Jesus. For one thing, were the authors of the Gospels even *able* to remember accurately what Jesus did and said? Exactly how much time had passed between the life of Jesus and the writing of the Gospels? What if the Gospels were written too late to be historically reliable? These questions take us straight into the topic of our next chapter: the dating of the Gospels.

The Dating of the Gospels

Not long ago, a friend of mine came to me upset because his son had come home from school telling him he had learned in religion class that the New Testament Gospels were written "over a hundred years after Jesus died." My friend's son wanted to know: Is this true? Were the Gospels really written *that long* after Jesus lived and died? How could they be reliable if so much time had passed between when Jesus lived and when they were written? And how could the apostles and their followers have written them? After all, a hundred years after Jesus, wouldn't all of the eyewitnesses to his life be long dead?

In other words, when it comes to the historical sources about Jesus, *chronological proximity matters*. The further in time you get away from the life of Jesus, the more likely it becomes that those who would remember what he did and said weren't around to tell what had happened and what hadn't. This is what Bart Ehrman refers to as the problem of the "time gap" between Jesus and the Gospels.[1] Most scholars these days agree that Jesus died sometime around AD 30–33. The majority of contemporary scholars also agree that the four Gospels were not written until the late first century. According to standard textbook introductions, like the one written by Ehrman himself,

Mark is usually dated roughly to around AD 70, Matthew and Luke to around AD 80–85, and John's Gospel to around AD 90–95. According to Ehrman, this means that some four to six decades transpired between the death of Jesus and the writing of the Gospels, during which time stories about Jesus were circulated by word of mouth, "year after year, decade after decade," by a long chain of anonymous storytellers.[2] These storytellers supposedly changed the details of Jesus's life and invented whole episodes about Jesus. (Remember the Telephone game?)[3] Then, finally, at the end of the first century, four equally anonymous authors decided to write down the stories they had heard. Only then did the Gospels as we know them start to come into existence.[4]

What are we to make of this scenario? When were the four Gospels actually written? How much time had passed between the death of Jesus and the moment the first evangelist set pen to papyrus? After all, ancient books weren't published with copyright dates as they are today. So how do scholars determine the date of the Gospels when the books themselves don't contain explicit information telling us when they were written? Most important of all, were the four Gospels written too late to be historically reliable?

In order to try to answer some of these questions, we need to go back and look carefully at what the evidence suggests about how memories of Jesus were transmitted and at exactly how wide the so-called "time gap" between the life of Jesus and the four first-century Gospels really is.

The Memories of Jesus's Students

In recent decades, an enormous amount of work has been done by New Testament scholars on the question of what happened during the years between the life of Jesus and the writing of the Gospels.[5] If we leave aside the imaginary scenario of an anonymous chain of storytellers and look instead at the actual *evidence* provided by the New Testament, the stages of development between Jesus and the Gospels can be outlined as follows (for references, see the endnotes):

THREE STAGES IN THE FORMATION OF THE GOSPELS

Stage 1. The Life and Teaching of Jesus

As a Jewish "rabbi" (*rabbi*), Jesus "taught" (*didaskō*) his "students" (*mathētai*) in the context of a *rabbi-student relationship*. His students lived with him and learned from him for some three years. During this time, Jesus expected his students to "remember" (*mnēmoneuō*) what he said and instructed them to begin "teaching" (*didaskō*) others while he was still alive (see Mark 4:1-20; 6:1-13, 30; 8:18; 9:5; 11:21; and parallels).[6]

Stage 2. The Preaching of Jesus's Students

After Jesus's death, the students of Jesus "remembered" (*mnēmoneuō*) what he had said and done, and they "taught" (*didaskō*) others about what they had seen and heard. Their preaching was based on the *skilled memories* of trained students and the *rehearsed memories* of disciples who repeatedly preached about what Jesus said and did (see John 2:22; 12:16; 15:20; 16:4; Acts 4:2-20; 20:35).[7]

Stage 3: The Writing of the Gospels

Eventually, the evangelists "wrote" (*graphō*) either what they themselves "witnessed" (*martyreō*) or what was "handed on" (*paradidōmi*) to them by "eyewitnesses" (*autoptai*) who were present with Jesus "from the beginning" (see Luke 1:1-4; John 21:24).[8]

If this description of the stages of tradition through which the life and teaching of Jesus have come down to us is basically correct, then three important implications follow.

First, Jesus's disciples were *students* who remembered what he did and what he said. Although nowadays we tend to use the word "disciple" to refer to a "believer," in the first century AD, it literally meant "student" (Greek *mathētēs*; Hebrew *talmid*).[9] Being a student in the ancient world was radically different from what it is like today, when it simply means you may (or may not) listen to a fifty-minute lecture three times a week for a semester. Being one of Jesus's students meant following him everywhere, and listening to him *all the time*, for anywhere between one and three *years*. As the Gospels make clear, it also meant remembering what he said (Matthew 16:9; Mark 8:18; John 15:20; 16:4). In the words of John Meier:

> Jesus called individuals to follow him literary, physically, as he undertook various preaching tours of Galilee, Judea, and surrounding areas. . . . Following Jesus as his disciple meant leaving behind one's home, parents, and livelihood. One could not follow Jesus simply by staying at home and studying his teachings or by going to his schoolhouse and attending his lectures.[10]

If we take seriously the evidence for the apostolic origins of the Gospels, then the four Gospels are not based on the memories of just *anybody*. They either contain the memories of Jesus's students (the Gospels of Matthew and John) or are based on the memories of Jesus's students that were passed on to their followers (such as Mark's record of Peter's preaching). Even Luke's Gospel claims to be based on the testimony of those who were eyewitnesses "from the beginning" of Jesus's public ministry (Luke 1:1).

Notice how different this is from the now widespread theory that our information about Jesus is primarily based on decade after decade of anonymous storytelling. Of course uncontrolled stories about Jesus circulated; the Gospel of Luke even mentions anonymous "reports" (Greek *ēchos*) making the rounds during Jesus's lifetime (Luke 4:37). However, as I have argued in earlier chapters, *that's not what the four Gospels claim to be*. They are not the last links in a long chain of anonymous rumors and stories. They are ancient biographies and authoritative accounts of the life of Jesus based on the testimony of his students. As such, they function in part precisely as controls over what was being said about Jesus.[11]

Second, in the years between Jesus's death and the writing of the Gospels, the disciples of Jesus would have frequently *rehearsed* their memories in the course of preaching and teaching. In fact, as Dale

Allison points out, the disciples would have likely begun "rehears-
ing" the teachings of Jesus already during his lifetime, starting with
the first time they were sent on mission by Jesus himself (see Matthew 10:1-23; Mark 6:7-12; Luke 9:1-10).[12] One reason this is important
is that, as Richard Bauckham states, "Frequent recall is an important
factor in both retaining the memory and retaining it accurately."[13]
Anyone who is a teacher knows this to be true. I might not be able to
tell you what I did last week, but I could give you a three-hour lecture
about Jesus and the Jewish roots of the Last Supper with zero prepa-
ration because I have been talking about it all the time for the last ten
years.[14] That's one key difference between rehearsed memories and
incidental memories.

Third, even if the Gospels weren't written until the late first century AD, they would still have appeared *well within the lifetime of Jesus's
apostles and their followers*. Think about it for a moment: if Mark and
Luke were in their twenties or thirties when they became disciples of
Peter and Paul in the 40s and 50s AD, then Mark would have been in
his forties in AD 65–70, and Luke in his fifties or sixties in AD 80–85.
There's nothing remotely implausible about them composing Gospels
at this age. In fact, Josephus tells us that he wrote his famous history of
the Jewish people in "the fifty-sixth year of my life" (Josephus, *Antiquities*, 20.267). Likewise, if Matthew and John were in their twenties
or thirties when they became disciples of Jesus around AD 30, then
Matthew would have been in his seventies or eighties in AD 80–85,
and John would have been in his eighties or nineties in AD 90–95. To
be sure, this is getting up there in years, especially for John. However,
the early church fathers actually tell us that the apostle John lived to
be "a very old man," dying sometime around AD 98 during the reign of
the emperor Trajan (Jerome, *Lives of Illustrious Men*, 9). Moreover, as
Irenaeus pointed out long ago and as anyone who spends time with the
elderly knows, the memories of one's formative years are often much
clearer than those of one's old age.[15]

Finally, if Matthew and John did outlive their fellow disciples,
then it makes sense that they would likely be asked to record their
memories of Jesus before their generation died off. To take an ancient

example: Josephus says that he wanted to write his own autobiography "while there are still persons living who can either disprove or corroborate my testimony" (*Antiquities*, 20.266). In our own times, in the last couple of decades, people who survived the Holocaust in the 1930s and '40s have been repeatedly interviewed precisely in order to record their memories of the events before their generation passes away. Yet some Holocaust survivors—such as Elie Wiesel, the famous author of *Night*—are still alive today, and we are well into the twenty-first century! In fact, Wiesel published two volumes of his memoirs in the late 1990s.[16] In other words, some people die young; other people live long and write books.

Perhaps most important of all, *although the four Gospels are often dated to the late first century, these proposed dates are by no means as certain as they are often made out to be.* Textbook introductions to the New Testament often simply list the dates of AD 65–70 for Mark, AD 80–85 for Matthew and Luke, and AD 90–100 for John as if they were *facts.*[17] However, as one textbook admits, these are just "rough estimates."[18] The question is: How rough are we talking? One decade? Two? Three? The answer is important, since the chronological proximity of the Gospels to the life of Jesus is a significant factor in evaluating them as historical sources. When we look carefully at the actual reasons given for dating all four Gospels to the late first century, we discover that there are some serious problems. In the pages that follow, we will focus primarily on the date of the Synoptic Gospels, since there is not much debate about the date of John's Gospel. Most of the early church fathers as well as contemporary scholars agree that John's Gospel was the last of the four to be written.[19]

The Destruction of the Temple in AD 70

The first major reason often given for dating the Synoptic Gospels to the late first century AD is based on how some scholars interpret Jesus's prophecies of the destruction of the Temple in Jerusalem. In each of the Synoptic Gospels, Jesus declares that the Temple will one day be completely destroyed:

Jesus left the temple and was going away, when his disciples came to point out to him the buildings of the temple. But he answered them, "You see all these, do you not? Truly, I say to you, there will not be left here one stone upon another, that will not be thrown down." (Matthew 24:1-2)

And as he came out of the temple, one of his disciples said to him, "Look, Teacher, what wonderful stones and what wonderful buildings!" And Jesus said to him, "Do you see these great buildings? There will not be left here one stone upon another, that will not be thrown down." (Mark 13:1-2)

And when he drew near and saw the city he wept over it, saying, ". . . [T]he days shall come upon you, when your enemies will cast up a bank about you and surround you, and hem you in on every side, and dash you to the ground, you and your children within you, and they will not leave one stone upon another in you; because you did not know the time of your visitation." (Luke 19:41-44)

But when you see Jerusalem surrounded by armies, then know that its desolation has come near. (Luke 21:20)

According to some scholars, Jesus's oracles about the destruction of the Temple in Jerusalem are not actual prophecies delivered almost forty years before the event. Instead, these scholars think these parts of the Gospel of Mark were written up after the fact by later Christians reflecting on their own experiences of the current events revolving around the destruction of the Temple in the year AD 70.[20] According to this theory, the reason the Gospels of Matthew and Luke contain more details about how Jerusalem will be destroyed—such as the fact that it will be "surrounded by armies" (Luke 19:43; 21:20) and "burned" (compare Matthew 22:7)—is that their accounts were written even longer after the destruction of the Temple than Mark's was.[21] As a result, Matthew and Luke's Gospels get dated to the 80s and 90s of the first century.

This is the primary foundation for dating the Synoptic Gospels to the late first century AD. The argument rests almost entirely on the claim that Jesus's oracles about the destruction of the Jerusalem Temple were written up *after the fact*. Read through the Synoptic Gospels for yourself and see. There is no other historical event on which to anchor the dating of the Gospels to the late first century.[22] Jesus's prophecies of the destruction of the Temple constitute the main "evidence." But this way of dating the Synoptic Gospels has several major weaknesses.

For one thing, the entire late-dating scheme is based on the *assumption* that Jesus of Nazareth could not actually have predicted the coming destruction of the Temple or described it in any detail. The problems with such an assumption are many, but one in particular stands out for me. If you know anything at all about the history of Israel, then you know that the Temple and the city of Jerusalem had *already been destroyed in 586 BC*—over five hundred years before the birth of Jesus. The first destruction of the Temple by the Babylonian Empire is described in the book of Kings:

> In the fifth month, on the seventh day of the month . . . Nebuzaradan, the captain of the bodyguard, a servant of the king of Babylon, came to Jerusalem. *And he burned the house of the Lord*, and the king's house and all the houses of Jerusalem; every great house he burned down. And all the army of the Chaldeans . . . *broke down the walls around Jerusalem*. (2 Kings 25:8-10)

Notice the exact kinds of details—such as the burning of the Temple and the siege of the city walls—details that some claim could only be described after AD 70. As if they had never happened before! As the British New Testament scholar C. H. Dodd pointed out long ago:

> So far as any historical event has colored the picture, it is not Titus' capture of Jerusalem in AD 70, but Nebuchadnezzar's capture in 586 BC. There is no single trait of the forecast which cannot be documented directly out of the Old Testament.[23]

In fact, Jesus of Nazareth apparently wasn't the only Jew in the first century AD who was using the Old Testament to warn that the Temple would be destroyed again. According to Josephus, around AD 66, a man named "Jesus the son of Ananias" also drew on the book of Jeremiah to predict that Jerusalem and the Temple would be destroyed (Josephus, *Jewish War*, 6.301; compare Jeremiah 7).[24] If Jeremiah could prophesy the destruction of Jerusalem, and Jesus the son of Ananias could prophesy the destruction of the Temple, then there is no reason that Jesus of Nazareth couldn't do the same. In fact, as I have written elsewhere (in a much longer book), there are plenty of compelling reasons for concluding that the oracles about the Temple destruction in Mark 13 originated with Jesus himself.[25] And if they do go back to him, they simply can't be used to "date" the Gospel. These passages aren't meant to tell you when the Gospel was written. They are meant to tell you what Jesus said about the eventual destruction of Jerusalem.

Equally important, the destruction of the Temple is never mentioned as a *past event* in any of the Gospels. If the Gospels were written after the destruction of Jerusalem in AD 70, then why don't the writers emphasize that Jesus's prophecy had been fulfilled? That would be the natural thing to do. In fact, that is exactly what Luke does in the Acts of the Apostles with regard to another prophecy that was actually fulfilled *before* his book was written:

> Now in these days prophets came down from Jerusalem to Antioch. And one of them named Agabus stood up and foretold by the Spirit that there would be a great famine over all the world; *and this took place in the days of Claudius.* (Acts 11:27-28)

Isn't it strange that Luke would go out of his way to emphasize that the prophecy of a little-known Christian prophet named Agabus had been fulfilled in the days of the emperor Claudius (the 40s AD) but fail to mention that Jesus's prophecy of the destruction of the Temple had been fulfilled in AD 70? Why doesn't he say that Jesus's word "took place in the days of the emperor Titus"? I'll give you one explanation: perhaps Luke does not mention the fulfillment of Jesus's prophecy because it had *not yet taken place.*

Finally, if you look carefully at Jesus's words about the destruction of the Temple, you will discover that certain parts make sense only if they are warnings delivered *before the event.* Remarkably, this is not just true of the Gospel of Mark; it is even more true of the Gospels of Matthew and Luke, which are supposed to have been written over a decade later. Compare Jesus's warnings about what to do when "the abomination of desolation"—an Old Testament expression related to the destruction of the Temple (see Daniel 9:24-27)—is set up in the Jerusalem Temple:

> But when you see the abomination of desolation set up where it ought not to be (let the reader understand), then let those who are in Judea flee to the mountains. . . . *Pray that it may not happen in winter.* (Mark 13:14,18)

> So when you see the abomination of desolation spoken of by the prophet Daniel, standing in the holy place (let the reader understand), then let those who are in Judea flee to the mountains. . . . *Pray that your flight may not be in winter or on a Sabbath.* (Matthew 24:15, 20)

> But when you see Jerusalem surrounded by armies, then know that its desolation has come near. Then let those who are in Judea flee to the mountains, *and let those who are inside the city depart, and let not those who are out in the country enter it.* (Luke 21:20-21)

Think about these quotations for a moment. Why would Mark exhort his readers to pray that the desolation of the Temple not happen "in winter" (Mark 13:18) if they knew it had already happened in the late *summer?* (The Temple was destroyed by the Romans in late July or early August of AD 70.)[26] And why would Luke add a warning for his audience not to "enter into the city" (Luke 21:21) if the city had already been destroyed? Finally, if the Gospel of Matthew really appeared over a decade later than Mark's Gospel, then why would Matthew *add* for his audience to pray that the desolation not take place in winter "or on a Sabbath" (Matthew 24:20) if it had already happened? Why add a command to pray that something not take place at a particular time if it had already happened, was widely known about, and could not be changed? In the words of W. D. Davies and Dale Allison: "What would be the point of inserting an imperative to pray about a past event, that it not take place at a particular time?"[27]

In the face of such evidence, the first major pillar for the late dating of the Synoptic Gospels—like the stones of the Temple— comes crashing to the ground. In the words of the Synoptic experts E. P. Sanders and Margaret Davies: "There is no material in Mark which must be dated after 70."[28] Along similar lines, in one recent study of the date of Mark's Gospel, James Crossley concludes that the Gospel could have been written "any time between the thirties CE and c. 70 CE."[29]

The Synoptic Problem

The second major reason for dating the Synoptic Gospels to the late first century AD is based on a particular theory about the order in which the Gospels were written. This theory is known as the *Two-Source Theory*.[30] According to this theory, the Gospel of Mark was the first to be written. Around the same time, a hypothetical gospel, which modern scholars refer to as "Q" (from the German *Quelle*, meaning "source"), also supposedly came into existence. Later on, the Gospels of Luke and Matthew used both Mark and "Q" as their two primary sources in writing their Gospels. Any other passages found only in Matthew's Gospel are attributed to a hypothetical source called "M," and any passages found only in Luke's Gospel are attributed to a hypothetical source called "L." The theory can be diagrammed as follows:

THE TWO-SOURCE THEORY

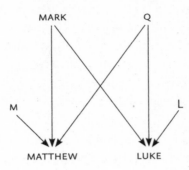

For many scholars, the Two-Source Theory plays a key role in the dating of the Synoptic Gospels to the late first century because if the Gospel of Mark was written around the time of the destruction of the Temple in AD 70, and if the Gospels of Matthew and Luke used Mark as a source, then that means Matthew and Luke's Gospels were written sometime after AD 70. By allowing ten to twenty years for the Gospel of Mark to circulate throughout the Roman Empire and find its way into the hands of the other two evangelists, proponents of this view arrive at the "rough estimate" of AD 80–85 for the Gospels of Matthew and Luke.[31]

Although at first glance this might seem like a logical way to date the Gospels, a closer look reveals several major weaknesses. For one thing, as we have seen previously, if the Gospel of Mark can't actually be dated to around AD 70 on the basis of Jesus's prophecies about the destruction of the Temple, then one of the primary reasons for claiming the Gospels of Matthew and Luke were written after the destruction of the Temple vanishes.

Moreover, if there is any subject that has been debated since the very beginnings of Christianity, it is the question of the order in which the Gospels of Matthew, Mark, and Luke were written.[32] As we have seen in chapter 3, although the early church fathers were unanimous on who wrote the Gospels, they did not agree about the *order* in which the Gospels were written. For example, Clement of Alexandria held that Matthew wrote first, Luke wrote second, Mark wrote third, and John wrote last (see Eusebius, *Church History*, 6.14.6–10). On the other hand, Origen of Alexandria argued that Matthew wrote first, Mark wrote second, and Luke wrote third, with John once again coming in last place (see Eusebius, *Church History* 6.25.3–6). Finally, Tertullian of Carthage states that Matthew and John were published first, and that Mark and Luke came later (Tertullian, *Against Marcion*, 4.5).

In modern times, the debate over the order of the Gospels has become so complex that it is now referred to as "the Synoptic *Problem*." Although many popular books on the Gospels mention only the Two-Source Theory, this hypothesis is by no means the only solution. As every New Testament scholar knows, in the last hundred years, there have been *multiple* theories about the order in which the Synoptic Gospels were written, theories that have been argued by well-respected scholars (see the chart entitled "The Synoptic Problem: Multiple Solutions").

THE SYNOPTIC PROBLEM: MULTIPLE SOLUTIONS

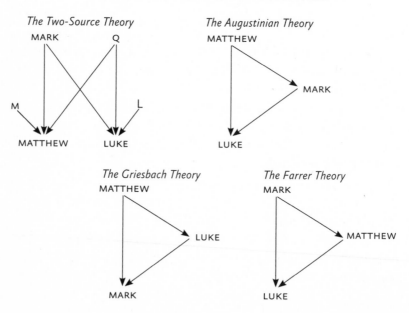

For example, a few modern scholars argue that Matthew wrote first, Mark wrote second, and Luke used them both. This is known as *the Augustinian theory*, after Saint Augustine of Hippo, who articulated this view around AD 400.[33] Other scholars argue that Matthew wrote first, Luke wrote second, and Mark used them both. This is known as *the Griesbach theory*, after Johan Jakob Griesbach, who first proposed it in the 1780s.[34] Finally, in recent decades, a number of scholars have argued that Mark wrote first, Matthew wrote second, and Luke used them both. From this point of view, there is no need for a hypothetical Gospel of "Q." This is known as *the Farrer theory*, after Austin Farrer, the English scholar who was the first to propose it in the 1950s.[35]

The reader will be relieved to know that I am not going to go into an analysis of the strengths and weaknesses of each of these theories. That would require a whole book. My point is simply this: if Gospel experts cannot agree on a solution to the Synoptic Problem—and there are literally *dozens* of theories, many more than I've mentioned here—then the Two-Source Theory should not be presented as if it were a *fact* that can be used to date the Gospels of Matthew and Luke to the late first century AD. In the words of Joseph Fitzmyer: "The history of Synoptic research reveals that the [Synoptic] problem is *practically insoluble*."[36] If the Synoptic Problem really is insoluble, then any solution—including the Two-Source Theory—cannot be a reliable starting point for dating the Gospels.

Furthermore, the Two-Source Theory has come under heavy fire in recent years. For example, the existence of "Q" has been called into question by scholars such as Mark Goodacre, whose 2002 book *The Case Against Q* changed my mind on the subject.[37] (I used to be a diehard "Q" believer.) One huge problem with the Two-Source Theory is that it relies on "Q," which exists only in the imagination of the scholars who believe in it. No manuscript of "Q" has ever been found. No reference to "Q" is ever made in the writings of the church fathers. Finally, there are so many internal problems with the Two-Source Theory that E. P. Sanders and Margaret Davies once concluded:

Of all the solutions, this one [the Two-Source Theory], which remains the dominant hypothesis, is *least satisfactory*.[38]

If Sanders and Davies are right, then the Two-Source Theory should certainly not be presented as if it were a factual basis for dating the Gospels to the late first century.

The Ending of the Acts of the Apostles

What then should we do? Should we just give up when it comes to dating the Gospels? I don't think so. Before bringing this chapter to an end, let's look at one point of agreement among the different theories about the order of the Synoptic Gospels that I think may help us in arriving at a general date. This point centers on the ending of the Acts of the Apostles.

Whichever solution to the Synoptic Problem you take, all of the major theories we have discussed so far agree that the Gospel of Luke was written *after* one (or both) of the Gospels of Matthew and Mark. The reason for this is simple: Luke tells us that other narratives of Jesus's life were already in existence when he decided to write his Gospel. He does this in the opening lines of the book:

> *Inasmuch as many have undertaken to compile a narrative* of the things which have been accomplished among us . . . *it seemed good to me also to write carefully* in order for you, most excellent Theophilus. . . . (Luke 1:1, 3)[39]

In light of these words and the extensive verbatim parallels between Luke and the Gospels of Mark and Matthew, many scholars agree that in writing the Gospel of Luke, the author used one or both of the Gospels of Mark and Matthew as sources.

The reason this is significant for dating the Gospels is that when we turn to the Acts of the Apostles, we discover evidence that this second volume by Luke (Acts 1:1) appears to have been written much earlier than is often supposed. For example, the book of Acts ends with Luke describing in the first person his arrival with the apostle Paul in the city of Rome and Paul's subsequent time under house arrest:

> *And so we came to Rome.* And the brethren there, when they heard of us, came as far as the Forum of Appius and Three Taverns to meet us. On seeing them Paul thanked God and took courage. And when we came into Rome, Paul was allowed to stay by himself, with the soldier that guarded him. . . . *And he [Paul] lived there two whole years at his own expense,* and welcomed all who came to him, preaching the kingdom of God and teaching about the Lord Jesus Christ quite openly and unhindered. (Acts 28:14-16, 30-31)

This is how the Acts of the Apostles ends. Now let me ask you a question: *Why does Luke stop so abruptly with Paul's imprisonment in Rome in AD 62?* If Acts was written in the late first century, then why doesn't Luke go on to tell about Paul's martyrdom under Caesar Nero in the late 60s? Although some people claim that the reason is that Acts was just supposed to tell the story of how Christianity got to Rome and then to stop there, the evidence doesn't support this claim.[40] For as the above quote from Acts shows, Luke himself tells you that there already *were* Christian "brethren" in Rome when he and Paul got there (Acts 28:14).[41] Moreover, throughout the book of Acts, Luke carefully highlights parallels between the life of Jesus and the lives of Peter and Paul.[42] Why then would Luke omit describing the most striking parallel of all—between the execution of Jesus and the executions of Peter and Paul?[43]

The most obvious answer to this question is simple: Luke stopped his story of Paul's life while Paul was in custody in Rome because *that's when the Acts of the Apostles was written*—around AD 62. In fact, it was precisely the ending of Acts that led the famous German scholar Adolf von Harnack, after a lifetime of research on the early Church, to change his mind and to conclude that both the Acts of the Apostles and the Synoptic Gospels were written while Paul was still alive:

We are accordingly left with the result: that the concluding verses of the Acts of the Apostles, taken in conjunction with the absence of any reference in the book to the result of the trial of St. Paul and to his martyrdom, make it *in the highest degree probable that the work was written at a time when St. Paul's trial in Rome had not yet come to an end.*[44]

And Harnack is not alone. After extensive study of Acts, other recent scholars, such as Alexander Mittelstaedt, have also concluded that Acts was written before Paul's execution.[45] I for one find the logic of this argument extremely persuasive—especially when we recall the flimsy reasons given for dating the Gospel of Luke to after the destruction of Jerusalem. Indeed, there's nothing at all implausible about Luke stopping his account once he got up to the present day. In the same way, why did the first-century historian Josephus bring his account of events to an end when he got "up to the present day" (*Antiquities*, 20.267)? Because there wasn't anything else to say. Or to use a more modern example: Why did the papal biographer George Weigel stop the first volume of his famous biography of Pope John Paul II without narrating the pope's dramatic decline and death from Parkinson's disease? Simple. None of that had happened yet. The book was originally published in 1999, when John Paul still had six years left to live. For the same reason, many biographies written during people's lifetimes stop when they get to the *present*. At that point, there isn't anything further to say.

The upshot of the ending of Acts is simple but significant: if the Acts of the Apostles was written before the death of Paul but after the Gospel of Luke, then that means that the Gospel of Luke was written *while Paul was still alive*. And if either the Gospel of Mark or the Gospel of Matthew was written before the Gospel of Luke (see Luke 1:1–4), then that means that either the Gospel of Mark or the Gospel of Matthew (or both) was also written *while Paul was still alive*. In other words, if we take the ending of the Acts of the Apostles as a clue to the date it was written, then we can make a good case that at least two of the three Synoptic Gospels, and perhaps all three, were written sometime before AD 62. If this is right, then the supposed "time gap" between the end of the life of Jesus and the writing of the Gospels shrinks by a few decades. Instead of dating the Synoptic Gospels to the 70s, 80s, and 90s of the first century, we would end up dating them sometime before the early 60s, within the first few decades after Jesus's death. At the very least, the lack of explicit internal evidence for dating the Synoptic Gospels after AD 70, the complexity of the Synoptic Problem, and the ending of Acts place a powerful question mark beside the common dating of the Gospels of Matthew, Mark, and Luke to the late first century.

In essence, there are compelling historical reasons to conclude that the Gospels are not the late-first-century end products of a long chain of anonymous storytelling. Instead, they are ancient biographies written by the students of Jesus and their followers, written well within the lifetimes of the apostles and eyewitnesses to Jesus. As such, they provide us with a sound basis for investigating the historical questions of what Jesus did, what he said, and who he claimed to be. It is to these questions that we now turn.

Jesus and the Jewish Messiah

With everything we've learned about the origins of the Gospels in mind, we can now take up the questions of Jesus's identity: *Who was Jesus of Nazareth?* According to the testimony of the four Gospels, who did he claim to be? Who did his first followers believe him to be? And, even more important, why did they believe in him?

As soon as we ask this question, we run into a bit of a problem—a paradox of sorts. I've noticed this paradox over the last ten years that I've been teaching the Bible as a professor in the classroom. On the one hand, if I ask my students *what kind of Messiah* the Jewish people were waiting for in the first century AD, they all seem to be very clear about the answer. Usually, their standard response goes something like this: "At the time of Jesus, the Jewish people were waiting for an earthly, political Messiah to come and set them free from the Roman Empire." On the other hand, if I ask students *which prophecies* led to this ancient Jewish hope for an earthly, political Messiah, they are often at a complete loss. The classroom quickly falls silent. They often get even quieter when I ask, "Which prophecies of the Messiah did Jesus actually fulfill?" or "What prophecies did the first Jewish Christians think he fulfilled?" Every time I pose these questions, the vast majority of the students (who are usually all Christians) can't answer them. They often can't name a single prophecy that Jesus fulfilled that would show that he was in fact the Messiah. Every now and then, one or two students may bring up the oracle of the virgin who bears a child (Isaiah 7) or the passage about the Suffering Servant (Isaiah 52–53). However, that's usually as far as it goes. If my experiences are any indication, many contemporary Christians believe *that* Jesus was the Messiah, but they don't necessarily know *why* they believe he was the Messiah, much less why his first followers thought he was the long-awaited king of Israel.

In light of this situation, it is important to begin this part of our investigation by looking carefully at certain biblical prophecies of the Messiah that Jesus was believed to have fulfilled. Of course, there are dozens of passages in the Old Testament that came to be interpreted as pointing to the Messiah.[1] We certainly don't have the space to go through all of them here, much less to try to show that Jesus of Nazareth fulfilled them all. But given our interest in who Jesus himself claimed to be, we can focus our attention on a few key prophecies about the *timing* of the coming of the Messiah—prophecies that Jesus seems to have considered to be some of the most important in Jewish Scripture. For when we turn to the Gospels, we find Jesus repeatedly referring to himself and his mission in terms of several prophecies from the book of Daniel (see Daniel 2, 7, 9). As we will see, these passages in Daniel give us the first clues that the Messiah would be not just the long-awaited king, but a divine being who would usher in a heavenly kingdom.

In order to see all of this clearly, we will have to go back to square one and put Jesus's otherwise familiar words in their original first-century Jewish context. Once we do this, we will be able to get a better grasp on what Jewish people in the first century AD were waiting for and why so many of them—starting with Jesus's own Jewish disciples—came to believe that he was indeed the Messiah.

The Kingdom of God

If there's anything Jesus loves to talk about in the Gospels, it is the coming of "the kingdom of God"—or, in Matthew's Gospel, "the kingdom of heaven."[2] For example, let's look at the very beginning of his public ministry:

> Now after John was arrested, Jesus came into Galilee, preaching the gospel of God, and saying, *"The time is fulfilled, and the kingdom of God is at hand;* repent, and believe in the gospel." (Mark 1:14-15)

Along similar lines, throughout the Gospels, Jesus speaks over and over again about the coming of the kingdom of God and the importance of entering into the kingdom so as to have eternal life. Dozens of examples of this could be given; for now, let the following suffice to make the point:

> These twelve Jesus sent out, charging them, . . . "Preach as you go, saying, *'The kingdom of heaven is at hand.'*" (Matthew 10:5, 7)

> But if it is by the finger of God that I cast out demons, then *the kingdom of God has come upon you.* (Luke 11:20)

> Jesus answered [Nicodemus], "Truly, truly, I say to you, unless one is born anew, he cannot see *the kingdom of God.*" (John 3:3)

Now, the question is: What does Jesus *mean* when he refers to "the kingdom of God"? And what does he mean when he says that it is "at hand"? He seems to assume that his Jewish audience will understand what he's talking about. Nowadays, many people think that the kingdom of God is just another way of talking about "life after death" or "going to heaven" when we die. And while it's certainly true that the kingdom of God is tied to eternal life, there's more going on here. The very fact that Jesus can talk about the kingdom as "coming" makes clear that he can't simply be referring to what happens after a person dies. So what does he mean when he speaks about "the time" being fulfilled and the coming of the kingdom being "at hand" (Mark 1:15)?

In this case—and in virtually every other passage we will look at for the rest of this book—the key to unlocking the meaning of Jesus's otherwise mysterious words can be found by going back to the Old Testament. When we do this, we discover something extremely significant. Although the exact expression "kingdom of God" almost never occurs in the Hebrew Scriptures, there is one prominent passage in the Jewish Bible that speaks about the future coming of the kingdom of God: the book of Daniel's famous prophecy of the four pagan kingdoms that are destroyed by the "kingdom" (Aramaic *malku*) of "the God of heaven" (Daniel 2:44).[3] So when Jesus talks about the coming of "the kingdom of God," he is alluding first and foremost to the fulfillment of this famous prophecy from Daniel.[4] Although this prophecy may be unfamiliar to modern-day readers, it was very popular among first-century Jews, because it gave them a *timeline* for when God would establish his kingdom on earth.

This is how the prophecy goes. According to the book of Daniel, in the sixth century BC, King Nebuchadnezzar of Babylon had a dream of a great "image" or statue made out of four precious metals. In the dream, the image is destroyed by a mysterious stone that grows into a great mountain and fills all the earth:

[Daniel said to King Nebuchadnezzar:] "You saw, O king, and behold, a *great image.* . . . The head of this image was of fine *gold*, its breast and arms of *silver*, its belly and thighs of *bronze*, its legs of *iron*, its feet partly of iron and partly of clay. As you looked, *a stone was cut out by no human hand, and it smote the image on its feet of iron and clay, and broke them in pieces*; then the iron, the clay, the bronze, the silver, and the gold, all together were broken in pieces, and became like the chaff of the summer threshing floors; and the wind carried them away, so that not a trace of them could be found. *But the stone that*

struck the image became a great mountain and filled the whole earth."
(Daniel 2:31-35)

What is the meaning of this mysterious dream? How would it have
been interpreted by Jewish people at the time of Jesus?

According to the book of Daniel, the four parts of the statue are *four
pagan kingdoms* (empires), beginning with the Babylonian Empire.
Daniel tells King Nebuchadnezzar that the king himself is "the head
of gold" and that after him shall arise "another kingdom inferior" to
Babylon, represented by silver. Then "a third kingdom of bronze" will
come, followed finally by "a fourth kingdom," which shall be "strong
as iron" at first but then gradually grow weaker, like a mixture of iron
and clay (Daniel 2:36-43). Most important, during the time of the fourth
kingdom—the one made of iron and clay—a fifth kingdom will finally
come, and this shall be the kingdom of God:

> "And in the days of those kings *the God of heaven will set up a king-
> dom which shall never be destroyed*, nor shall its sovereignty be
> left to another people. *It shall break in pieces all these kingdoms
> and bring them to an end, and it shall stand for ever;* just as you saw
> that *a stone was cut from a mountain by no human hand*, and that
> it broke in pieces the iron, the bronze, the clay, the silver, and the
> gold. A great God has made known to the king what shall be here-
> after. The dream is certain, and its interpretation sure." (Dan-
> iel 2:44-45)

It should go without saying that lots could be said about this mysterious oracle. For our purposes, the main point is that according to the
most ancient Jewish interpretations we possess, in the first century
AD, the four pagan kingdoms described by the book of Daniel were interpreted as the four empires that had reigned over the Jewish people
since the time of King Nebuchadnezzar: (1) the Babylonian Empire, (2)
the Medo-Persian Empire, (3) the Greek Empire, and (4) the Roman
Empire.[5]

The reason this ancient Jewish interpretation is important for us is that for many first-century Jews who were following the prophecy of Daniel, the fifth kingdom—the kingdom of God—was expected to come during the time of the Roman Empire. In the following chart, compare the four empires represented in the dream of Nebuchadnezzar with the empires whose rule the Jewish people had experienced:

THE PROPHECY OF THE KINGDOM OF GOD (DANIEL 2)

Nebuchadnezzar's Dream	Daniel's Interpretation	Five Empires	Dates
1. Gold head	1st Kingdom	Babylonian	6th cent. BC
2. Silver chest and arms	2nd Kingdom	Medo-Persian	5th cent. BC
3. Bronze belly and thighs	3rd Kingdom	Greek	4th cent. BC
4. Iron/clay legs and feet	4th Kingdom	Roman	1st cent. BC
5. Stone →mountain	5th Kingdom	Kingdom of God	1st cent. AD?

As this chart makes clear, the implication of Daniel's prophecy is simple but explosive: *the long-awaited kingdom of God will come sometime during the reign of the Roman Empire.* That's what Daniel says: "in the days" of the fourth kingdom, "the God of heaven will set up a kingdom which shall never be destroyed" (Daniel 2:44). Notice also that while the kingdom of God will start out seemingly small and powerless—like a little stone—it will somehow miraculously overthrow the Roman Empire. Then, from the very foot of the "statue" of the fourth kingdom, the kingdom of God will spread throughout the world until the little stone becomes a "great mountain"—that is, a worldwide kingdom.[6]

Imagine the effect this oracle would have had on Jewish people living at the time of Jesus—living, that is, during the time of Daniel's fourth kingdom! Once you understand this biblical prophecy, it comes as no surprise that Jewish expectations about the coming of the kingdom of God were at a fever pitch during the first century AD. In the words of New Testament scholar N. T. Wright:

> The passage [about the stone in Daniel 2] was regularly interpreted, from at least as early as the first century, to refer to the Messiah, and to the kingdom that would be set up through him.[7]

In short, in the first century AD, it was believed that the kingdom of God spoken of by Daniel would come sometime during the reign of the Roman Empire.[8] In other words, it would come *soon*. According to Daniel, it was this kingdom that would somehow overthrow the Roman Empire and then, from the "foot" of the statue symbolizing that empire, the kingdom of God would spread throughout the world.

This is the kingdom Jesus has come to announce. This is the kingdom Jesus is talking about when he declares, *"The time is fulfilled,* and *the kingdom of God is at hand"* (Mark 1:15). What time? What kingdom? The time spoken of by the prophet Daniel. The kingdom spoken of by the prophet Daniel. This is what many Jews were hoping for, and this is what Jesus says he's bringing—with one important point of clarification. Notice that the kingdom in Daniel is not a man-made kingdom; it is represented as a stone "cut out by no human hand" (Daniel 2:34)—that is, a *supernatural kingdom* made by God himself. And this is the context in which everything Jesus says about himself needs to be understood.

The Son of Man

But the prophecy of the coming of the kingdom of God isn't the only oracle from the book of Daniel that is essential for understanding Jesus. For if the "kingdom of God" was one of Jesus's favorite ways of referring to the coming age of salvation, the expression "the Son of Man" was one of his favorite ways of referring to himself.[9] To take but a few examples:

"For John [the Baptist] came neither eating nor drinking, and they say, 'He has a demon'; *the Son of Man* came eating and drinking, and they say, 'Behold, a glutton and a drunkard, a friend of tax collectors and sinners!' " (Matthew 11:18-19)

As they were going along the road, a man said to him, "I will follow you wherever you go." And Jesus said to him, "Foxes have holes, and birds of the air have nests; but *the Son of Man* has nowhere to lay his head." (Luke 9:57-58)

For *the Son of Man* goes as it is written of him, but woe to that man by whom *the Son of Man* is betrayed! It would have been better for that man if he had not been born. (Mark 14:21)

Just as with the kingdom of God, so too with the Son of Man: throughout the Gospels, over and over again Jesus uses this expression to speak about himself. What does Jesus *mean* when he refers to himself as "the Son of Man"? Why does he speak about himself in the third person in this way? As with the expression "kingdom of God," Jesus once again seems to assume that his original Jewish audience will understand what he's talking about. He never says: "Now here's what the expression 'the Son of Man' means and here's why I'm referring to myself this way." He just uses it. So what does it mean?

On the one hand, the basic expression "son of man" in both Hebrew and Greek can simply be used to refer to *a human being*. For example, one of the prayers from the book of Psalms says: "When I look at your heavens [God], the work of your fingers, the moon and the stars which you have established; what is man that you are mindful of him, the son of man that you care for him?" (Psalm 8:4-5). In this case, "son of man" (Hebrew *ben 'adam*) is simply a synonym for "man" (Hebrew *'enosh*)—that is, a human being. On the other hand—and this is important—when Jesus uses the expression, he does so in such a way that he seems to be referring to a specific person: literally, "*the* Son of Man" (Greek *ho huios tou anthrōpou*). Who is this particular "Son of Man"?

Once again, the answer seems to lie in the Old Testament. As scholars widely agree, when Jesus speaks about "the Son of Man," he is referring to another prophecy from the book of Daniel: the famous vision of the four beasts and the coming of "one like a son of man" (Daniel 7).[10] In this passage, Daniel has a dream about a sequence of four pagan empires that will be followed by the coming of the kingdom of God. In this case, the four empires are not described as four kinds of metal but as four kinds of "beasts":

> "I [Daniel] saw in my vision by night, and behold, the four winds of heaven were stirring up the great sea. And *four great beasts* came up out of the sea, different from one another. *The first was like a lion* and had eagles' wings. Then as I looked its wings were plucked off, and it was lifted up from the ground and made to stand upon two feet like a man; and the mind of a man was given to it. And behold, *another beast, a second one, like a bear.* It was raised up on one side; it had three ribs in its mouth between its teeth; and it was told, 'Arise, devour much flesh.' After this I looked, and lo, *another, like a leopard,* with four wings of a bird on its back; and the beast had four heads; and dominion was given to it. After this I saw in the night visions, and behold, *a fourth beast,* terrible and dreadful and exceedingly strong; and it had great iron teeth; it devoured and broke in pieces, and stamped the residue with its feet." (Daniel 7:2-7)

Once again, lots could be said about this mysterious vision. For our purposes here, the main point is that the four beasts of Daniel's dream also symbolize a sequence of four pagan empires, beginning with the Babylonian Empire. In this case, the book of Daniel makes clear that "these four great beasts are *four kings* who shall arise out of the earth" (Daniel 7:17). In other words, although the beasts represent the various empires, they first and foremost symbolize the pagan *rulers* of those empires.[11]

The reason Daniel's vision is important for understanding who Jesus claimed to be is that the vision doesn't end with the coming of the fourth beast; it ends with the victorious coming of a heavenly "son of man":

As I looked,
thrones were placed,
and one that was ancient of days took his seat;
his raiment was white as snow,
and the hair of his head like pure wool;
his throne was fiery flames,
its wheels were burning fire. . . .
. . . Behold, with the clouds of heaven
there came *one like a son of man,*
and he came to the Ancient of Days
and was presented before him.
And to him was given dominion
and glory and kingdom,
that all peoples, nations, and languages
should serve him;
his dominion is an everlasting dominion,
which shall not pass away,
and his kingdom one
that shall not be destroyed. (Daniel 7:9, 13-14)

We'll come back to this passage more than once before the end of this book. For now, we just need to highlight one main point. *In order to understand who the son of man is, you have to remember who the four beasts are.* As the angel tells Daniel: the four beasts are four kings (Daniel 7:17). Once this is clear, then the identity of the son of man also becomes clear: *the son of man is the king of the fifth kingdom*—the everlasting kingdom of God.[12] This kingdom will be established when the fourth beast is destroyed. The following chart compares the symbols in Daniel's dream with the five empires.

THE PROPHECY OF THE SON OF MAN (DANIEL 7)

Daniel's Dream	Angel Interpretation	Five Empires	Dates
1. Lion	1st king	Babylonian	6th century BC
2. Bear	2nd king	Medo-Persian	5th century BC
3. Leopard	3rd king	Greek	4th century BC
4. Fourth beast	4th king	Roman	1st century BC
5. Son of Man	5th king	Kingdom of God	1st century AD?

Once again, the implications of this prophecy are enormous, for it makes clear that *the long-awaited kingdom of God and the heavenly "son of man"*—who will reign over the kingdom of God—*will come sometime during the reign of the Roman Empire*. It wouldn't take much for a first-century Jew to realize that if the "son of man" in Daniel will be the ruler of the kingdom of God, then he must also be the long-awaited Messiah. Indeed, the fact that the son of man is a king is made clear not only by his being contrasted with the pagan kings (the "beasts"), but also by the fact that he is seated on a heavenly "throne" (Daniel 7:9–14).[13]

Should there be any doubt about the messianic identity of the "son of man" in Daniel, it's critical to note that this is exactly how he was identified by early Jewish interpreters, going all the way back to the first century AD.[14] For example, in the ancient writing known as *1 Enoch*—a very popular book in first-century Judaism—the "Son of Man" is explicitly identified as "the Messiah" (*1 Enoch* 48:10; 52:4). Along similar lines, another first-century Jewish writing interprets Daniel's vision of "the figure of a man" flying with "the clouds of heaven" as a reference to the "Son" of God (see *4 Ezra* 13:1–52). Finally, even the later rabbis identified the "son of man" in Daniel as the Messiah (see Babylonian Talmud, *Sanhedrin* 98a; *Numbers Rabbah* 13:14).

In light of these Jewish parallels, it seems clear that if Jesus of Nazareth went around proclaiming that the kingdom of God was at hand and referring to himself as the Son of Man, then he was saying, in effect: "The time for the fulfillment of the prophecies of Daniel is at hand. The time for the coming of the Messiah is *now*." Every Jew in Jesus's audience who knew the book of Daniel would have known he might be right. For, as we have seen previously, the long-awaited kingdom of God and the messianic Son of Man were supposed to come during the time of the Roman Empire. And that, of course, is precisely when Jesus began his public ministry: during "the reign of Tiberius Caesar" (Luke 3:1). In other words, it is the book of Daniel's kingdom of God that Jesus proclaims. And it the book of Daniel's Son of Man whom Jesus implicitly claims to be.[15]

If we accept these conclusions, then something significant follows: if Jesus is claiming to be the messianic Son of Man from the book of Daniel, then that means that he is no mere earthly Messiah, no mere earthly king. For in the book of Daniel, the son of man is a *heavenly* king ruling over a *heavenly* kingdom. As we will see later on, some scholars even suggest that the son of man in Daniel is a divine being. But we'll have to wait until a later chapter to deal with that issue. For now, there is one last prophecy from the book of Daniel that we need to take a look at so that we can understand the words and deeds of Jesus in their context. I am speaking about Daniel's mysterious prophecy of the *death* of the Messiah.

The Death of the Messiah

Anyone familiar with the four Gospels will recall that on several occasions, Jesus speaks about eventually being handed over to the authorities and put to death. What sometimes goes unnoticed is that when Jesus predicts that he will suffer and die, he repeatedly refers to himself as "the Son of Man." For example, according to the Gospel of Mark, after Peter confesses Jesus to be the Messiah, this is what happens:

> And he began to teach them that *the Son of Man must suffer many things*, and be rejected by the elders and the chief priests and the

scribes, *and be killed*, and after three days rise again. And he said this
plainly. (Mark 8:31-32)

We'll get to the question of the resurrection in a later chapter. For now,
I simply want to emphasize that when Jesus speaks about his own future suffering and death, he alludes once again to the book of Daniel.
It is as the messianic Son of Man spoken of by Daniel that he must suffer and die. In fact, the word "must" here indicates that Jesus is referring to the fulfillment of biblical prophecy.[16]

   If Jesus is referring to a specific prophecy, then an important question arises: Where does he get the idea that the messianic Son of Man
must suffer and die? What passage in the Bible is he talking about? If
you go back to the Old Testament, you will discover that there is no explicit prophecy of the death of the Son of Man anywhere to be found.
The book of Isaiah contains prophecies of the death of the Suffering
Servant, but that figure is never explicitly identified as "the Son of
Man" (see Isaiah 52–53). Why then does Jesus seem to think that the
Bible foretells the suffering and death of the Son of Man?

   Once again, the answer lies in the book of Daniel. Although the
"son of man" in Daniel 7 is not described as being put to death, the future "messiah" in Daniel 9 *is* described as being put to death. In fact,
this is the only explicit prophecy of the death of the "messiah" (Hebrew
mashiach) in the Old Testament. Although the passage is somewhat
obscure, it is worth reading carefully:

[The angel Gabriel said to Daniel:] "*Seventy weeks of years* [=490
years] *are decreed* concerning your people and your holy city, to fin-
ish the transgression, to put an end to sin, and to atone for iniquity,
to bring in everlasting righteousness, to seal both vision and prophet,
and to anoint a most holy [one]. Know therefore and understand that
*from the going forth of the word to restore and build Jerusalem to the
coming of a messiah*, a prince, there shall be seven weeks. Then for
sixty-two weeks it shall be built again with squares and moat, but in
a troubled time. And after the sixty-two weeks, *a Messiah shall be
cut off*, and shall have nothing; and *the people of the prince who is to*

come shall destroy the city and the sanctuary. Its end shall come with a flood, and to the end there shall be war; desolations are decreed. And he shall make a strong covenant with many for one week; and for half of the week he shall cause sacrifice and offering to cease; and upon the wing of abominations shall come one who makes desolate, until the decreed end is poured out on the desolator." (Daniel 9:24-27)[17]

It should go without saying that we can't go into every issue raised by this admittedly difficult passage.[18] All I want to do here is highlight three reasons it has been interpreted since ancient times as telling not only *that* the Messiah would come, but *when* the Messiah would come.

First, the prophecy declares that there will be 490 years ("seventy weeks of years") between the restoration of the city of Jerusalem and the coming of a "messiah" (Hebrew *mashiach*). In other words, this passage gives a remarkably specific timeline for the arrival of a future king of Israel. Because kings were "anointed" with oil, they were sometimes referred to as "messiahs" (see 1 Samuel 24:6; Psalm 2:2). Second, and equally important, the prophecy also declares that this future Messiah will be "cut off"—a common Hebrew expression for being *put to death.*[19] This is where Jesus appears to derive the idea that the Son of Man must be put to death. As I have argued elsewhere in more detail, Jesus is treating the Son of Man in Daniel 7 and the Messiah in Daniel 9 as if they were *the same person:* the first prophecy describes the heavenly enthronement of the Messiah; the second describes the earthly suffering and death of the Messiah.[20] Third and finally, the prophecy links the death of the future Messiah to the destruction of the "city" of Jerusalem and the Temple "sanctuary," resulting in the end of sacrifice and a mysterious "abomination" that "makes desolate" (Daniel 9:27). Significantly, Jesus elsewhere explicitly refers to this passage from Daniel when he warns the disciples about the coming of the "abomination of desolation" and the destruction of Jerusalem (see Matthew 24:15; Mark 13:14).

In short, it is almost impossible to overestimate the importance of Daniel's prophecy of the death of the Messiah for understanding Jesus. According to the book of Daniel, the Messiah will not just come in glory; he will also suffer and die. Perhaps even more striking, Daniel gives a timeline for the coming of the Messiah: he will come some 490 years after the rebuilding of the city of Jerusalem, which had been destroyed by the Babylonian Empire (ca. 587 BC). but which King Artaxerxes of Persia, in the "seventh year" of his reign (ca. 457 BC), had ordered to be rebuilt under the leadership of Ezra the Jewish priest (see Ezra 7:1-28).[21] I don't want to lose any readers by getting into a numbers game here, but suffice it to say that since ancient times, interpreters have calculated Daniel's prophecy as placing the coming of the Messiah sometime during the first century AD.[22] Consider the following chart:

THE PROPHECY OF THE MESSIAH'S DEATH (DANIEL 9)

Daniel's Prophecy	Historical Events	Dates
"Going forth of the word to restore and build Jerusalem."	Decree to rebuild the Temple by King Artaxerxes of Persia	ca. 457 BC
"Seventy weeks of years"	70 x 7 years = 490 years	457 BC–AD 33
"Messiah" will be "cut off"	Jesus is crucified	ca. AD 33
"City and sanctuary" will be destroyed	Temple and Jerusalem destroyed by Romans	AD 70

I expect some readers may be thinking at this point: "What?! The Old Testament actually *predicts* the timing of the death of the Messiah? Why haven't I heard this before?"

This reaction is understandable. I for one had never seen any of these passages from the book of Daniel before I started studying first-century Judaism seriously. For whatever reason, modern-day Christians are often far less familiar with these passages than were ancient Jews and Christians. Indeed, many have never even heard of these prophecies, much less reckoned with the claim that Jesus fulfilled them.

But you don't have to take my word (or my math!) when it comes to Daniel's prophetic timeline for the coming of the Messiah. These ideas have been around for a long, long time. Listen to the words of the first-century Jewish historian Josephus, the fourth-century Church historian Eusebius, and the famous seventeenth-century French mathematician Blaise Pascal:

> We are convinced . . . that Daniel spoke with God, for he did not only prophesy future events, as did the other prophets, but *he also determined the time at which these would come to pass.* (Josephus, *Antiquities*, 10.267–68)[23]

> [W]e must count the numbers, that is to say the seventy weeks, which are 490 years, from the going forth of the word of answer and from the building of Jerusalem. *This took place in the twentieth year of Artaxerxes, King of Persia.* For Nehemiah his cup-bearer made the request, and received the answer that Jerusalem should be rebuilt, and the order went forth to carry it out. . . . *And from that date to the coming of Christ is seventy weeks.* (Eusebius, *The Proof of the Gospel*, 8.2.389)[24]

> One must be bold to predict the same thing in so many ways. It was necessary that the four idolatrous or pagan monarchies, the end of the kingdom of Judah, and *the seventy weeks*, should happen at the same time, and *all this before the second temple was destroyed.* (Pascal, *Pensées*, 11.709)[25]

In short: however one calculates the exact dates spoken of by Daniel, the 490 years between the restoration of Jerusalem and the coming of the Messiah are undeniably completed before the destruction of the Temple in Jerusalem in AD 70. In other words, Daniel's prophecy clearly points to a fulfillment in the *first century*.

This background from the book of Daniel explains one aspect of what many Jewish people in the first century were actually waiting for. They were waiting for the coming of the kingdom of God and the messianic Son of Man. It also explains why Josephus, writing after the Temple's destruction, is so amazed at the accuracy of Daniel's predictions. And it explains why a first-century Jew like Jesus of Nazareth could describe his own coming passion and death—along with the destruction of Jerusalem and the Temple—as the fulfillment of biblical prophecy. For Daniel had not only prophesied that the Messiah would come; he predicted when he would come, what would happen to him, and what would happen to Jerusalem and its Temple. *And it happened.* In the first century. Two thousand years ago. Jesus of Nazareth, proclaimer of the Kingdom of God and coming of the Son of Man, was "cut off" by the Romans when he was crucified, some 490 years after the restoration of Jerusalem under King Artaxerxes.

But we can't stop there. The messianic prophecies of the Old Testament give us only the beginnings of an answer to the question: Who did Jesus claim to be? For not only did the first Christians believe that Jesus was the long-awaited Messiah; they also very early on began proclaiming he was *divine*. Where did they get this idea? Did Jesus only claim to be the Messiah? Or did he also say he was God?

Did Jesus Think He Was God?

We come now to the question at the heart of this book: *Did Jesus of Nazareth claim to be God?* The answer to this question has enormous historical and theological implications. If Jesus did not think he was God, then it is reasonable to conclude that he wasn't. And if Jesus wasn't God, then one of the central claims of Christianity, indeed, arguably *the* central claim—that the one true God became man in Jesus of Nazareth—comes crashing to the ground. But if Jesus did speak and act as if he were the one God, then we are forced to make a decision. Either he was a liar who knew he was just a man but spoke as if he were divine; or he was a lunatic who thought he was God but was grossly mistaken; or he was who he claimed to be—the one true God come in person. What does the historical evidence suggest?

As we will see, the evidence in the Gospels suggests that Jesus did in fact claim to be God. He did so, however, in a very Jewish way. That is, Jesus used riddles and questions that were intended to both reveal and conceal his identity at the same time. These riddles were designed to force his audience to ask the question "Who is this man?" Jesus also performed signs and wonders that were intended to reveal his identity. As with his parables, however, the full meaning of these actions can only be fully understood in the context of ancient Jewish Scripture and tradition. I cannot stress the point enough: just because Jesus did not go around Galilee shouting, "I am God!" does not mean that he didn't claim to be divine. As I hope to show, one of the primary reasons some scholars argue that Jesus did not think he was God is because they do not interpret his teachings and actions in their first-century Jewish context. In other words, they fail to take seriously the Jewish roots of Jesus's divine identity.

In order to see all of this clearly, we need to look briefly at why some people doubt that Jesus thought he was God. Let's begin with the claim that the Synoptic Gospels—our earliest biographies of Jesus—do not depict him as divine.

Is Jesus Divine in the Synoptic Gospels?

Perhaps the most widespread and persuasive argument against the idea that Jesus thought he was God is the claim that three out of the four Gospels—Matthew, Mark, and Luke—do not depict Jesus as God. According to this argument, although Jesus speaks and acts as if he were God in the Gospel of John, the same thing is not true for the Jesus of the Synoptic Gospels. While the Synoptic Gospels describe Jesus as a wonder-worker, a great rabbi, a true prophet, and even the Messiah, they do not portray him as the one God come in the flesh. Consider, for example, the recent words of Bart Ehrman:

> If Jesus went around Galilee proclaiming himself to be a divine being sent from God . . . could anything else that he might say be so breathtaking and thunderously important? And yet none of these earlier sources [Matthew, Mark, and Luke] says any such thing about him. Did they (all of them!) just decide not to mention the one thing that was most significant about Jesus? Almost certainly the divine self-claims in John are not historical.[1]

Elsewhere, Ehrman admits that the Synoptic Gospels do not depict Jesus as an ordinary man.[2] However, he also insists that Jesus in the

Synoptic Gospels is not a pre-existent being and is in no way equal to the God of Israel, the Creator of the universe. Instead, Ehrman suggests that the idea of Jesus's "divinity" is something that only came into existence in the wake of Jesus's resurrection, after which his followers began ascribing honors to him that he never claimed for himself.[3]

Now, if it were true that Jesus never speaks or acts as if he is divine in the Synoptic Gospels, that three of the earliest biographies of Jesus do not provide any evidence that he claimed to be divine, then a major historical argument could be made against the ancient Christian belief that Jesus thought he was God. And this would quite understandably lead to doubts about whether the Gospel of John is historically accurate in portraying Jesus as claiming to be God.

The problem is that the claim that Jesus is not depicted as God in the Synoptic Gospels is flat-out wrong. The only way to hold such a claim is to completely *ignore* both the miracles of Jesus in which he acts as if he is the one God, as well as the sayings of Jesus in which he speaks as if he is the one God. We will look at the sayings of Jesus in the next chapter. For now, let us focus on three of Jesus's most startling deeds—(1) the stilling of the storm, (2) the walking on water, and (3) the Transfiguration—in which he acts precisely as if he is the God described in the Jewish Scriptures.

Before we begin, three caveats are necessary. First, in the following chapters, I will not go into the detailed arguments for or against the historicity of the various actions or sayings in the Gospels in which Jesus reveals his divine identity. That would require a much longer and different kind of book.[4] My goal here is much more modest: I simply want to show that the Synoptic Gospels do in fact repeatedly refer to Jesus making divine claims about himself.[5] Second, for the sake of space, I will normally quote from only the version of events recorded in the Gospel of Mark. Yet for every episode, I will base my arguments primarily on what the Gospel accounts have in common. Remember that we are not looking for the exact words of Jesus but for the *substance* of what he reportedly said and did.[6] Readers interested in the differences in detail between the various accounts are invited to consult the endnotes. Finally, in what follows, whenever I use the expression "the LORD" (all caps), I am referring to the Hebrew name of God (YHWH). It's important to be clear about this because, as we will see, Jesus is identifying himself not just with any "god," but with the LORD,[7] the God of the universe.

With this in mind, we can turn now to the accounts of Jesus's miracles.

The Stilling of the Storm: "Who Is This?"

The first episode in which Jesus begins to reveal his divine identity in the Synoptic Gospels is related in the famous account of the stilling of the storm, which is recorded in the Gospels of Matthew, Mark, and Luke. Consider the following account:

> On that day, when evening had come, [Jesus] said to [his disciples], "Let us go across to the other side." And leaving the crowd, they took him with them just as he was in the boat. And other boats were with him. And a great storm of wind arose, and the waves beat into the boat, so that the boat was already filling. But he was in the stern, asleep on the cushion; and they woke him and said to him, "Teacher, do you not care if we perish?" And he awoke and rebuked the wind, and said to the sea, "Peace! Be still!" And the wind ceased, and there was a great calm. He said to them, "Why are you afraid? Have you no faith?" And they were filled with awe, and said to one another, *"Who then is this, that even wind and sea obey him?"* (Mark 4:35-41)

Despite a few minor differences in details and formulation, the three accounts of this event are substantially the same (see Matthew 8:23-27; Luke 8:22-25).[8] A storm rises up on the Sea of Galilee, and the disciples become afraid of perishing and wake Jesus from his sleep. In response, Jesus rebukes the wind and sea, calming the storm, leading the disciples to ask: "Who is this?" Given our focus, two questions immediately leap out: What would the stilling of the storm have meant to first-century Jews like Jesus's disciples? And what does this episode reveal about Jesus's identity?

On the one hand, a person could argue that all we have here is an account of a miracle performed by a Jewish prophet. Taken by itself, a miracle alone does not necessarily point to Jesus's divine identity. As anyone familiar with the Bible knows, various people in the Old Testament perform wonders, and that doesn't lead anyone to claim the miracle worker was divine. For example, Moses uses his staff to part the waters of the Red Sea (Exodus 14:21-31), but no one claims that he was the one true God. Likewise, when Joshua and the Israelites cross over into the promised land, the Jordan River is parted when the priests' feet touch the water (Joshua 3:14-17). But nobody seems to have taken this to mean that the priests were divine. Finally, the prophet Elijah prays for the rain to stop, and it stops for three years; then he prays for the rain to come again, and the three-year drought ends (see 1 Kings 17–18). But this doesn't seem to have led anyone to think that Elijah was God.

On the other hand, it is not just *any* miracle Jesus performs here. And it is not just any power that he displays in the stilling of the storm. If you go back to the Jewish Scriptures and read them with this account in mind, you will discover something extremely important. Over and over again, the Old Testament emphasizes how the God of the universe displays his power by controlling two of the most powerful forces in creation: *the wind and the sea.*[9] For example, in the book of Job, God shows his might when at his "rebuke" and "by his power" he "stilled the sea" (Job 26:11-12). Likewise, the book of Psalms shows how "great" the LORD is by declaring that he has power over the "winds" and that he "rebuked" the "waters" of the sea when he made the world (Psalm 104:1-7). Along similar lines, the God of Israel revealed his "mighty power" when he "rebuked the Red Sea" in the exodus from Egypt (Psalm 106:8-9). Finally, and most striking of all, Psalm 107 describes the LORD as having the power to save his people by stilling a storm and calming the waves of the sea:

Some went down to the sea in ships,
    doing business on the great waters;

they saw the deeds of the LORD,
his wondrous works in the deep.
For he commanded, and raised the stormy wind,
which lifted up the waves of the sea.
They mounted up to heaven, they went down to the depths;
their courage melted away in their evil plight;
they reeled and staggered like drunken men,
and were at their wits' end.
Then they cried to the LORD in their trouble,
and he delivered them from their distress;
he made the storm be still,
and the waves of the sea were hushed.
Then they were glad because they had quiet,
and he brought them to their desired haven. (Psalm 107:23-30)

The parallels between what the God of Israel does in this psalm and what Jesus does in the stilling of the storm are truly remarkable:

THE STILLING OF THE STORM AND THE DIVINITY OF JESUS

The LORD Stills the Storm	*Jesus Stills the Storm*
1. Sailors in ships	1. Disciples in boats
2. Stormy wind and waves	2. Stormy wind and waves
3. Courage melts away	3. Disciples are afraid
4. Cry out to the LORD	4. Cry out to Jesus
5. The LORD stills the storm	5. Jesus stills the storm
6. Waves of the sea "quiet"	6. There was a "great calm"
(Psalm 107)	(Matthew 8; Mark 4; Luke 8)

Can this many parallels really be chalked up to coincidence? I think not. Instead, it seems clear that the Gospels of Matthew, Mark, and

Luke are depicting Jesus as possessing God's own power over the sea and water. In the words of New Testament scholars Joseph Fitzmyer and John Meier:

> As YHWH established order over chaos and rescued his people from watery disasters, so now Jesus is presented as having a similar role in their destiny.[10]

> In short, what YHWH does to save the crew of the ship on the sea in Psalm 107, Jesus does to save his disciples in the ship on the sea of Galilee.[11]

How can the man Jesus of Nazareth have such power and mastery over creation—a power that the Old Testament reserves to the LORD alone? The best explanation is that Jesus is the God of Israel come in person.

Should there be any doubt about the implication of Jesus's actions, we need only turn to the reaction of Jesus's Jewish disciples: *"Who then is this, that even wind and sea obey him?"* (Mark 4:41). In context, this question implies that Jesus has not merely performed a remarkable miracle. Even more, he has displayed a power that the Old Testament repeatedly attributes to God alone. As New Testament scholar François Bovon writes:

> They [the disciples] know from Scripture that *only God* has a word that is effective to this extent. . . . [T]he range of messianic power is broadened here: the lord of the congregation is even *Lord of the cosmos.*[12]

The divine implications of Jesus's action become even clearer when we realize that he does not pray to God to make the wind and sea stop. He gives no impression that he depends on any outside force to supply this divine power.[13] Instead, he simply commands the wind and sea himself. And they obey him. In the words of Joel Marcus:

[N]ow obedience is rendered to the Messiah not only by human beings but also by inanimate powers. The one so acknowledged is *not
just a human but a cosmic figure;* if he is the Messiah, he is a Messiah
who bears *the marks of divinity.*[14]

Contrary to what some claim, the accounts of the stilling of the storm
reveal Jesus's identity as the LORD, the Creator of the universe. And
this happens in all three Synoptic Gospels. To be sure, Jesus reveals
his divine identity in a very *Jewish* way: by manifesting the same power
over the wind and the sea that God showed when he created the world
and saved Israel in the exodus. But it remains a manifestation of divinity nonetheless.

Finally, it is worth pointing out that Jesus's actions during the
storm do not imply that he isn't fully human. After all, he does fall
asleep in the boat! But the stilling of the storm does raise a central
question his followers will have to reckon with on more than one
occasion—the question of Jesus's identity. As the disciples say in the
Gospel of Matthew: "*What sort of man* is this, that even the winds and
sea obey him?" (Matthew 8:27).

The Walking on Water: "I Am"

The next important miracle in the Synoptic Gospels is the equally un-
forgettable account of Jesus walking on the water. Once again, the
episode is recorded in three Gospels. But this time, one of them is the
Gospel of John (see Matthew 14:22-33; Mark 6:45-52; John 6:16-21).
Given that scholars widely recognize that Jesus is depicted as divine in
John's Gospel, we will focus our attention once again on the Synoptic
evidence, since that is what is in question. Consider the account in the
Gospel of Mark:

> Immediately [Jesus] made his disciples get into the boat and go before
> him to the other side, to Bethsaida, while he dismissed the crowd.
> And after he had taken leave of them, he went up into the hills to pray.
> And when evening came, the boat was out on the sea, and he was

alone on the land. And he saw that they were distressed in rowing, for the wind was against them. And about the fourth watch of the night he came to them, walking on the sea. *He meant to pass by them, but when they saw him walking on the sea they thought it was a ghost, and cried out; for they all saw him, and were terrified.* But immediately he spoke to them and said, *"Take heart, I am; do not be afraid."* And he got into the boat with them and the wind ceased. And they were utterly astounded. (Mark 6:45-51)[15]

While there are several differences in detail and unique features in the three accounts, it is the substantial agreement among them that demands our attention.[16] In all three accounts, Jesus does and says two very remarkable things. First, he walks on the Sea of Galilee in the midst of wind and waves (Matthew 14:25; Mark 6:48; John 6:19). Second, in all three accounts, when the disciples see him and become afraid, he says to them: "I am; do not be afraid (Greek *egō eimi mē phobeisthe*)" (Matthew 14:27; Mark 6:50; John 6:20). What is the meaning of this miracle? Why does Jesus say "I am" to the disciples?

At first glance, you could argue that Jesus's words "I am" (Greek *egō eimi*) simply mean "It's me." Indeed, that's exactly how the expression is translated in various English versions of the Bible: "Take heart, *it is I*" (Matthew 14:27; Mark 6:50; John 6:20) (see RSV, NAB). And, to be sure, the Greek expression "I am" (*egō eimi*) can be used simply as a way to identify oneself. For example, elsewhere in the Gospels, Jesus speaks about false messiahs who will come and say, "I am," meaning, by implication, "I am the Messiah" (Mark 13:6).[17] According to this interpretation, Jesus would simply be identifying himself to the disciples.

On the other hand, while it's certainly true that Jesus is identifying himself, there are several problems with the idea that he's *only* identifying himself.[18] For one thing, in the original Greek, Jesus does not actually say "It is I" (as some English translations suggest). He literally says "I am" (Greek *egō eimi*). This is different from other occasions when Jesus simply wants to identify himself. For example, after the resurrection, when the disciples don't recognize him, Jesus says: "It is I myself" (Greek *ego eimi autos*), meaning "It's really me" (Luke 24:39).

In other words, whenever the expression "I am" (Greek *ego eimi*) occurs *by itself*, then its meaning must be determined *by the context*. In certain contexts, the expression "I am" by itself means much more than just "It's me." In the Old Testament, "I am" is often used for the divine name of God (see Exodus 3:14; Deuteronomy 32:39; Isaiah 41:4; 43:10-11). For our purposes, by far the most important of these passages is the famous account of the appearance of God to Moses in the burning bush on Mount Sinai:

> Then Moses said to God, "If I come to the people of Israel and say to them, 'The God of your fathers has sent me to you,' and they ask me, 'What is his name?' what shall I say to them?" God said to Moses, "*I AM WHO I AM*." And he said, "Say this to the people of Israel, '*I AM has sent me to you*.'" God also said to Moses, "Say this to the people of Israel, 'The LORD, the God of your fathers, the God of Abraham, the God of Isaac, and the God of Jacob, has sent me to you': *this is my name for ever*, and thus I am to be remembered throughout all generations." (Exodus 3:13-15)

Notice two things here. First, in both the Hebrew and the Greek versions of this passage, "I am" (Hebrew *'ehyeh*; Greek *ego eimi*) is a name. It is another name for "the LORD" (Hebrew YHWH), the God of the universe. Second, and equally important, this name reveals something important about the God of Moses: he is eternal. He has no beginning; he has no end; he simply "is." Indeed, the sacred name YHWH can be translated as "He who Is."[19] This is the God who is appearing to Moses and speaking to him from the miraculous bush that burns but is not consumed.

Once this Old Testament background is clear, we can go back to Jesus's words to the disciples in the boat and interpret them in the context of the miracle he is performing. In light of Jesus's miraculous display of power over the wind and sea, when he says to the disciples, "*I am* (Greek *ego eimi*); do not be afraid," he is not just saying "It's me."

He is *revealing his divine identity* to them. Just as the LORD revealed his divine name to Moses in the context of his display of power over creation in the burning bush, so too Jesus reveals his divine name to the disciples in the context of his display of power over creation when he walks on water. In the words of John Meier and Joel Marcus:

> [W]hile the "surface meaning" of *egō eimi* in the Gospel narrative is "It is I," the many OT allusions . . . intimate a secondary, solemn meaning: the divine "I am." Ultimately this solemn utterance goes all the way back to YHWH's revelation of himself to Moses in the burning bush.[20]

> The OT texts in which God identifies himself by means of *egō eimi* . . . are especially relevant for our passage [the walking on water]. . . . God identifies himself by means of *egō eimi ho ōn*, "I am the One who is," a name denoting his active, upholding, uncircumscribed, everlasting presence, which allows no rival force to withstand it.[21]

In other words, in a first-century Jewish context, Jesus's act of walking on the water is nothing less than a *theophany*—an appearance of God—the same God who appeared to Moses on Sinai.[22] That is why Jesus refers to himself by the mysterious expression "I am." Because he is revealing his divine identity as the LORD come in person.

Should there be any doubts about this interpretation, there are two further points that will support it.

First, notice that Mark's account says that Jesus "meant to pass by" the disciples when he was walking on the water (Mark 6:48). This is rather odd. Where was Jesus going? The key to unlocking this otherwise baffling detail lies in Jewish Scripture. In the Old Testament, the expression "passing by" is repeatedly used to describe what God does when he appears to human beings.[23] Consider the biblical accounts of God appearing to Moses and Elijah:

> [The LORD said to Moses:] "I will make all my goodness *pass before you*, and will proclaim before you *my name 'The LORD.'* . . . [A]nd

while my glory *passes by* I will put you in a cleft of the rock, and I will cover you with my hand until I have *passed by*. . . ." The LORD *passed before him*, and proclaimed, "*The LORD, the LORD*, a God merciful and gracious, slow to anger, and abounding in steadfast love and faithfulness. (Exodus 33:19, 22; 34:6)

[God said to Elijah:] "Go forth, and stand upon the mount before the LORD." And behold, *the LORD passed by*. (1 Kings 19:11)

Notice here that in the theophany to Moses, God not only "passes by"; he also proclaims his divine name. In the light of this Old Testament background, the emphasis on Jesus's "passing by" signals that he is not just a prophet performing a miracle. He is a divine person revealing his power and his name. As New Testament scholar Adela Yarbro Collins writes of Mark's account: "Jesus is being portrayed here as *divine*."[24]

Second, the Gospel of Matthew contains its own unique clue that Jesus is revealing his divine identity. For Matthew also tells us how Simon Peter and the disciples react to seeing Jesus walking on the water:

And Peter answered him, "Lord, if it is you, bid me come to you on the water." He said, "Come." So Peter got out of the boat and walked on the water and came to Jesus; but when he saw the wind, he was afraid, and beginning to sink he cried out, "Lord, save me." Jesus immediately reached out his hand and caught him, saying to him, "O man of little faith, why did you doubt?" And when they got into the boat, the wind ceased. *And those in the boat worshiped him*, saying, "Truly you are the Son of God." (Matthew 14:28-33)

Note well that the disciples' response to the wonder they have just witnessed is to fall down and *worship* Jesus. It is true that the Greek word for "worship" (*proskyneō*) can be used to refer either to homage given to human beings (such as kings) or the worship given to the one God alone. In any given case, the meaning depends on the context.

However, as Larry Hurtado and other scholars have shown, in the Gospel of Matthew, the word "worship" (Greek *proskyneō*) is used "only in the sense of genuine worship of Jesus," the kind of Jewish worship ordinarily given only to "the one God."[25] In other words, the disciples recognize that Jesus has just manifested divine power over the sea, and, as a result, they worship him as divine. As W. D. Davies and Dale Allison write: "What matters is not that Jesus has done the seemingly impossible but that he has performed actions which the Old Testament associates with *YHWH alone*."[26] In the words of the recent *Jewish Annotated New Testament:* the disciples' reference to Jesus here as the "Son of God" is an indication of "Jesus's *divine nature*."[27]

Does this mean that the disciples grasp the full implications of who Jesus is after the stilling of the storm? Not at all. As their responses to the eventual crucifixion and resurrection of Jesus show, they still have a lot to learn.[28] But what it does mean is that the Synoptic Gospels *do* in fact depict Jesus as "having existed in eternity past," as "the creator of the universe," and as equal with "the one true God."[29] For, as any first-century Jew would have understood, Jesus's pre-existence and identity with the one Creator God are precisely what follow from him using as his own the divine name "I am" that had been revealed to Moses on Mount Sinai (Exodus 3:14). Perhaps that is why the Gospel tells us that when his Jewish disciples see Jesus walking on water and saying "I am," they fall down and worship him.

The Transfiguration on the Mountain

The third and for our purposes final instance in which Jesus reveals his divine identity is the Transfiguration, which is recorded in all three Synoptic Gospels. Once again, for the sake of space, we will focus primarily on the account in the Gospel of Mark:

> And after six days Jesus took with him Peter and James and John, and led them up a high mountain apart by themselves; and *he was transfigured before them, and his garments became glistening, intensely white, as no fuller on earth could bleach them. And there appeared to*

them Elijah with Moses; and they were talking to Jesus. And Peter said
to Jesus, "Master, it is well that we are here; let us make three booths,
one for you and one for Moses and one for Elijah." For he did not
know what to say, for they were exceedingly afraid. *And a cloud over-
shadowed them, and a voice came out of the cloud, "This is my beloved
Son; listen to him."* And suddenly looking around they no longer saw
any one with them but Jesus only. And as they were coming down the
mountain, he charged them to tell no one what they had seen, until
the Son of Man should have risen from the dead. (Mark 9:2-9)

Although there are several differences in detail among the accounts
(compare the passage in Mark with Matthew 17:1-8 and Luke 9:28-
36),[30] all three agree on the basics of the event. Jesus takes his disciples
Peter, James, and John up a mountain and is "transfigured" (Greek
metemorphōthē) before them. Moses and Elijah appear as well, and
Peter responds by offering to build "booths" or "tents" for Jesus and
the two prophets. At this point, a cloud overshadows them and a voice
from heaven identifies Jesus as God's "Son" and commands the disciples to listen to him. Afterward, Jesus commands the disciples not to
tell anyone about anything they have seen or heard.

Like every other episode we have examined so far, the Transfiguration generates a whole host of questions. For our purposes, I want
to focus on just one: *Why do Moses and Elijah appear on the mountain
with Jesus?* Why these two figures, and not, say, Abraham, Isaac, or
Jacob? The most common explanation is a symbolic one. According
to this interpretation, Moses represents the Law, the first five books of
the Bible, and Elijah represents the Prophets, the second major part
of the Jewish Scriptures.[31] In support of this, interpreters often point
out that by the first century AD, "the Law and the Prophets" was a common way of referring to the Scriptures (compare Matthew 5:17).

But it seems to me that there is a better explanation for why Moses
and Elijah appear, one more deeply rooted in the Old Testament.[32]
If you go back to the Jewish Scriptures, you will discover that both
Moses and Elijah experience *theophanies*—that is, appearances of
God—in which God comes to them on a mountain and reveals his

glory. Yet neither Moses nor Elijah is able to see God's face. Compare the following:

> Moses said, "I beg you, show me your glory." And he said, "I will make all my goodness pass before you, and will proclaim before you my name 'The LORD'; and I will be gracious to whom I will be gracious, and will show mercy on whom I will show mercy. But," he said, *"you cannot see my face;* for man shall not see me and live." And the LORD said, "Behold, there is a place by me where you shall stand upon the rock; and while my glory passes by I will put you in a cleft of the rock, and I will cover you with my hand until I have passed by; then I will take away my hand, and *you shall see my back; but my face shall not be seen."* (Exodus 33:18-23)[33]

> And there he [Elijah] came to a cave, and lodged there; and behold, the word of the LORD came to him. . . . And he said, "Go forth, and *stand upon the mount before the Lord." And behold, the Lord passed by,* and a great and strong wind rent the mountains, and broke in pieces the rocks before the LORD, but the LORD was not in the wind; and after the wind an earthquake, but the LORD was not in the earthquake; and after the earthquake a fire, but the LORD was not in the fire; and after the fire a still small voice. *And when Elijah heard it, he wrapped his face in his mantle and went out and stood at the entrance of the cave.* (1 Kings 19:9, 11-13)

Notice that both theophanies occur on the same mountain, Mount Sinai, the mountain of divine revelation. Notice also that neither Moses nor Elijah could look at God. They can hear him and see manifestations of his power, but they cannot see his face. What does all of this have to do with the Transfiguration? The answer is simple but profound. *On the mountain of the Transfiguration, Moses and Elijah are finally allowed to see what they could not see during their earthly lives: the unveiled face of God.* How is this possible? Because the God who appeared to them on Mount Sinai has now become man. *In Jesus of Nazareth, the one God now has a human face.*

In other words, whereas the face of Moses shone with light after coming down the mountain because he reflected the light of the LORD (Exodus 34:29-35), Jesus, in the words of Pope Benedict XVI, now "shines *from within;* he does not simply receive light, but he himself is light from light."[34] And just as God descends upon Mount Sinai in a "thick cloud" and speaks to Moses and the people (Exodus 19:16), so now "a cloud" overshadows Jesus on the mountain of the Transfiguration and a voice speaks: "This is my beloved Son; listen to him" (Mark 9:7). By means of these words, Jesus's true identity is being revealed. Not only does Jesus speak and act as if he is God, but God speaks and acts as if Jesus is his divine Son. In his recent study of Jesus's divinity, M. David Litwa writes:

> By introducing the voice from the cloud . . . Mark reveals that the transformed Jesus was more than an angel and higher than glorified saints (i.e., Moses and Elijah). The account indicates that Jesus was revealed specifically *as a deity.*[35]

Here then we see the beginnings (but just the beginnings) of what would only later become clear: a plurality of persons in the one God. In the Transfiguration of Jesus, we begin to see that there is both God the Father and God the Son.

Ignoring the Evidence Won't Make It Disappear

Before we end this chapter, let's quickly look at one last issue. At this point you might be wondering: In the face of so much evidence—and there is more[36]—how can some people claim with a straight face that the Synoptic Gospels do not depict Jesus as divine?

There are lots of different ways to get around the evidence. Consider, for example, the words of Bart Ehrman:

> [E]ven in the Gospels Jesus appears to have a heavenly body during his earthly life—one that can walk on water, for example, or be

transfigured into a radiating glow in the presence of some of his disciples. But it is important to remember: these Gospels were written by believers in Jesus decades later who already "knew" that Jesus had been exalted to heaven. As storytellers told the stories of Jesus' earthly career, year after year and decade after decade, they did not separate who Jesus was after his death—the one who had been exalted to heaven—from who he was during his life. And so their belief in the exalted Jesus affected the ways that they told their stories about him.[37]

Do you see what Ehrman just did? He knows full well that there are accounts of Jesus in the Synoptic Gospels that reveal that Jesus was "a divine human." (In fact, he names two of the three episodes discussed in this chapter!) But when faced with evidence, in order to maintain the theory that Jesus does *not* claim to be God in the earliest sources, Ehrman plays up the idea of a "time gap" between the events in the life of Jesus and the writing of the Gospels and includes the theory of anonymous storytellers (the Telephone game strikes again). He does this precisely in order to make the Synoptic Gospels' evidence for Jesus's divinity effectively disappear. In this way, the accounts of Jesus's disciples and eyewitnesses are transformed into tales told later by followers who made up stories about Jesus in which he spoke and acted as if he were divine.

But, as we have seen in earlier chapters, there's no evidence that the four Gospels are the end products of an anonymous chain of storytellers. There's no evidence that the Gospels are the last link in an ancient game of Telephone. Instead, the evidence is that the Gospels are based on the testimony of "eyewitnesses" to the life and ministry of Jesus (see Luke 1:1-4; John 21:24). And the Gospels—including the Synoptic Gospels—are very clear that during the stilling of the storm, the walking on water, and the Transfiguration, Jesus of Nazareth did and said things that only the LORD, the Creator of the universe, the God of Israel, could do and say.

With that said, we are still left with the question: Is Jesus's divine identity something that he reveals only privately, to his closest disciples? Or does he ever speak about his divinity in his public teaching? And why does Jesus command the disciples not to tell about what happened during the Transfiguration? Why the secrecy? In order to answer these questions, in the next chapter we will look more carefully at the "secret" of Jesus's divinity.

The Secret of Jesus's Divinity

If you've ever sat down and read the Gospels of Matthew, Mark, or Luke from beginning to end, one of the most striking things you might have noticed is how Jesus often instructs the demons, his disciples, and others *not to tell anyone who he is*.

For example, during his many exorcisms, Jesus "would not permit the demons to speak, because they knew him" (Mark 1:34). In one case, when the demons cry out, "You are the Son of God," Jesus "strictly ordered them not to make him known" (Mark 3:11-12). After he heals a man of leprosy, he "sternly charged him" to "say nothing to any one" about what had happened (Mark 1:43-44). Likewise, when he heals the man with a speech impediment, he does so "aside from the multitude, privately," and then afterward "charged them to tell no one" (Mark 7:36). When the apostle Peter confesses Jesus to be the Christ at Caesarea Philippi, Jesus charges the disciples "to tell no one about him" (Mark 8:30). And after the voice of God identifies Jesus as his beloved Son during the Transfiguration, Jesus commands the disciples "to tell no one what they had seen, until the Son of Man should have risen from the dead" (Mark 9:9). This secrecy about Jesus's identity is present in all three Synoptic Gospels (see Matthew 8:4; 12:16; 16:20; Luke 4:41; 9:21).

Why does Jesus do this? Why the secrecy?

The Messianic Secret

Whole books have been written attempting to explain what scholars have come to refer to as "the Messianic secret."[1] Some don't know what to make of Jesus telling everybody to keep quiet. If we assume that Jesus came to bring the good news of who he is, then his insistence on silence about his identity and his most memorable miracles seems counterintuitive, to say the least. Others suggest Jesus may have been using "reverse psychology"—what he really wanted was for his disciples and those he healed to tell everybody. So, knowing human nature, he tells them not to tell anybody who he is. The result: "the more he charged them, the more zealously they proclaimed it" (Mark 7:36).

But the best explanation is that he is biding his time. Because the truth about his identity is so potentially explosive, Jesus keeps it as secret as possible until the time is right to bring his mission to a climax. In the words of New Testament scholar Craig Keener:

> [A]t least one important reason for allowing claims of his messiahship only toward the end of his ministry was a matter of *practical strategy*. Messianic acclamations could (and did) lead the authorities wrongly to classify Jesus as a revolutionary and seek his execution; thus Jesus presumably delays his martyrdom until the appropriate time and place (Passover in Jerusalem). . . . If Jesus knew anything at all about the political situation in Jerusalem, he would know that a public messianic claim would lead to his almost immediate execution.[2]

It is difficult to overemphasize the importance of this insight into Jesus's practical strategy for revealing who he is. Many scholars accept the idea that Jesus keeps his messianic identity secret for strategic reasons. However, they often fail to apply the same logic to his divine identity. In short: the reason Jesus does not repeatedly and explicitly proclaim himself to be *the Messiah* is also the reason Jesus does not repeatedly and explicitly proclaim himself to be *divine*. Because the truth about his divine identity is even more momentous than his messianic identity, during his public ministry he only speaks about it in riddles until the time is come for him to reveal it fully.

This is precisely what some readers of the Gospels fail to see. For some, the fact that Jesus does not repeatedly and explicitly identify himself as God during his public ministry in the Synoptic Gospels shows that he did not think he was divine. As we saw in the last chapter, one of the major reasons given by some scholars for doubting that Jesus thought he was God is that he (supposedly) does not make the same kind of "exalted claims" about himself in the Synoptic Gospels as he does in the Gospel of John.[3] But this idea is wrong on two counts.

For one thing, as several scholars have shown, *even in the Gospel of John*, when Jesus speaks about his divine identity, he does not go around proclaiming, "I am God!" Instead, he uses riddles, parables, and words that can be interpreted in more than one way.[4] In fact, on more than one occasion in the Gospel of John, Jesus's Jewish audience and his disciples refer to the elusive way in which Jesus speaks about his identity:

> So the Jews gathered round him and said to him, *"How long will you keep us in suspense?* If you are the Christ, *tell us plainly."* (John 10:24)

> His disciples said, "Ah, *now you are speaking plainly*, not in any figure [of speech]!" (John 16:29)

Because of these and other passages, some scholars even talk about "a form of the Messianic Secret" in the Gospel of John.[5] Moreover, in contrast to the common claim, the Synoptic Gospels do in fact provide evidence that Jesus claimed to be divine. But Jesus reveals his divine identity in the same way he reveals his messianic identity—not explicitly, but implicitly—using riddles and questions, partly in order to bide his time.[6]

In other words, just as Jesus sometimes practices a kind of secrecy about his messianic identity, so too he sometimes practices a kind of secrecy about his divine identity. As Joseph Ratzinger (Benedict XVI) writes: "This was the idea to which even Jesus could only slowly and gradually lead people."[7] However, this secrecy does not mean that Jesus never taught that he was God; it just means that he did so in a strategic way, by using *riddles* and *questions* designed to *reveal* his identity to those who were open to believing and to *conceal* his identity from those who would oppose him. In this chapter, we will look at three episodes in the Synoptic Gospels in which Jesus speaks in this way about his divine identity: (1) the healing of the paralytic, (2) Jesus's question about the Messiah, and (3) his encounter with the rich young man.

The Healing of the Paralytic: Who Can Forgive Sins but God Alone?

The first example of how Jesus reveals his divinity comes from one of the first miracles recorded in the Synoptic Gospels: the famous account of the healing of the paralytic. In response to the extraordinary effort of the men who let down their paralyzed friend through the roof, Jesus says and does something even more extraordinary:

> And when he returned to Capernaum after some days, it was reported that he was at home. And many were gathered together, so that there was no longer room for them, not even about the door; and he was preaching the word to them. And they came, bringing to him a paralytic carried by four men. And when they could not get near him because of the crowd, they removed the roof above him; and when they had made an opening, they let down the pallet on which the paralytic lay. And when Jesus saw their faith, he said to the paralytic, "My son, your sins are forgiven." Now some of the scribes were sitting there, questioning in their hearts, *"Why does this man speak thus?*

It is blasphemy! Who can forgive sins but God alone?" And immediately Jesus, perceiving in his spirit that they thus questioned within themselves, said to them, "Why do you question thus in your hearts? Which is easier, to say to the paralytic, 'Your sins are forgiven,' or to say, 'Rise, take up your pallet and walk'? *But that you may know that the Son of Man has authority on earth to forgive sins"*—he said to the paralytic—"I say to you, rise, take up your pallet and go home." And he rose, and immediately took up the pallet and went out before them all; so that they were all amazed and glorified God, saying, *"We never saw anything like this!"* (Mark 2:1-12)

As with other passages we've looked at, there are various differences in detail among the versions in the Synoptic Gospels (compare Matthew 9:1-8; Luke 5:17-26). However, all three accounts agree in substance on the paralyzed man being brought to Jesus; the declaration by Jesus that the man's sins are "forgiven"; the scribes' reacting to Jesus's declaration by accusing him of blasphemy; and Jesus's response, in which he heals the paralytic precisely to show that "the Son of Man" has authority to "forgive sins."[8] The question for us is this: What does all this reveal about who Jesus thinks he is? How would his words and actions have been understood in a first-century Jewish context?

First, notice that Jesus's initial words to the paralytic are focused exclusively on the forgiveness of his sins. At first, Jesus does not say anything about the healing of the man's body. Now, I don't know about you, but if *I* were the paralytic, I could imagine thinking: "Thanks for letting me know about my sins being forgiven. However, that's not *exactly* what I came here for!" In other words, from the start, Jesus exceeds the expectations of those who seek him, surprises those whom he encounters, and shows that his ministry is focused above all on healing the broken relationship between sinful human beings and God.

Second, in all three Synoptic Gospels, the Jewish scribes react by accusing Jesus of "blasphemy" (Matthew 9:3; Mark 2:7; Luke 5:21). In a first-century Jewish context, the word "blasphemy" could be used to describe any number of offenses against God, the Temple, the Scriptures, and even holy men (see Acts 6:11).[9] Direct blasphemy against God was punishable by death (Exodus 20:7). In this instance, the Jewish scribes clarify the specific nature of Jesus's supposed blasphemy when they ask: "*Who can forgive sins but God alone?*" (Mark 2:7). A more literal translation of the original Greek would be: "Who can forgive sins but *the one God* (Greek *heis ho theos*)?" Significantly, this expression "the one God" alludes to the most well-known passage in the Old Testament:

> "Hear, O Israel: *The LORD our God, the LORD is one;* and you shall love the LORD your God with all your heart, and with all your soul, and with all your might." (Deuteronomy 6:4-6)[10]

This passage is known in Jewish tradition as the Shema (from the Hebrew word for "hear"). In the first century, it was likely recited by Jews like Jesus at least twice a day.[11] It was certainly the foundation of Jewish monotheism: the belief that the LORD is the one true God. This means that when the scribes accuse Jesus of doing something that only "the one God" can do, they are accusing him of blasphemy of the gravest sort. In the words of Adela Yarbro Collins:

> [T]here is no precedent for a human being making a simple declaration that God is at this moment forgiving another human being's sin. . . . What Jesus has said calls the unity of God into question.[12]

From the scribes' point of view, by declaring the paralytic's sins forgiven, Jesus is acting as if *he* were the one God of the Shema—the God who "forgiv[es] iniquity and transgression and sin" (Exodus 34:7).

With this Old Testament background in mind, it is remarkable that Jesus does not back down from the charge that he is acting as if he were the one God. Instead, he declares that he will heal the paralytic precisely so that the scribes might know that "the Son of Man" *does* have authority on earth "to forgive sins" (Mark 2:10). With these words, Jesus implicitly reveals himself to be "the Son of Man," since he is the one who goes on to heal the paralytic. Even more important, he is also alluding to one of the few passages in the Old Testament that appears to describe two divine beings in heaven—the Ancient of Days, and the one like a son of man:

> As I looked,
> thrones were placed,
> and *one that was ancient of days* took his seat;
> his raiment was white as snow,
> and the hair of his head like pure wool;
> his throne was fiery flames,
> its wheels were burning fire. . . .
> . . . *Behold, with the clouds of heaven*
> *there came one like a son of man,*
> and he came to the Ancient of Days
> and was presented before him.
> And to him was given dominion
> and glory and kingdom,
> that all peoples, nations, and languages
> should serve him;
> his dominion is an everlasting dominion,
> which shall not pass away,
> and his kingdom one
> that shall not be destroyed. (Daniel 7:9, 13-14)

In chapter 8, I showed how ancient Jews identified the figure of the "son of man" in Daniel as the Messiah. But there's more going on here. Many modern-day readers may think that when Jesus refers to himself as "the Son of Man" he is emphasizing his humanity, but in a first-century Jewish context, the opposite may have been true. Several scholars have argued that the "son of man" in Daniel 7 is not only a messianic king, but a *divine being.*[13]

Two observations are necessary in order to see the divinity of the son of man in the book of Daniel. First, he "comes on the clouds of heaven"—something *only God* does in the Old Testament.[14] Second, the book of Daniel says that he is *"like* a son of man"—that is, he *appears* to be a merely human figure but is in fact a heavenly being (Daniel 7:13). In light of these points, the contemporary Jewish scholar Daniel Boyarin draws the following striking conclusion about the identity of the son of man in Daniel:

> What this text [Daniel 7] projects is *a second divine figure* to whom will be given eternal dominion of the entire world. . . . In other words, a simile, *a God who looks like a human being* (literally Son of Man) has become the name for that God, who is now called "Son of Man," a reference to his human-appearing divinity.[15]

In other words, the son of man in the book of Daniel is a divine figure who appears as a human being—a mysterious blend of both God and man. As Rabbi Boyarin puts it, the son of man is "a human-divine combination."[16] That's why the one like a son of man has a heavenly throne and reigns over an everlasting kingdom. Those are the kinds of things God does.

Once you have this Old Testament background in mind, all of a sudden, not only does Jesus's response to the accusation of blasphemy make perfect sense; it also begins to reveal the secret of his divine identity. Jesus forgives the sins of the paralytic, acting as if he were God. The scribes charge him with blasphemy for claiming to do something only the one God can do. Jesus responds by posing a riddle that challenges the scribes to recognize his identity as the Son of Man described in the book of Daniel, who looks mysteriously like a divine being. As the heavenly Son of Man, Jesus has the power "on earth" to forgive sins. Finally, in order to back up his claim to divine power, Jesus performs the *visible* act of healing the paralytic in order to prove that he can also perform the *invisible and divine act* of forgiving the man's sins. And he does all this without ever having to publicly or explicitly say, "I am God" or "I am divine"—something which would have gotten him quickly stoned to death.

In short: Jesus uses the expression "the Son of Man" to both conceal and reveal his identity. In the words of Adela Yarbro Collins:

[T]he use of the epithet "the Son of Man" conceals as much as it re-
veals about who Jesus is. . . . The phrase alludes to Daniel 7:13, but in
a very indirect and cryptic way. Its use by Jesus in his dialogue with the
scribes is, in effect, *a riddle.* Jesus issues them a challenge to discern
his identity, a challenge they apparently failed to meet.[17]

By means of this riddle, Jesus is issuing a challenge to the scribes to
discern his *divine* identity as the heavenly Son of Man. And this isn't
the only time he hints at the secret of his divinity.

Jesus and the Pre-existent Messiah

Another instance is when Jesus speaks of the mysterious riddle about
the son of David. This episode is particularly important because it is
the only passage in all four Gospels in which Jesus explicitly poses a
question about "the Messiah" (Greek *ho Christos*). According to all
three Synoptic Gospels, while Jesus is teaching in the Temple in Jerusalem, he raises this question about the identity of the Messiah:

> And as Jesus taught in the temple, he said, "How can the scribes say
> that the Messiah is the Son of David? *David himself, inspired by the*
> *Holy Spirit, declared,*
>
> *'The Lord said to my Lord,*
> *Sit at my right hand,*
> *till I put thy enemies under thy feet.' [Psalm 110:1]*
>
> *David himself calls him Lord; so how is he his son?"* And the great
> throng heard him gladly. (Mark 12:35-37)

Once again, although there are a few minor differences in detail,
the three Synoptic accounts are substantially the same: Jesus raises a
question about why "the Messiah" is referred to by some as "the Son of
David"; he quotes the first line of Psalm 110 to show that David himself
referred to the Messiah as "Lord"; and then he leaves his audience to

figure out how the two statements can be reconciled (compare Matthew 22:41-46; Luke 20:41-44).[18] For our purposes, this evidence raises several questions: Why does Jesus question the custom of referring to the Messiah as the Son of David? Why does Jesus quote the words of David in Psalm 110 about "the Lord" saying to David's "Lord" to sit at his right hand? Above all, what does Jesus's reference to this particular psalm reveal about his view of the Messiah?

First, despite what some claim, Jesus is *not* rejecting the idea that the Messiah is a descendant of King David.[19] The Old Testament makes abundantly clear that the future king of Israel—who by the first century came to be known as "the Messiah"—will in fact be descended from David (see 2 Samuel 7; Isaiah 11; Jeremiah 33; Ezekiel 37). What Jesus *is* questioning is the scribal tradition of referring to the Messiah by the *title* "the Son of David." Why? Because the title "Son of David" is never found in Jewish Scripture; it comes from later in Jewish tradition. For this reason, Jesus is saying that the scriptural title for the Messiah is actually "Lord (Greek *kyrios*) of David." He does this by referring to Psalm 110, in which David, inspired by the Holy Spirit, refers to the future king—which Jesus identifies as the Messiah—as his "Lord" (Hebrew *'adon;* Greek *kyrios*) (Psalm 110:1). By juxtaposing the traditional scribal title for the Messiah with David's reference to "my Lord" in Psalm 110, Jesus is saying that, according to Scripture, *the Messiah is more than just the descendant of David. The Messiah is also David's lord.* From a biblical point of view, the Jewish scribes should be going around referring to the Messiah as "the Lord of David."[20]

But that's not all that's going on here. If you go back to Psalm 110 and read it carefully, you will discover that the figure identified by Jesus as the Messiah is not only referred to as David's "Lord." He is also described as being seated on a heavenly throne and as being begotten by God from the beginning of creation! You can see this clearly if you read the first several verses of the psalm:

> A Psalm of David.
> *The LORD says to my lord:*
> *"Sit at my right hand,*

till I make your enemies your footstool."
The scepter of your power the LORD will stretch forth from Zion:
Yours is princely power in the day of your birth, in holy splendor;
From the womb of the dawn, like the dew, I have begotten you.
the LORD has sworn and will not repent:
"You are a priest forever according to the order of Melchizedek."
    (Psalm 110:1-4)[21]

By choosing Psalm 110 to describe the identity of "the Messiah" (Greek *ho Christos*), Jesus gives us a crucial window into his own "Christology"—his own teaching about who the Messiah really is. The king in the psalm is not just a descendant of David; he is in some way greater than David, since David addresses him as "lord" (Hebrew *'adon;* Greek *kyrios*). Moreover, the Messiah in Psalm 110 is not just greater than King David; he is a *heavenly* king who is depicted in some way as *equal* with the LORD, the one true God. Although modern readers might miss the point, such equality is implied because the Messiah sits "at the right hand" of God. In the words of Joel Marcus:

> A seated position at the right hand of a deity implies co-regency with him. . . . The imagery of the quoted portion of the psalm, then, implies that "my lord" stands in a relation of *near-equality with God.*[22]

Finally, a case can be made that the Messiah in Psalm 110 is not just the heavenly Lord of David. According to the most ancient Jewish translation that we possess, he is also described as having been "begotten" (Hebrew *yalad*) by God "from the womb of the dawn" (Hebrew *merechem mishchar*) (Psalm 110:3).[23] This may be the final point of contrast implied by Jesus: while the scribes say the Messiah is begotten of David, the psalm says the Messiah is "begotten" by the LORD from the very dawn of creation. So by choosing Psalm 110, Jesus is also implying that the Messiah is the *pre-existent* Son of God.[24]

The reason this Old Testament background matters so much is simple but enormously significant. *Since Jesus thought he was the Messiah, he is using Psalm 110 to reveal what he thinks about himself.*

Jesus is implying that he is not just a descendant of David; he is David's "Lord." He is implying that he is a heavenly king who will be "seated at the right" of God, and thus is equal to him. Finally, and most staggering of all, Jesus is implying that he himself was "begotten" by the LORD from "the womb of the dawn." And he does all this by using a riddle—a question intended to tease the minds of his audience—in order to get them to ask: "Who is the Messiah really?" And most of his Jewish audience loved it: as the Gospel of Mark tells us, "the great throng heard him gladly" (Mark 12:37). They delighted in being taught by these kinds of parables, riddles, and questions. Others, however, are stopped short by the magnitude of Jesus's claim. As Matthew tells us: "No one was able to answer him a word, nor from that day did any one dare to ask him any more questions" (Matthew 22:46).

Thus Jesus is using the question about the Messiah in Psalm 110 to reveal the mystery of his own divine identity. He is both a descendant of King David and the Lord of King David. He is both the long-awaited Messiah and the pre-existent Son of God. In other words, he is both human and divine. And he reveals all this without ever coming out and explicitly declaring, "I am the Messiah," or "I am David's Lord," or "I existed from before the dawn of creation." Jesus uses the question about the Messiah in Psalm 110 just as he used the riddle about the Son of Man in Daniel 7: to reveal and conceal his messianic and divine identity—until the time was right. As we will see in the next chapter, it is precisely because Jesus will later quote these same two passages— Daniel 7 and Psalm 110—in the presence of the Jewish high priest that he will be accused of blasphemy and handed over to be executed. For when the time comes, he will use them again to reveal his identity to the high priest and the Jewish Sanhedrin.

Jesus and the Rich Young Man: "No One Is Good but God Alone"

The last example from the Synoptic Gospels of Jesus revealing the secret of his divinity is the famous story of his encounter with the rich young man. Unlike the other passages we've looked at so far, this evidence has often been used to argue that Jesus *denied* he was divine. So let's look at it carefully:

> And as he was setting out on his journey, a man ran up and knelt before him, and asked him, "Good Teacher, what must I do to inherit eternal life?" And Jesus said to him, *"Why do you call me good? No one is good but God alone.* You know the commandments: 'Do not kill, Do not commit adultery, Do not steal, Do not bear false witness, Do not defraud, Honor your father and mother.'" And he said to him, "Teacher, all these I have observed from my youth." And Jesus looking upon him loved him, and said to him, *"You lack one thing;* go, sell what you have, and give to the poor, and you will have treasure in heaven; *and come, follow me."* At that saying his countenance fell, and he went away sorrowful; for he had great possessions. (Mark 10:17-22)

Unlike the other episodes we've examined, the Gospel accounts of this incident are notably different (compare Matthew 19:17-22; Luke 18:18-23). While Mark and Luke are virtually identical, in Matthew's account, the young man asks about what "good deed" he must do to have eternal life, and Jesus replies, "Why do you ask me about what is good?" (Matthew 19:16-17). Over the centuries, various proposals for how to reconcile these differences have been put forward.[25] I for one see no way to reconstruct the *exact* words of Jesus, but I don't think we need to. For our purposes, what matters is that in all three accounts, the substance is the same: Jesus declares there is only "one" who is "good," namely, God (Matthew 19:17; Mark 10:18; Luke 18:19). He also commands the young man to keep the commandments, and then ends by telling him that the only thing he's lacking is to go and sell everything and "come follow" him. At this, the man goes away sad. What are we to make of Jesus's words? Is he denying that he is good? And, if so, is he also denying that he is God?

That's exactly how many people have interpreted Jesus's words.

For example, all the way back in the fourth century AD, Arius—a priest in Alexandria who denied that Jesus was fully divine and went on to become the most famous heretic in Church history—used Jesus's declaration that "no one is good but God alone" to argue that Jesus was not fully God.[26] In more recent times, the famous German scholar Adolf von Harnack used the story of Jesus and the rich young man to claim that the message of Jesus was focused on God, not himself. At the beginning of the twentieth century, Harnack wrote: "Not the Son, but the Father only, has a place in the Gospel which Jesus proclaimed. . . . He characterized the Lord of heaven and earth as his God and Father, as greater than he, and as *the only one who is good*."[27] And, if I may speak for myself, for many years the story of the rich young man was one of the key passages in the Synoptic Gospels that made me wonder if Jesus really claimed to be divine or if he himself insisted that he was just a man.

I can now see that there were three things about Jesus's exchange with the rich young man that I did not yet understand. First and foremost, *Jesus does not deny that he himself is good.* He does not say, "I am not good." If he had said this, then we would have to admit that he did not regard himself as God. Yet all Jesus affirms is that there is only "one" (Greek *heis*) who is truly "good"—God. And he does this by alluding to the Shema—the same Old Testament passage he alluded to in the account of the healing of the paralytic!

> Hear, O Israel: *The LORD our God, the LORD is one;* and you shall love the LORD your God with all your heart, and with all your soul, and with all your might. (Deuteronomy 6:4-6)

Jesus's allusion to "the one God" of the Shema is no coincidence.[28] It is an important clue that he is leading the rich young man to the same conclusion to which he was leading the Jewish scribes when he healed the paralytic. As Joel Marcus states: "Our passage does not deny Jesus' goodness but ascribes it to its divine origin."[29] Likewise, Simon Gathercole writes that in both accounts "we have the phrase 'except God alone,' and in both places Jesus does not constitute a second exception alongside God but rather stands, in his goodness, on the divine side of reality over against humanity."[30] If these interpretations are right, then Jesus is using the young man's knowledge of the Shema to go straight to the heart of the question: Who is Jesus?

Second, *Jesus uses questions and riddles to lead his audience into the mystery of who he is.* That's what he does with the healing of the paralytic. That's what he does with the question about the Messiah. And that's what he's doing with the rich young man. New Testament scholar Sigurd Grindheim writes:

> The most natural way to read the first part of this saying is that Jesus wants the rich man to make clear what he means. In other words, *Jesus wants to elicit from the man what he thinks about Jesus. . . .* The diverging interpretations of this saying continue to demonstrate the openness of Jesus' words. He does not make a statement about himself, but provokes the audience to *make their own judgment.*[31]

This is an extremely important insight: Jesus does not go around shoving the mystery of his divinity down people's throats. He wants *them* to freely come to believe in him. He wants *them* to freely arrive at their own conclusions about who he is and how they are going to respond to him. And in the case of the rich young man, Jesus poses a question that is meant to lead the young man to follow out the implications of his own words. If Jesus is "good," and God alone is "good," then who exactly is Jesus? That is the question.

Third and finally, Jesus ends by telling the rich young man that the "one thing" he still lacks is to sell all he has and follow him. *This ending is essential for unlocking the riddle of his words.* Yet it is constantly overlooked by those who claim Jesus is denying that he is God. After making his declaration about the goodness of God, Jesus does something stunning: he adds a command to follow *him* to the obligation to keep the Ten Commandments. In a first-century Jewish context, this would have been shocking. In Jewish Scripture, the Ten Commandments are written by the very "finger of God" (Exodus 31:18). Yet here is Jesus adding the command to follow him as if that was on par with keeping the commandments.[32] As Simon Gathercole writes:

> [W]hat is most striking is that having established the one good God as the one who defines what is required of human beings, in the final analysis Jesus is the one who defines what is ultimately commanded. . . . *If God alone is good and able to give commandments, then Jesus does so as well. By implication then, he is also good.* And he is good not in the sense implied by the rich man, but in the absolute, divine sense used by Jesus himself.[33]

In other words, when it comes to the question of "eternal life," following Jesus is an essential part of the equation. The only way to interpret Jesus's statement that "No one is good but God alone" as a denial of his divine identity is to wrench his words completely out of context. In context, these words are preceded by a riddle-like question and followed by Jesus's striking injunction to the rich man to sell everything and follow him.

Thus, when we interpret the story of Jesus and the rich young man in its first-century Jewish context, we discover that the passage most frequently used to argue that Jesus does not claim to be divine upon closer inspection turns out to be powerful evidence that Jesus does claim to be God. However, he is communicating in a way that is both very Jewish (alluding to the Shema) and very consistent with the messianic secret of his identity. During his public ministry, Jesus wants his audience to ask for themselves: Who is this man? And what is his relationship with the one God?

The Church Fathers and the Secret of Jesus's Divinity

Before I wrap up this chapter, it's important for readers to know that none of the interpretations that I have given here are really anything new. Since ancient times, these passages in the Gospels have been interpreted just as I have suggested: as riddle-like revelations of Jesus's divine identity.

For example, both orthodox and heretical ancient Christian writers agree that when Jesus declared that the paralytic's sins were forgiven, he was also acting as if he were God. Consider the words of Novatian of Rome (third century AD) and John Chrysostom (fourth century AD):

> If Christ forgives sins, Christ must be truly God because no one can forgive sins but God alone. (Novatian, *The Trinity*, 13)[34]

> He confirmed this [his divinity] through his own actions. . . . The scribes themselves had devised this definition. They themselves had introduced the precept. But he proceeded to entangle them in their own words. In effect he said: it is you yourselves who have confessed that forgiveness of sins is given to God alone. (John Chrysostom, *The Paralytic Let Down Through the Roof*, 6)[35]

Along similar lines, way back in the fifth century AD, Augustine of Hippo recognized that Jesus's question about the "Son of David" in Psalm 110 does not deny that the Messiah is descended from David. Instead, Jesus uses the question about the Messiah to reveal the mystery of his divinity:

> He did not say, "He is not his Son," but "How is He his son?" *When he says "How," it is a word not of negation, but of enquiry.* . . . [It] is a great thing to know *the mystery of how He is David's Son and David's Lord: how one Person is both Man and God.* . . . Seeing this is a great mystery, our conduct must be fashioned, that it may be comprehended. For to the unworthy is it closed up, [but] it is opened to those who are ready for it. (Augustine, *Sermons on Selected Lessons of the New Testament*, 91.2)[36]

Unlike some modern interpreters, Augustine recognizes Jesus's question as an *invitation* to inquire into the mystery of how the Messiah can be both David's son and David's Lord. And precisely because this *is* a "great mystery," not everyone is going to comprehend the implications of Jesus's words.[37] But that doesn't mean Jesus isn't teaching that he's God. He's just doing so in the form of a question.

Finally, even Jesus's declaration that "No one is good but God alone" was recognized by church fathers such as Ambrose of Milan and John Chrysostom as an invitation to the rich young man to follow the implications of his own words:

> The Lord, then, does not deny His goodness. . . . For when the scribe said, "Good Master," the Lord answered, "Why do you call me good? . . ." (Ambrose, *Exposition of the Christian Faith*, 2.1.19)[38]

> When he [Jesus] says, "No one is good," *he does not say this to show that he is not good;* far from it. *For he does not say,* "Why do you call me good? *I am not good*" but *"No one is good,"* that is, no human being. (John Chrysostom, *Homilies on the Gospel of Matthew*, 63.1)[39]

The upshot of this evidence is simple: for centuries, readers have recognized that Jesus is not denying that he is divine in the Synoptic Gospels. Instead, in keeping with his parabolic method of teaching, he is using questions and riddles precisely in order to lead people into the mystery of his divinity.

Of course, this still leaves us with the question: Did Jesus's teachings about his identity have anything to do with why he was eventually put to death? How does a man who claims to be the divine Son of God end up as a crucified Messiah? To that question we now turn.

11

The Crucifixion

If there's any aspect of the life of Jesus that has given rise to doubts about whether he really was the Messiah and the divine Son of God, it is the fact that he was *crucified*. Already in the first century AD, the apostle Paul could refer to the crucifixion of Christ as a "stumbling block (Greek *skandalon*) to the Jews and folly (Greek *mōria*) to Gentiles" (1 Corinthians 1:23). If you look carefully at the two Greek terms Paul uses here, you can see that we get the English words "scandal" and "moron" from them. In other words, Paul is saying that the very idea of "Christ crucified"—a crucified Messiah—was scandalous to first-century Jews and moronic to ancient pagans (known as "Gentiles"). That should give you some idea of just how foolish the idea of a crucified Savior really was. The reason: in the first century AD, Roman crucifixion was nothing less than the most brutal, most shameful, most despicable way to die that could be imagined. In the words of both Jewish and Roman writers: crucifixion was "the most wretched of deaths" (Josephus, *War* 7.203) and "the most severe punishment" possible (Paulus, *Sententiae*, 5.21.3).[1]

Because Jesus of Nazareth met his end on the wood of a Roman cross, the question has to be asked: *Why was Jesus crucified?* What did he do and say that led to his being condemned to death by the Jewish leaders and executed by the Roman authorities? Moreover, if Jesus was divine, how could he have uttered the words: "My God, my God, why have you forsaken me?" (Matthew 27:46; Mark 15:34). Is this the kind of thing the divine Son of God would say? Doesn't it sound as if Jesus is despairing at the very end? In short, if you're trying to make the case that Jesus of Nazareth was not only the Messiah but the divine Son of God, then you have to be able to explain the historical fact and the theological significance of his crucifixion.

That's what we'll try to do in this chapter. We'll begin by looking carefully at the reason Jesus was crucified.

Why Was Jesus Crucified?

If we know anything about Jesus of Nazareth, it is that he was put to death by crucifixion. Both the writings of the New Testament and ancient Jewish and Greco-Roman sources like Josephus, Tacitus, and Lucian of Samosata agree that Jesus was executed by the Roman authorities of his day.[2] As a result, many scholars emphasize that any truly historical investigation of the life of Jesus has to be able to explain why, from a historical perspective, he was crucified.

As Bart Ehrman notes, sometimes the popular answers to the question "Who was Jesus?" don't do justice to the fact of the crucifixion:

> [If] Jesus had simply been a great moral teacher, a gentle rabbi who did nothing more than urge his devoted followers to love God and one another, or an itinerant philosopher . . . then he would scarcely have been seen as a threat to the Romans and nailed to a cross. Great moral teachers were not crucified—unless their teachings were considered subversive.[3]

This is a great point. Although people nowadays are sometimes tempted to paint Jesus as a great teacher or a harmless rabbi who just wanted everyone to love each other, such caricatures fail as history because they cannot explain how Jesus ended up crucified. In the words of John Meier: "[O]ne of the most striking things about Jesus was his crucifixion or execution by Rome. A Jesus whose words and deeds would not alienate people, especially powerful people, is not the historical Jesus."[4]

So why was Jesus crucified? Different theories have been put forward over the years. In recent decades, perhaps the most popular explanation is that Jesus's predictions of the destruction of the Temple (Mark 13:2; 14:58), combined with his overturning of the money changers' tables in the Temple (Mark 11:15-16; John 2:14-16), is what ultimately got him killed. According to this theory, it was primarily Jesus's words against the Temple that angered the Jewish leaders and led them to arrest him and hand him over to the Roman authorities as a troublemaker.[5]

What are we to make of this explanation? At first glance, it seems plausible. For one thing, it's true that Jesus's prophecies about the Temple and his act of overturning the tables in the Temple played a key role in his being arrested and tried by the Jewish leaders in Jerusalem. One Gospel clearly says that after Jesus overturned the money changers' tables, "the chief priests and scribes heard it and sought a way to destroy him" (Mark 11:18). Moreover, as we'll soon see, Jesus's (alleged) threat to "destroy the Temple" and in three days raise it up again is brought up against him later when he is being questioned by the chief council of Jewish leaders (Mark 14:58). But there's one big problem with the theory that he was crucified because of what he prophesied about the Temple. On closer inspection, there's no actual evidence of this. According to the first-century Gospels, the Jewish leaders do not condemn Jesus because of what he says about the Temple. *They condemn him to death because of who he claims to be.* According to the evidence, Jesus was condemned for blasphemy.

Jesus Was Condemned for Blasphemy

In order to see this clearly, we have to look carefully at Jesus's exchange with the high priest, Caiaphas, in the presence of the council of Jewish leaders known as the Sanhedrin. This episode, which is re-corded in all three Synoptic Gospels (Matthew 26:59-66; Mark 14:53-64; Luke 22:66-71), may be the most important evidence in any historical attempt to explain why Jesus was crucified.[6] Consider Mark's account:

> Now the chief priests and the whole Sanhedrin sought testimony against Jesus to put him to death; but they found none. For many bore false witness against him, and their witness did not agree. And some stood up and bore false witness against him, saying, "We heard him say, 'I will destroy this temple that is made with hands, and in three days I will build another, not made with hands.'" Yet not even so did their testimony agree. And the high priest stood up in the midst, and asked Jesus, "Have you no answer to make? What is it that these men testify against you?" But he was silent and made no answer. Again the high priest asked him, *"Are you the Christ, the Son of the Blessed?"* And Jesus said, *"I am; and you will see the Son of Man seated at the right hand of Power, and coming with the clouds of heaven."* And the high priest tore his garments, and said, "Why do we still need wit-nesses? *You have heard his blasphemy.* What is your decision?" *And they all condemned him as deserving death.* (Mark 14:55-64)

There are a number of differences in detail among the Synoptic Gos-pels, but the essential content of Jesus's response to Caiaphas before the Sanhedrin is the same.[7] Although Jesus is accused of threatening to destroy the Temple, that's not what leads to his being condemned to death. Instead, he is condemned for how he answers Caiaphas's question about his identity. In two of the three accounts, Jesus is found guilty of the sin of "blasphemy" (Greek *blasphēmias*), based on what he has said to the Jewish leaders about himself (Matthew 26:65; Mark 14:64). No other charge is ever mentioned. Jesus is sentenced to death for who he claims to be.

As soon as we say this, a problem arises. Was it really blasphemy to claim to be the Messiah? Of course not.[8] Think about it for a moment: if the Messiah is simply the long-awaited king of Israel, then how could it be blasphemy to claim to be him? Likewise, if it were somehow against the law to claim to be the Messiah, then how would anyone ever know who the Messiah was? Clearly, something more is going on here. Who exactly is Jesus claiming to be?

In order to answer these questions, we need to explore four key points.

First, in his response to Caiaphas, *Jesus openly claims to be the Messiah.*[9] When Caiaphas asks Jesus, "Are you the Christ (Greek *Christos*), the Son of the Blessed?" (Mark 14:61), that's what he is asking. And that is what Jesus affirms, whether his exact words were "I am" or "You have said so" or "You say that I am" (compare Mark 14:62 with Matthew 26:64; Luke 22:70). Either way, he is answering Caiaphas in the *affirmative:* he is saying, in effect: "You said it. I am the Messiah."[10] As we have seen previously, during his public ministry, Jesus was reluctant to explicitly identify himself as the Messiah. However, now that the end of his life is at hand, he formally affirms his messianic identity. In the words of Gerhard Lohfink:

> Naturally, the reader of the gospel wonders how Jesus can accept in the presence of the Sanhedrin a title of authority . . . he has long avoided in public and even forbidden his disciples to use openly. . . . The answer can only be that now, in the presence of the highest authority in Israel, the hour has come to speak openly. Now the possibility of misunderstanding and deliberate misinterpretation must be accepted.[11]

In other words, the time for keeping the messianic secret is over. Notice also that in the exchange between Caiaphas and Jesus, the question of the Temple never comes up. Jesus's identity is the real issue.[12]

Second—and this is crucial—Jesus not only explicitly claims to be the Messiah; *he also implicitly claims to be divine*. He does so by quoting from two passages in Jewish Scripture: the vision of the heavenly "son of man" in Daniel 7 and the description of the pre-existent king in Psalm 110. Although we've looked at these passages before, let's examine them once again with Caiaphas's question about Jesus's identity in mind:

> Behold, *with the clouds of heaven*
> *there came one like a son of man,*
> and *he came to the Ancient of Days*
> *and was presented before him.*
> And to him was given dominion
> and glory and kingdom,
> that all peoples, nations, and languages
> should serve him. (Daniel 7:13-14)

> A Psalm of David.
> *The LORD says to my lord:*
> *"Sit at my right hand,*
> till I make your enemies your footstool."
> The scepter of your power the LORD will stretch forth from Zion:
> Yours is princely power in the day of your birth, in holy splendor;
> *From the womb of the dawn, like the dew, I have begotten you.*
>   (Psalm 110:1-3)[13]

In both passages alluded to by Jesus, the royal figure is described as if he were divine. In Daniel 7, the son of man ascends to the heavenly "throne" to sit beside the Ancient of Days. He also comes "on the clouds of heaven"—something that only God does in Jewish Scripture.[14] Likewise, in Psalm 110, the Davidic king sits on a heavenly throne at the "right hand" of the LORD. Even more, the king is described as having been "begotten" by God before the dawn of history. In other words, the person being described is no ordinary human, but the pre-existent Son of God. As Adela Yarbro Collins puts it:

> In this saying, Jesus claims to be a messiah of the heavenly type, who will be exalted to the right hand of God (Ps 110:1). *Being seated at the right hand of God implies being equal to God,* at least in terms of

authority and power. The allusion to Dan[iel] 7:13 reinforces the heavenly messianic claim.[15]

It is no coincidence that Jesus answers Caiaphas's question about his identity by quoting two passages from the Old Testament in which the Messiah appears to be divine. In this way, Jesus is using the Scriptures to reveal that he is not just the Messiah, but the divine Son of God.[16]

Third, *the reaction of Caiaphas and the Sanhedrin confirms the divine implications of Jesus's answer.* Caiaphas immediately tears his garments and declares Jesus guilty of "blasphemy" (Matthew 26:65; Mark 14:63). Strikingly, this is precisely the same reaction described in early rabbinic literature when someone blasphemes against God by pronouncing the divine name: "the judges stand up on their feet and rend their garments" (Mishnah, *Sanhedrin* 7.5). Not surprisingly, the Sanhedrin condemns Jesus to "death" (Matthew 26:66; Mark 14:64). Recall once again that simply claiming to *be* the Messiah was not blasphemy.[17] But if Jesus is claiming to be a *divine* Messiah who will be seated on a heavenly throne (like God) and come in on the clouds of heaven (also like God), then the charge of blasphemy makes sense. In the words of W. D. Davies and Dale Allison:

> [I]t is also possible that Jesus himself was in fact accused of blasphemy—not for claiming to be the Messiah, nor for speaking against the temple, nor for things done during the course of his ministry, but for seating himself on a throne . . . in heaven.[18]

This suggestion finds support in first-century Judaism. For example, Philo of Alexandria, a Jewish contemporary of Jesus, described as "blasphemy" the words of any "man" who "has dared to compare himself to the all blessed God" (*On Dreams*, 2.130).[19] Equally striking are the words of Josephus, the first-century Jewish historian:

> Let him that blasphemes God (Greek *blasphēmēsas theon*) be stoned, *then hung for a day*, and buried ignominiously and in obscurity. (Josephus, *Antiquities*, 4.202)[20]

In other words, when it comes to a case of blasphemy against God him-self, execution alone is not enough. The offense requires crucifixion—being "hung" so that all can see the shame of the one who has dared to blaspheme God. Although under Rome it was not "lawful" for the Jewish leaders to put Jesus to death by stoning (John 18:31), they can still hand him over to be "hung" on a tree by the Romans. And that is what they do.

Fourth and finally, it's important to remember that Jesus's dec-laration before Caiaphas isn't the first time Jesus is accused of blas-phemy. Both the Synoptic Gospels and the Gospel of John testify to previous incidents when Jesus is accused of blasphemy during his public ministry:

> And behold, some of the scribes said to themselves, *"This man is blas-pheming."* (Matthew 9:3)

> Now some of the scribes were sitting there, questioning in their hearts, "Why does this man speak thus? *It is blasphemy!* Who can for-give sins but God alone?" (Mark 2:6-7)

> [Jesus said:] "I and the Father are one." The Jews took up stones again to stone him. Jesus answered them, "I have shown you many good works from the Father; for which of these do you stone me?" The Jews answered him, *"We stone you for no good work but for blasphemy; be-cause you, being a man, make yourself God."* (John 10:30-33)

These other charges of blasphemy are consistently ignored by those who claim that Jesus was condemned to death for speaking against the Temple.[21] The reason: this evidence poses great difficulties for those who contend that Jesus never claimed to be God. And that is one reason why such an idea fails as a historical explanation. In order to work, it has to ignore or dismiss key pieces of evidence.[22] According to the Gospels, Jesus of Nazareth was accused of and, ultimately, con-demned for blasphemy because of who he claimed to be.

By the way, the evidence that Jesus was condemned for blasphemy isn't just in the Synoptic Gospels; it's also in the Gospel of John.[23] Although John's Gospel does not contain an account of Jesus's proclamation before Caiaphas, it does report that the chief priests and scribes publically accused Jesus of blasphemy on the day of his crucifixion:

> So Jesus came out, wearing the crown of thorns and the purple robe. Pilate said to them, "Here is the man!" When the chief priests and the officers saw him, they cried out, "Crucify him, crucify him!" Pilate said to them, "Take him yourselves and crucify him, for I find no crime in him." The Jews answered him, *"We have a law, and by that law he ought to die, because he has made himself the Son of God."* (John 19:5-7)

What is this law to which the chief priest and scribes are referring? It is the biblical law against blasphemy: "He who blasphemes the name of the LORD shall be put to death" (Leviticus 24:16).[24] Thus, both the Synoptics and the Gospel of John agree that it is the charge of blasphemy that lands Jesus on the cross.

The evidence presented here suggests that the now popular idea that Jesus never claimed to be anything more than an ordinary human being totally fails to deal with the actual historical evidence. Jesus's words and actions regarding the Temple might have got him hauled into the Jewish court, but it was what he said about himself that got him crucified. As Joseph Ratzinger (Benedict XVI) has written: "It is during Jesus' trial before the Sanhedrin that we see what was actually scandalous about him. . . . He seemed to be putting himself on an equal footing with the living God himself."[25]

"My God, My God, Why Have You Forsaken Me?"

As soon as we say this, a possible objection arises. If Jesus really claimed to be the pre-existent Messiah and the divine Son of God, then how do we explain his final words on the cross? How could he have been condemned for claiming to be divine, and then turn around and utter the words he reportedly spoke from the cross?

And when the sixth hour had come, there was darkness over the whole land until the ninth hour. *And at the ninth hour Jesus cried with a loud voice, "Eloi, Eloi, lama sabachthani?" which means, "My God, my God, why [have you] forsaken me?"* . . . And Jesus uttered a loud cry, and breathed his last. (Mark 15:33-35, 37; compare Matthew 27:45-50)[26]

What are we to make of Jesus's words on the cross just before he dies? What is the meaning of his so-called "cry of dereliction"?

Over the course of the last decade or so of teaching students in the classroom, it has become apparent to me that this is one of the most difficult passages in the Gospels to explain for those who believe in Jesus's divinity. Many of my Christian students have admitted to me that they don't understand how and why Jesus could say such a thing if he himself was God. And to be sure, on the surface, it certainly *seems* like Jesus is declaring that God has abandoned him in his final agony. At the very least, Jesus's cry of dereliction raises serious questions about his divine identity. How can he cry out to God for forsaking him if he himself is divine? Over a hundred years ago, the famous and influential German scholars Albert Schweitzer and Rudolf Bultmann concluded based on this passage that Jesus ended his life in despair. In the words of Bultmann: "We may not veil from ourselves the possibility that [Jesus] suffered a collapse."[27]

But this is completely wrong. If we've learned anything in this book so far, it's that Jesus's teachings—especially the most mysterious ones—must be interpreted in their *ancient Jewish context.* The same thing is true when it comes to his words: "My God, my God, why have you forsaken me?" (Matthew 27:46; Mark 15:34). As any first-century Jew would have known, these words are not just a spontaneous "cry of dereliction." Instead, they are a deliberate quotation of

Scripture. To be specific, Jesus is quoting the first line of Psalm 22, which begins:

> A Psalm of David.
> *My God, my God, why have you forsaken me?*
> Why are you so far from helping me, from the words of my groaning?
> O my God, I cry by day, but you do not answer;
> and by night, but find no rest. (Psalm 22:1-2)[28]

In ancient Judaism, it was customary to invoke an entire psalm just by quoting the first line.[29] We still do something like this today, when we invoke a well-known song or poem simply by quoting the first line or the chorus. (In Catholic circles, entire papal encyclical letters are customarily invoked by using the first line in Latin.) In other words, in order to understand *why* Jesus is quoting the first line of Psalm 22, we have to go back and look at *what the entire psalm is about*. When we do this, suddenly, Jesus's cry of dereliction gives us an important window into how Jesus understood his crucifixion.

First, Psalm 22 is a song of trust that God will save his suffering servant despite the appearance that God has abandoned him. For example, immediately after the opening lines, the psalm declares that the ancestors of Israel—the "fathers"—trusted in God and were saved. "To you they cried, and were saved; in you they trusted, and were not disappointed" (Psalm 22:5). Even more important, the psalm explicitly affirms that God does *not* turn his back or hide his face from the one who is suffering. Reread the following lines with Jesus's death in mind:

> You who fear the Lord, praise him!
> all you sons of Jacob, glorify him,
> and stand in awe of him, all you sons of Israel!
> *For he has not despised or abhorred the affliction of the afflicted;*
> and *he has not hid his face from him,*
> but has heard when he cried to him. (Psalm 22:23-24)

If Jesus breathed his last breath with this psalm in mind, then these verses alone prove that he did not die thinking that God the Father had "hid his face" from him. Instead, Psalm 22 shows that Jesus sees his suffering and death as a fulfillment of Scripture. When the whole psalm is taken into account, Jesus's words make crystal clear that although he *appears* to be forsaken in his suffering and death, in the end, God will hear him and save him.

Second, although Psalm 22 is attributed to King David, there are aspects of the psalm that never actually happened to David during his lifetime. As a result, this and other psalms came to be viewed by ancient Jews as prophecies of the Messiah.[30] We've already seen Jesus himself interpret Psalm 110 as a prophecy of the pre-existent "Messiah" (Mark 12:35-37). In the same vein, it's not hard to see why Jesus would quote Psalm 22 as a kind of prophecy of his death, since the psalmist describes the experience of being executed in what appears to be a crucifixion:

> Yea, dogs are round about me;
> a company of evildoers encircle me;
> *they have pierced my hands and feet—*
> *I can count all my bones—*
> *they stare and gloat over me;*
> *they divide my garments among them,*
> *and for my raiment they cast lots.*
> But you, O LORD, be not far off!
> O my help, hasten to my aid! (Psalm 22:16-19)

Although scholars continue to debate exactly how to translate the Hebrew expression for the "piercing" of his "hands and feet" (Psalm 22:16), the ancient Greek Septuagint—the oldest Jewish translation of the Hebrew Scriptures we possess—clearly states: "They have gouged my hands and feet" (Psalm 21:17 LXX).[31] At the very least, these lines from the psalm describe the mockery, persecution, and execution of the suffering psalmist. Yet none of these things ever happened to David. But by quoting this particular psalm in his final moments,

Jesus is identifying the sufferings described in the psalm with his own passion and death on the cross.

Finally, and perhaps most significant of all, although Psalm 22 *begins* with David's experience of feeling abandoned by God, it *ends* with the conversion of the non-Jewish peoples and the coming of the kingdom of God. This is how the psalm ends:

> The afflicted shall eat and be satisfied;
> those who seek him shall praise the LORD!
> *All the ends of the earth shall remember*
> *and turn to the LORD;*
> *and all the families of the nations*
> *shall worship before him.*
> For dominion belongs to the LORD,
> and he rules over the nations. (Psalm 22:26-29)

In order to grasp the magnitude of these final verses, it's important to remember that whenever you see the word "nations" in the Old Testament, that is an English translation of the Hebrew word for all non-Jewish peoples—the Gentile "nations" (Hebrew *goyim*). Thus, Psalm 22 begins with the persecution and execution of the king of Israel, but it ends with the miraculous conversion of the pagan "nations" to the worship of the LORD, the God of Israel! In light of this, the contemporary Jewish scholar Judith Newman writes: "Jesus' words on the cross from Ps. 22:1 . . . may thus not simply lament divine abandonment, but point to the end of the psalm with its praise for divine restoration."[32]

Even in his dying breath, Jesus poses one last riddle: the riddle of Psalm 22. On the one hand, it looks and sounds as if he has been abandoned by the very God whose Son he has claimed to be. On the other hand, if you know the Jewish Scriptures, you will also know the end of the story.[33] For though Jesus appears to be forsaken by God, he is revealing that not only is his death part of the divine plan; it is also the event that will trigger the conversion of "all the families of the nations" to the worship of the one God of Israel. And that's exactly what begins to happen, at the foot of the cross, when the Roman centurion sees what occurs:

> And Jesus uttered a loud cry, and breathed his last. And the curtain of the temple was torn in two, from top to bottom. And when the centurion, who stood facing him, saw that he thus breathed his last, he said, *"Truly this man was the Son of God!"* (Mark 15:37-39)

And so the prophecies begin to be fulfilled. Far from being evidence that Jesus died a failure, the cry of dereliction is evidence that he saw his death as the fulfillment of the prophecies that would bring about the conversion of the pagan peoples of the world to the worship of the God of the Jews. And look around you now. What are literally billions of non-Jews from the Gentile nations doing? Worshiping the one God of the Jewish people. And when did this phenomenon begin? With the passion and death of Jesus of Nazareth on the cross.

The Temple of Jesus's Body

Before bringing this chapter to an end, it's important to point out that just because Jesus wasn't condemned for speaking against the Temple doesn't mean that what he had to say about the Temple isn't significant for the question of his divinity. As we have seen previously, during his hearing before the Sanhedrin some people accused him of having threatened to "destroy this temple that is made with hands" and in "three days" he would "build another, not made with hands" (Mark 14:58). Even more important is Jesus's response to the Jews in Jerusalem who question him for overturning the tables of the money changers in the Temple:

> The Jews then said to him, "What sign have you to show us for doing this?" Jesus answered them, *"Destroy this temple, and in three days I will raise it up."* The Jews then said, "It has taken forty-six years to build this temple, and will you raise it up in three days?" But he spoke of *the temple of his body.* (John 2:18-21)

Jesus's words imply that *he himself* is the "temple" that will be destroyed and then "raised up" "in three days" (Mark 14:58; John 2:19).
We'll look at the bodily resurrection that is implied here in the next
chapter. For now, the important point is that Jesus describes his passion and death as the destruction of a temple.[34]

If we fast-forward to the ending of the Gospel of John, something
happens during Jesus's crucifixion that sheds one last ray of light on
the question of Jesus's identity. Immediately after Jesus dies, one of
the Roman soldiers pierces his heart with a spear in order to make
sure he is dead. When he does so, something mysterious takes place:

> Since it was the day of Preparation, in order to prevent the bodies
> from remaining on the cross on the sabbath (for that sabbath was a
> high day), the Jews asked Pilate that their legs might be broken, and
> that they might be taken away. So the soldiers came and broke the
> legs of the first, and of the other who had been crucified with him; but
> when they came to Jesus and saw that he was already dead, they did
> not break his legs. *But one of the soldiers pierced his side with a spear,
> and at once there came out blood and water.* He who saw it has borne
> witness—his testimony is true, and he knows that he tells the truth—
> that you also may believe. (John 19:31-35)

Clearly something momentous just happened. Nowhere else does
John interrupt his Gospel like this to insist that what he is saying is
based on eyewitness testimony. So why is he so emphatic in insisting that the "blood and water" flowed from the side of Jesus crucified
and that "he who saw it" is telling the truth? What would this flow of
blood and water from Jesus's side have meant in a first-century Jewish
context?[35]

In order to answer the question, remember that Jesus was put to
death not just during any time, but during the Jewish "feast of the Passover" (John 13:1).[36] In our day, it has become customary for Jews (and
many Christians) to celebrate the Passover meal (known as a *Seder*)
anywhere in the world. But in the first century AD, that's not how the
occasion was observed. At the time of Jesus, the Passover was not just a

meal; it was a *sacrifice*. And sacrifices could be offered only in the city of Jerusalem.[37] Because of this requirement, once a year multitudes of Jews would travel to the city of Jerusalem in order to sacrifice the Passover lamb in the Temple. In fact, Josephus, who was himself a priest in the first century AD, describes the sacrifice of the Passover lambs as follows:

> So these High Priests, upon the coming of their feast which is called the Passover, when they slay their sacrifices, from the ninth hour to the eleventh . . . found the number of sacrifices was 256,500; which, upon the allowance of no more than ten that feast together, amounts to 2,700,200 persons that were pure and holy. (Josephus, *War*, 6.423–37)[38]

Most modern-day people have never seen a single lamb sacrificed, much less tens of thousands! This background is important for understanding what happens to Jesus on the cross because of the way in which the blood of the Passover lambs was disposed of. Think about it: if thousands of lambs were sacrificed in the Temple in one day, then where did all the blood go?

According to ancient Jewish tradition, before the Temple was destroyed in AD 70, the blood of the sacrifices used to be poured into a drain that flowed down from the altar of sacrifice to merge with a spring of water that flowed out the side of the mountain on which the Temple was built:

> At the south-western corner [of the Altar] there were two holes like two narrow nostrils by which *the blood that was poured* over the western base and the southern base *used to run down and mingle in the water-channel and flow out into the brook Kidron*. (Mishnah *Middoth* 3:2)[39]

So at the time when Jesus lived, if you were approaching the Temple during the feast of Passover from the vantage point of the Kidron

Valley, what might you have seen? *A stream of blood and water,* flowing out of the side of the Temple Mount.

Once you've got this first-century Jewish context in mind, all of a sudden John's emphasis on the blood and water flowing out of the side of Jesus makes sense. This seemingly small detail about his death actually reveals something deeply significant about who Jesus really is. He is not just the messianic son of God; he is the true Temple. In other words, *Jesus is the dwelling place of God on earth.* For that's what the Temple was to a first-century Jew. As Jesus himself says elsewhere: "He who swears by the Temple, swears by it and by him who dwells in it" (Matthew 23:21). In the words of E. P. Sanders:

> *The Temple was holy not only because the holy God was worshipped there, but because he was there.* . . . . Jews did not think that God was there and nowhere else, nor that the Temple in any way confined him. Since he was creator and Lord of the universe, he could be approached in prayer at any place. Nevertheless, he was in some special sense present in the Temple.[40]

Given this first-century Jewish context, the piercing of Jesus's side after his death reveals that he was the presence of God on earth. His body was the true Temple. That's why Jesus responds elsewhere to the Pharisees' accusations of Sabbath breaking with the following shocking declaration:

> Have you not read in the law how on the sabbath the priests in the temple profane the sabbath, and are guiltless? *I tell you, something greater than the temple is here.* (Matthew 12:5-6)

How can Jesus say such a thing? For a first-century Jew, what could possibly be greater than the Temple? What could be greater than the dwelling place of God on earth? Only *God himself,* present in the flesh.[41]

And if Jesus is the true Temple of God—the living presence of God on earth—then that means that his death on the cross was not just one more bloody execution. If his body is the true Temple of God, the true place of sacrifice, then the true altar from which the blood and water flow *is his heart*. That is what makes the crucifixion redemptive. As first-century Jews would have known, according to the Old Testament: "Hatred stirs up strife, but *love covers all offenses*" (Proverbs 10:12). Or, as the apostle Peter puts it: "Love covers a multitude of sins" (1 Peter 4:8). And if this is true, then the crucifixion of Jesus, by which he willingly offered "his life as a ransom for many" (Mark 10:45)—changes everything. *For if love covers a multitude of sins, then divine love—infinite love—covers an infinite multitude of sins*. Even your sins. Even my sins. Indeed, that is what converted the first Jewish Christians (and the first pagans, for that matter). And that is why the apostle Paul, after his conversion, could write these words: "We preach Christ crucified, a stumbling block to Jews and folly to Gentiles, but to those who are called, both Jews and Greeks, Christ the power of God and the wisdom of God. For the foolishness of God is wiser than men, and the weakness of God is stronger than men" (1 Corinthians 1:23-25).

The Resurrection

In some ways, the sheer power of "Christ crucified" (1 Corinthians 1:23) almost makes it tempting to stop at the foot of the cross. But as anyone familiar with the Gospels knows, the story of Jesus of Nazareth by no means ends with his death and burial. We have to press on and ask the question: What about the resurrection? Why did the closest disciples of Jesus come to believe that he had been raised from the dead? And what did it mean for them, as first-century Jews, to say that Jesus was "resurrected"? What is resurrection?

One reason it is necessary to ask these questions is because, in recent years, there has been an extraordinary amount of confusion about what it means to say that Jesus of Nazareth was "raised from the dead." For some people, the resurrection of Jesus means that, although he died on the cross, his "spirit" somehow "lives on" in the hearts of his followers. According to this point of view, whatever happened to Jesus's body in the tomb doesn't really matter. Other people—including a number of scholars who should know better—argue that the resurrection of Jesus means that his earliest followers believed that his spirit "went to heaven" after he died, that he was somehow exalted or taken up into the presence of God. People who hold this point of view tend to be ambiguous about exactly what happened to his body. They will often claim that it doesn't really matter. Still others see the resurrection primarily as a kind of divine vindication of Jesus, by which God confirmed the truth of everything Jesus had said about himself. Finally, there are those who simply do not believe that Jesus was raised from the dead. After all, ordinarily dead people *stay dead*. Why should we believe anything different about the man from Nazareth?

In this chapter, we will take up the question of the resurrection. Given the limited space we have, this can't of course be a comprehensive investigation.[1] Instead, I want to stay focused on two basic questions. First, *what* did it mean for Jesus's disciples to claim that he had been "raised" from the dead? Second, *why* is it that so many Jews in the first century AD believed that Jesus really was raised from the dead? According to the Acts of the Apostles, within a couple years after Jesus's death, some "five thousand" Jews came to believe in his "resurrection" (see Acts 4:1-4). What was it that convinced them that the tomb of Jesus really was empty on Easter Sunday? How do we explain the historical fact of early Christian belief in the resurrection?

What the Resurrection Is Not

In order to understand what it means for the disciples of Jesus to have claimed that he was "raised" from the dead, it is crucial to clarify exactly what resurrection did and did not mean in a first-century Jewish context. Otherwise, we can't even begin to discuss whether or not *the* resurrection of Jesus happened, much less why so many Jews came to believe that he had been raised. We'll begin by clearing the air and focusing on what the disciples did not mean when they claimed that Jesus had been resurrected.

First, when the Jewish disciples of Jesus spoke about his resurrection, *they were not claiming that he had simply come back to ordinary earthly life*.[2] This is what we would call "resuscitation."[3] Think here of the prophet Elijah raising the widow's son from the dead (1 Kings

17:17-24); or of Jesus bringing Jairus's twelve-year-old daughter back to life (see Matthew 9:18-26; Mark 5:21-43; Luke 8:40-56); or of Jesus raising his friend Lazarus from the dead after he had been "four days" in the tomb (John 11:38-44). In all of these cases, the person is miraculously brought back to life. Eventually, however, each one of them—the widow's son, Jairus's daughter, and Lazarus—would die again.[4]

Second, when the Jewish disciples of Jesus spoke about his resurrection, *they were also not claiming that Jesus's soul or spirit was "alive" with God.*[5] This is perhaps the most common mistake modern people make when they talk about the resurrection of Jesus. Many first-century Jews believed that death was the separation of the "soul" (Greek *psychē*) from the body, and that the soul could live on in a state of "immortality" (Greek *athanasia*).[6] For example, the book of Wisdom declares, "The souls of the righteous are in the hand of God," and that "their hope is full of immortality" (Wisdom 3:1-4). Likewise, Jesus talks about how Abraham, Isaac, and Jacob are still "living," even though the remains of their bodies were still on earth and long since corrupted (Luke 20:37-38). *But the disciples of Jesus were not just talking about the immortality of Jesus's soul.* They did not go around proclaiming, "The spirit of Jesus is with God!" or "Jesus is alive to God!" Instead, they went around proclaiming the "resurrection" (Greek *anastasis*) of Jesus's "body" (Greek *sōma*).[7] This means that something happened to Jesus's corpse—something radically, fundamentally different from what was believed to have happened to the bodies of all the other people who had ever died.[8]

Finally, when Jesus's followers spoke about his resurrection, *they were not claiming that he was "exalted to heaven" after he died.* It's remarkable how popular some form of this idea has become nowadays, especially among scholars who do not believe in Jesus's bodily resurrection.[9] Nevertheless, this idea is (literally) dead wrong. It is true that the Gospels and the book of Acts describe Jesus ascending into heaven to be seated at the right hand of God (Mark 16:19; Luke 24:50-51; Acts 1:6-11). But the ascension of Jesus into heaven clearly takes place after his bodily resurrection. In other words, the resurrection of Jesus and his ascension into heaven are two different events. This distinction is particularly clear in the account of Jesus's appearance to Mary Magdalene:

> Jesus said to her, "Mary." She turned and said to him in Hebrew, "Rabboni!" (which means Teacher). Jesus said to her, *"Do not hold me, for I have not yet ascended to the Father;* but go to my brethren and say to them, I am ascending to my Father and your Father, to my God and your God." (John 20:16-17)

Notice that there is a clear distinction here between the resurrection of Jesus from the tomb and the ascension of Jesus into heaven. The resurrection has to do with what happened to Jesus's *dead* body as it lay in the tomb; the ascension has to do with what happened to Jesus's *living* body after it exited the tomb. The resurrection and the ascension are not two ways of describing the same event.[10]

What the Resurrection Is

What then does the resurrection mean? Let's turn to the Gospel accounts and look at three points that are essential for understanding what the disciples were actually claiming when they said that Jesus had been "raised from the dead."[11]

First, the resurrected Jesus has *a body*. He is not a ghost.[12] This is perhaps clearest in Luke's account of Jesus's appearance to the disciples in the Upper Room:

> As they were saying this, Jesus himself stood among them, and said to them, "Peace to you." *But they were startled and frightened, and supposed that they saw a spirit.* And he said to them, "Why are you troubled, and why do questionings rise in your hearts? *See my hands and my feet, that it is I myself; handle me, and see; for a spirit has not flesh and bones as you see that I have."* And when he had said this he showed them his hands and his feet. And while they still disbelieved for joy, and wondered, he said to them, "Have you anything here to

eat?" They gave him a piece of broiled fish, and he took it and ate before them. (Luke 24:36-43)

Note well that the disciples' first reaction is to assume that Jesus is a
"spirit" (Greek *pneuma*). This shows us, for one thing, that they believed in ghosts! It also shows us that they were familiar with the idea
of encountering the disembodied "spirit" of a dead person. In order
to correct this misunderstanding, Jesus insists that he has "flesh and
bones"—that is, that he has a real human body. And just in case the
disciples have any doubts about the reality of his body, he asks them
for something to eat! Although spirits might be able to do lots of things,
because they lack bodies, sitting down to a nice meal of broiled fish
is not one of them. There are few things more bodily than the act of
eating.

Second, the resurrected Jesus has *the same body* that he had while
he was alive. That's why he still bears the wounds of the cross.[13] Jesus
implies as much when he shows his disciples "his hands and his feet"
(Luke 24:40). The Gospel of John's account of Jesus's appearance to
Thomas makes this explicit:

> Now Thomas, one of the twelve, called the Twin, was not with them
> when Jesus came. So the other disciples told him, "We have seen the
> Lord." But he said to them, *"Unless I see in his hands the print of the
> nails, and place my finger in the mark of the nails, and place my hand
> in his side, I will not believe."* Eight days later, his disciples were again
> in the house, and Thomas was with them. The doors were shut, but
> Jesus came and stood among them, and said, "Peace be with you."
> Then he said to Thomas, *"Put your finger here, and see my hands; and
> put out your hand, and place it in my side; do not be faithless, but be-
> lieving."* Thomas answered him, "My Lord and my God!" Jesus said
> to him, "Have you believed because you have seen me? Blessed are
> those who have not seen and yet believe." (John 20:24-29)

As this account makes very clear, the risen Jesus has not discarded his
human body like an old garment. The crucifixion has literally left its

THE CASE FOR JESUS

marks on him, forever, but without conquering his life. Moreover, notice also that when Thomas is confronted with the reality of the resurrection, his response is an unequivocal affirmation of Jesus's divinity: "My Lord and my God! (Greek *ho kyrios mou kai ho theos mou*)" (John 20:28).[14] For Thomas, the resurrection of Jesus after his death vindicates the claims that Jesus made about his divinity during his life.

Third and finally, the resurrected Jesus has *a transformed body*. Although it is the same body, it now possesses new, extraordinary qualities.[15] For example, in his resurrected body, Jesus can walk through walls, veil his presence, and appear when and how he will. Consider his appearance to the two disciples on the road to Emmaus and to the apostles when they were hiding for fear:

> That very day two of them were going to a village named Emmaus, about seven miles from Jerusalem, and talking with each other about all these things that had happened. While they were talking and discussing together, Jesus himself drew near and went with them. *But their eyes were kept from recognizing him.* (Luke 24:13-16)

> On the evening of that day, the first day of the week, *the doors being shut where the disciples were,* for fear of the Jews, *Jesus came and stood among them* and said to them, "Peace be with you." (John 20:19)

Contrary to what some readers assume, the disciples on the road to Emmaus do not fail to recognize Jesus. It's not as if they've forgotten what he looked like after only three days! The Gospel says very clearly that their eyes are "kept" from recognizing him (Luke 24:16). In other words, the resurrected Jesus can change or veil his appearance. Likewise, in the account of the disciples on Easter Sunday, the risen Jesus passes through the "shut" doors. How can he do this? Because after the resurrection, he possesses what the apostle Paul refers to as a "glorified" body—one that has been radically "changed" (1 Corinthians 15:42-51).

In short, when the disciples say that Jesus was "raised from the dead," they did not mean that he was restored to earthly life. Nor did they mean that his soul was exalted to heaven after he died. Instead, they meant that Jesus had been restored to bodily life—a new, glorified bodily life. And in this glorified body, Jesus would never die again. Ever.

Why Did Anyone Believe in the Resurrection of Jesus?

Now that the meaning of Jesus's resurrection is clear, the next obvious question is *Why would anyone believe such a thing?* Even if you personally don't believe Jesus was raised from the dead, you still have to be able to explain historically how it is that the first disciples—and thousands of Jews after them, as well as countless Gentiles—came to believe in his resurrection. How is it that belief in Jesus's bodily resurrection swept like wildfire through the ancient Jewish synagogues, beginning in Jerusalem, then on through Judea and Samaria, and to the ends of the earth?

Before we work through the answers, I have to insist on one prior point. Belief in the resurrection of Jesus did not spread because ancient people—Jewish or pagan—were any more gullible or credulous about miracles than are modern-day people.[16] In fact, the New Testament repeatedly informs us that the resurrection of Jesus was met with doubts, suspicion, and even ridicule by Jesus's own disciples, other Jews, and pagans as well:

> Now the eleven disciples went to Galilee. . . . And when they saw him they worshiped him; *but some doubted.* (Matthew 28:16-17)

> After this he appeared in another form to two of them. . . . And they went back and told the rest, but *they did not believe them.* (Mark 16:12-13)

> Now it was Mary Magdalene and Joanna and Mary the mother of James and the other women with them who told this to the apostles; but these words seemed to them *an idle tale,* and *they did not believe them.* (Luke 24:10-11)

[Thomas] said to them, "Unless I see in his hands the print of the nails, and place my finger in the mark of the nails, and place my hand in his side, *I will not believe.*" (John 20:25)

So Paul, standing in the middle of the Areopagus, said: "Men of Athens, . . . [God] has fixed a day on which he will judge the world in righteousness by a man whom he has appointed, and of this he has given assurance to all men by raising him from the dead." *Now when they heard of the resurrection of the dead, some mocked.* (Acts 17:22, 31-32)

These passages demolish any argument that the first Christians—whether Jew or Gentile—believed in the resurrection of Jesus because they were particularly gullible. Once again, ancient people knew full well that ordinarily dead people stay dead.[17] So if the fact of the resurrection was such a hard pill for so many people to swallow, why then did the disciples come to believe it? The Gospels describe three major reasons they believed.

First, the disciples came to believe in the resurrection of Jesus because of *the empty tomb.*[18] As Bart Ehrman writes: "All of our sources agree that Jesus was dead and buried, and that on the third day his tomb was empty."[19] Ehrman is entirely correct. All four of the first-century Gospels tell us that on the Sunday of Passover week, the tomb in which Joseph of Arimathea had laid Jesus's body was empty (see Matthew 28:1-8; Mark 16:1-8; Luke 24:1-12; John 20:1-10). Perhaps the most striking eyewitness account of the discovery of the empty tomb is from the Gospel of John:

Now on the first day of the week Mary Magdalene came to the tomb early, while it was still dark, and saw that the stone had been taken away from the tomb. So she ran, and went to Simon Peter and *the other disciple, the one whom Jesus loved,* and said to them, "They have taken the Lord out of the tomb, and we do not know where they have laid him." Peter then came out with the other disciple, and they went toward the tomb. They both ran, but the other disciple outran Peter and reached the tomb first; and stooping to look in, he saw the linen cloths lying there, but he did not go in. Then Simon Peter came, following him, and went into the tomb; he saw the linen cloths lying, and the napkin, which had been on his head, not lying with the linen cloths but rolled up in a place by itself. Then the other disciple, who reached the tomb first, also went in, and he saw and believed; for as yet they did not know the scripture, that he must rise from the dead. Then the disciples went back to their homes. (John 20:1-10)

It's important to highlight how unlikely it would be for the discovery of the empty tomb to be attributed to a female disciple like Mary Magdalene if Jesus's other disciples had wanted anyone to believe it.[20] As a number of scholars have shown, in the first century AD, the testimony of women was widely regarded as unreliable.[21] In fact, the Gospels themselves report that some of the male disciples regarded the women's account of Jesus's resurrection as an "idle tale" or "nonsense" (Greek *lēros*) (Luke 24:10-11). Nevertheless, finding the empty tomb was the disciples' first step toward grasping the fact that Jesus had been raised. Something had happened to his body. It wasn't in the grave anymore.

Of course, it wasn't the empty tomb *alone* that led to belief in the resurrection. There are other ways to explain an empty tomb.[22] As we just saw, Mary Magdalene's first response is to assume someone has "taken away" the body of Jesus (John 20:13). Moreover, according to the Gospel of Matthew, when the Jewish elders of Jerusalem learn about the empty tomb, they begin spreading the rumor that Jesus's disciples "came by night and stole him away" while the soldiers were sleeping (Matthew 28:12-13). Notice that the Jewish elders and the Romans *do not deny the fact of the empty tomb*. Instead, they simply try to *explain* the empty tomb. The problem with their explanation, however, is that it is extremely difficult to believe that the disciples came together at night to a sealed tomb guarded by a cohort of Roman soldiers, rolled the stone away, and hauled off Jesus's corpse—and all without anyone ever waking up! It's especially implausible when you recall that the Roman penalty for failing on guard duty was death (see Acts 12:18-19).[23] Nevertheless, because the empty tomb could be explained in different ways, more was needed to convince people that Jesus had been raised.

The second reason people came to believe in the resurrection is because of *the appearances of the risen Jesus to those who knew him*. Significantly, there are so many accounts of Jesus's appearances to his disciples that we do not have the space to even quote them all here, much less discuss them.[24] Instead, I'll just summarize the evidence in the form of a list.

The Appearances of the Resurrected Jesus

1. Jesus appears to Mary Magdalene
   (Matthew 28:1-10; John 20:14-18)

2. Jesus appears to several female disciples
   (Matthew 28:1-10; Mark 16:1-8; Luke 24:1-11)

3. Jesus appears to Simon Peter
   (Luke 24:34; 1 Corinthians 15:5; John 21:1-24)

4. Jesus appears to James, John, Thomas, Nathanael, and two others
   (John 21:1-24)

5. Jesus appears to the eleven disciples as a group
   (Matthew 28:16-20; John 20:19-29)

6. Jesus appears to Cleopas and one unnamed disciple
   (Luke 24:13-35)

7. Jesus appears to more than five hundred "brothers" at once
   (1 Corinthians 15:6)

8. Jesus appears to James (a.k.a. "the Lord's brother")
   (1 Corinthians 15:7; compare Galatians 2:19)

9. Jesus appears to Saul of Tarsus (a.k.a. Paul)
   (1 Corinthians 15:8)

Two observations about this evidence are in order.

First, contrary to what some claim, two of the Gospels that report Jesus's appearances after the resurrection claim to be firsthand eyewitness testimony: the Gospel of Matthew records Jesus's appearance to the eleven disciples, which would of course include Matthew himself (Matthew 28:16-20); and the Gospel of John records the appearance of Jesus to John the Beloved Disciple, along with several other apostles, while fishing in the Sea of Galilee (John 21:1-24).[25] And that is to say nothing of the accounts contained in the Gospel of Luke, who describes the material in his Gospel as also being based on the testimony of "eyewitnesses from the beginning"—though he does not name them (Luke 1:1-4). Of course, none of this means you have to accept the truth of the accounts of Jesus's appearances. What it does mean is that there is no historical basis for claiming that there are no eyewitness accounts of the appearances of the risen Jesus. You can reject those accounts if you'd like, but you can't say they don't exist.

Second, some scholars reject the historicity of Jesus's resurrection appearances because "they differ in detail at almost every level."[26] For example, if you compare the various accounts, it can be quite difficult (if not impossible) to answer certain questions, such as: How many women are present at the initial discovery of the empty tomb (one, two, three?)? How many angels are present (one? two?)? When and where does Jesus appear to his disciples (Jerusalem? Galilee? both?)? (See Matthew 28:1-10; Mark 16:1-8; Luke 24:1-11; John 20:1-24). To be sure, there are differences in detail, and scholars have proposed various ways to reconcile them.[27] But *the presence of differences in details in the various accounts does not mean that the resurrected Jesus did not actually appear to his disciples.* To say so would be like claiming that the discrepancies between the eyewitness accounts of the sinking of the *Titanic* mean that the ship didn't actually sink. It just doesn't follow.

Instead, what matters from a historical perspective—in the case of both the resurrection of Jesus and the sinking of the *Titanic*—is that there are primary claims on which the eyewitnesses clearly *agree*.[28] And all of the historical evidence we possess agrees that on the third day after his death (and several times thereafter), Jesus of Nazareth appeared to multiple disciples in bodily form. It is the fact of these appearances—and not the precise enumeration of how many women and how many angels were present—that is the second major reason people came to accept that Jesus was indeed risen.

The third and final reason that people came to believe in the resurrection of Jesus is one of the most important but most overlooked. It is this: Jesus's resurrection from the dead was *the fulfillment of Jewish Scripture*. Over and over again, the New Testament writings insist on this point:

> Then he opened their minds to understand the scriptures, and said to them, *"Thus it is written, that the Christ should suffer and on the third day rise from the dead.* (Luke 24:45)

> Then the other disciple, who reached the tomb first, also went in, and he saw and believed; for as yet they did not know *the scripture, that he must rise from the dead.* (John 20:8-9)

> For I delivered to you as of first importance what I also received, that Christ died for our sins in accordance with the scriptures, that he was buried, *that he was raised on the third day in accordance with the scriptures.* (1 Corinthians 15:3-4)

Remarkably, this third reason for believing in the resurrection—the fulfillment of Scripture—is neglected in many modern-day books on the resurrection.[29] Nowadays, writers often like to point out how many of Jesus's disciples were willing to suffer and die for their faith in the resurrection. Peter and Paul, for example, were both executed by the Roman authorities—one by being crucified upside down and the other by being decapitated—as witnesses to the resurrection of Jesus.

Intriguingly, however, that's *not* the kind of proof we find in the New Testament. The writers of the New Testament do not go to great lengths to explain why it's reasonable to trust the claims of Peter, or James, or John, or Matthew, or Paul, or Mary Magdalene, or the more than five hundred disciples to whom Jesus reportedly appeared alive. Instead, the writers of the New Testament point repeatedly to the fact that Jesus's resurrection was the fulfillment of Scripture. But what Scriptures did Jesus's resurrection fulfill?

The Sign of Jonah

This is where contemporary scholars often fall silent. Indeed, many admit that they *aren't sure* what Scripture is being referred to when it is said that Jesus was raised on the third day "in accordance with the scriptures" (1 Corinthians 15:4). If you go back to the Old Testament, there is no explicit prophecy of the Messiah being resurrected on the third day. The closest you get is perhaps an obscure passage from the book of Hosea, which speaks about a group of people ("we") being raised up to life "on the third day" (Hosea 6:1-2). The problem with citing this passage is that it seems to refer to the resurrection of the people of Israel, using the image of coming back to life to describe the regathering of the twelve tribes (see Hosea 5–6).

So what Scripture is Jesus's resurrection on the third day supposed to fulfill? In order to answer this, we have to go back to the teachings of Jesus. In the Gospels, there is only *one passage* from Jewish Scripture that Jesus cites as a direct prophecy of his resurrection on the third day: the so-called sign of Jonah (Matthew 12:38-41; Luke 11:29-32).[30] Consider Matthew's account:

> Then some of the scribes and Pharisees said to him, "Teacher, we wish to see a sign from you." But he answered them, "An evil and adulterous generation seeks for a sign; but *no sign shall be given to it*

except the sign of the prophet Jonah. For as Jonah was three days and three nights in the belly of the whale, so will the Son of Man be three days and three nights in the heart of the earth. The men of Nineveh will arise at the judgment with this generation and condemn it; for they repented at the preaching of Jonah, and behold, something greater than Jonah is here. (Matthew 12:38-41)

What is the meaning of this mysterious "sign of Jonah"? And what does it have to do with the resurrection of the Son of Man after three days in the "heart of the earth"?[31]

True confession: for years, when I read this passage, I went away somewhat underwhelmed. With all due respect to Jesus, I always felt like the comparison between Jonah being in the belly of the whale for three days and the Son of Man being in the "heart of the earth" for three days was, well, somewhat *forced*. Don't get me wrong—I got the parallel: three days and three nights. But this didn't seem to me to be the most impressive prophecy of the resurrection you could come up with. Moreover, lots of readers find the story in the book of Jonah to be so unbelievable. How could anyone actually stay alive for "three days and three nights" in the belly of a whale, or a fish, or whatever it was?

And then one day I went back and actually *read* the book of Jonah, carefully, and in its original Hebrew. And do you know what I found? I found that the problem wasn't with Jesus; it was with me. (I'm learning that this is usually the case.) For if you read the book of Jonah carefully, you will discover something interesting: the author of the book never claims that Jonah remained *alive* for three days and three nights in the fish. Sure, that's what all the children's Bibles and movies and sermons say, but not the text itself. In fact, it pretty explicitly says that *Jonah died and went to the realm of the dead.* Don't take my word for it; go back and look for yourself, without skipping Jonah's prayer (like I used to do):

And the Lord appointed a great fish to swallow up Jonah; and *Jonah was in the belly of the fish three days and three nights.*

Then Jonah prayed to the Lord his God from the belly of the fish, saying,

> "I called to the Lord, out of my distress,
> and he answered me;
> *out of the belly of Sheol I cried*
> *and thou didst hear my voice.*
> The waters closed in over me,
> the deep was round about me;
> weeds were wrapped about my head
> at the roots of the mountains.
> *I went down to the land*
> *whose bars closed upon me for ever;*
> *yet you brought my life from the Pit,*
> *O Lord my God.*
> *When my soul fainted within me,*
> I remembered the LORD;
> and my prayer came to you,
> into your holy temple."
> And the Lord spoke to the fish, and it
>   vomited out Jonah upon the dry land.

Then the word of the LORD came to Jonah the second time, saying, "*Arise*, go to Nineveh, that great city, and proclaim to it the message that I tell you." So Jonah *arose* and went to Nineveh, according to the word of the LORD. (Jonah 1:17–3:3)

Notice three key points here. First, when Jonah says that he cried out to God from "the belly of Sheol" and "the Pit," these are standard Old Testament terms for the realm of the dead (Psalm 139:7-8; Job 17:13-16; 33:22-30).[32] Second, when Jonah says that his "soul" (Hebrew *nephesh*) fainted within him, this is another way of saying that he died. In other words, Jonah's prayer is the last gasp of a dying man. Thus, when the fish vomits Jonah out onto the land, it is vomiting up his *corpse*.[33] Finally, with all this in mind, notice what God's first word to

Jonah is: "Arise" (Hebrew *qûm*). This is the same Semitic word that Jesus uses when he raises Jairus's daughter from the dead and says to her: "Talitha *cumi*," meaning "Little girl, I say to you, *arise*" (Mark 5:41). In other words, *the story of Jonah is the story of his death and resurrection.*

But that's not all. For as any first-century Jew would have known, the climax of the book of Jonah is not his miraculous "arising" after being vomited out by the fish; it is the even more miraculous *repentance of the Gentile city of Nineveh.* In response to the preaching of Jonah, "the people of Nineveh believed God; they proclaimed a fast, and put on sackcloth, from the greatest of them to the least of them" (Jonah 3:5). Even the pagan king of Nineveh is said to have "covered himself with sackcloth, and sat in ashes" before commanding his entire people to "cry mightily to God" (Jonah 3:6-8). It is hard to overstate how staggering this would be to a first-century Jewish reader, who would have known that Nineveh was the capital city of the Assyrian Empire, one of Israel's fiercest pagan enemies (see 2 Kings 15-17; Tobit 13). Once the identity of the Ninevites is clear, it becomes apparent that the real miracle in the book of Jonah is the repentance—one might even say the "conversion"—of the Gentiles.

What does all this mean for how Jesus understands his own death and resurrection? Once the biblical background of his proclamation about Jonah is clear, everything he says makes perfect sense. To begin with, the scribes and Pharisees demand a "sign" from Jesus—that is, a miracle of some sort meant to prove who he really is (Matthew 12:38). In response, Jesus declares that the only "sign" that will be given to his generation is the sign of the prophet Jonah. What is this miraculous sign? Scholars debate whether it refers to the miraculous rescue of Jonah or the miraculous repentance of the Gentiles.[34] The answer is both. And the same thing is true of the sign of the Son of Man. The "sign of Jonah" is both the resurrection of the Son of Man on the third day and the repentance of the Gentiles that will follow his resurrection. Consider the parallels:

THE SIGN OF JONAH AND THE RESURRECTION OF JESUS

The Sign of Jonah	*The Sign of the Son of Man*
1. Death and resurrection after three days in Sheol.	1. Death and resurrection after three days in the tomb.
2. Repentance of the Ninevites in response to his preaching.	2. Repentance of the Gentiles in response to his preaching.

What do these parallels mean for what Jesus is saying about his own resurrection?[35] The answer is simple but significant. *According to Jesus, it is not just his resurrection from the dead that will be a reason for believing in him. It is also the inexplicable conversion of the pagan nations of the world—the Gentiles.* As Jesus says: the pagans "repented at the preaching of Jonah, and behold, something greater than Jonah is here" (Matthew 12:41; Luke 11:32). In Jonah's case, only one Gentile city repents, and that only for a time. In Jesus's case, countless Gentile nations, cities, even empires would go on to repent, cast away their idols, and turn to the God of Israel.

For whatever reason, many modern Christians have forgotten this point. We seem to take for granted that literally billions of non-Jews— that is, Gentiles—have abandoned centuries of idol worship and turned to the worship of the one God of Israel. But the same cannot be said for ancient Christians. Over and over again, whenever the early church fathers wanted to make the case for the messiahship, divinity, and resurrection of Jesus, they did not (as a rule) point to the evidence for the empty tomb, or the reliability of the eyewitnesses. They did not get into arguments about historical probability and evidence and such. Instead, they simply pointed to the pagan world around them that was crumbling to the ground as Gentile nations that had worshiped idols and gods and goddesses for millennia somehow inexplicably repented, turned, and began worshiping the God of the Jews. In the words of the fourth-century writer Ambrose of Milan:

The mystery of the Church is clearly expressed [in Jesus's words about the sign of Jonah]. Her flocks stretch from the boundaries of the whole world. They stretch to Nineveh through penitence. . . . *The mystery is now fulfilled in truth.* (Ambrose of Milan, *Exposition of the Gospel of Luke,* 7.96)[36]

Even more stunning are the observations of the fourth-century historian Eusebius of Caesarea, who penned these unforgettable words:

Behold how today, yes, in our own times, our eyes see not only Egyptians, but every race of men who used to be idolaters . . . released from the errors of polytheism and the demons, and calling on the God of the prophets! . . . *Yes, in our own time the knowledge of the Omnipotent God shines forth and sets a seal of certainty on the forecasts of the prophets. You see this actually going on, you no longer only expect to hear of it, and if you ask the moment when the change began, for all your inquiry you will receive no other answer but the moment of the appearance of the Savior.* . . . And who would not be struck by the extraordinary change—that men who for ages have paid divine honor to wood and stone and demons, wild beasts that feed on human flesh, poisonous reptiles, animals of every kinds, repulsive monsters, fire and earth, and the lifeless elements of the universe should after our Savior's coming pray to the Most High God, Creator of Heaven and earth, the actual Lord of the prophets, and the God of Abraham and his forefathers? (Eusebius of Caesarea, *The Proof of the Gospel,* 1.6.20–21)[37]

Many other church fathers could be cited to the same effect, but these suffice to make the point. From the ancient Christian point of view, not only was the tomb empty. Not only did Jesus appear to many disciples after he died. He also saved what is in many ways the greatest miracle of all for last. The Gentiles began to repent, and convert, and convert. And they are still converting today. The Church is still here, after two thousand years, spreading throughout the world. What began as a little stone "cut out by no human hand"—with one Jew from Nazareth and his tiny band of followers—has indeed become, as the prophet Daniel foretold, "a great mountain and filled the whole earth" (Daniel 2:34-35).

Indeed, how does one explain the universality of the Church? I guess you could argue that it was a coincidence. I guess you could claim that the many passages in the Old Testament prophesying that one day the pagan nations of the world would turn and worship the God of Abraham just happened to take place after the death and resurrection of Jesus (see Isaiah 2:1-3; 25:6-8; 66:18-21; Jeremiah 3:15-18; Micah 4:1-2; Zechariah 8:20-23). I guess you could also claim that these mass conversions among the pagans just happened to coincide with the life, death, and resurrection of Jesus of Nazareth, who just happened to live and die at the very time that the book of Daniel said the Messiah would come. And I guess you could believe that after Jesus was crucified, the tomb just happened to be inexplicably empty and hundreds of disciples of Jesus began claiming to have seen him alive again in his body. I guess you could claim all this. I, for one, prefer the simpler explanation. Jesus of Nazareth was right. The Son of Man was crucified. The Son of Man was buried. The Son of Man was raised on the third day. The tomb was empty. It still is. And the Gentiles turn to the God of Israel in droves. Because something greater than Jonah *is* here.

13

At Caesarea Philippi

In order to bring this book to an end, let's go back to where we began: with C. S. Lewis's famous Liar, Lunatic, or Lord trilemma. According to Lewis: Jesus claimed to be God. Therefore either he was a liar (who knew he wasn't God but said he was), a lunatic (who thought he was God but wasn't), or the Lord (who was who he claimed to be).

As we have seen in chapter 1, as compelling as Lewis's argument may seem at first glance, it depends on two assumptions: (1) that the Gospels are historically reliable and (2) that they all depict Jesus as claiming to be God. Take either of these assumptions off the table and the argument no longer works. It is precisely these two points that have been called into question in the half a century or so since Lewis penned *Mere Christianity*. According to many scholars these days, there is a "fourth option": Jesus never actually claimed to be God. According to one prominent version of this theory, all of the passages in which Jesus claims to be divine—which are supposedly found only in the Gospel of John—are not historically accurate. Instead, they are "legends" created by later Christians who believed Jesus to be divine and put into the mouth of their Master something he never claimed for himself.

What now are we to make of this fourth option? What should we think of the theory that Jesus of Nazareth never claimed to be God?

In light of everything we've seen in this book, one thing is clear: if you are going to hold to the theory that Jesus never claimed to be God, *you had better be committed to eliminating a lot of historical evidence.* In fact, eliminating evidence may be the most consistent feature of the theory. Think about it: in order to hold on to the idea that the Gospels are the anonymous end products of an early Christian game of Telephone, you have to eliminate all of the manuscript evidence for the titles of the Gospels; eliminate the external evidence from ancient Christians and their pagan opponents; eliminate the literary parallels between the Gospels and ancient biographies; eliminate the passages in which the Gospels themselves insist that they are telling you what Jesus actually did and said; and eliminate the internal and external evidence that the Gospels were written within the lifetime of the apostles.

Likewise, in order to hang on to the theory that Jesus never claimed to be divine, you have to eliminate the entire Gospel of John and what it tells us about who Jesus claimed to be; eliminate the passages in the Synoptic Gospels in which Jesus takes the divine name "I am" and speaks as if he is the divine Son of Man; eliminate all the miracles in which Jesus does what only the God of the Old Testament can do; and eliminate all the evidence that Jesus was both repeatedly accused of blasphemy and condemned to death for blasphemy because of who he claimed to be. (And that is to say nothing of eliminating the evidence that Jesus's tomb was actually empty, that he actually appeared to his disciples after the resurrection, and that he fulfilled biblical prophecies about the coming of the Messiah, the kingdom of God, and the conversion of the Gentile nations.) In other words, in order for the theory that Jesus never claimed to be God to be correct, you have to keep eliminating all of the evidence that doesn't fit the theory.

Now, of course, there's nothing to stop a person from trying to make all of this evidence disappear. Lots of people do it. Some of them are scholars. But I for one can't. It just isn't good history. It makes far more historical sense to me to conclude that the reason the idea that

Jesus never claimed to be divine has to eliminate so much evidence for the theory to work is that the theory is wrong. And not just wrong about the details. It's wrong about the big questions: how we got the Gospels, who Jesus claimed to be, and why it matters.

Which means, of course, that we are thrown back onto the horns of C. S. Lewis's trilemma. His basic point was right: according to all the actual historical evidence we possess, Jesus of Nazareth *did* claim to be God. At least, that's what all four first-century biographies of Jesus say. In both the Gospel of John *and the Synoptic Gospels*, Jesus claims to be God by identifying himself with the heavenly Son of Man and by taking the divine name "I am." In both the Gospel of John *and the Synoptic Gospels*, Jesus acts as if he is God when he performs miracles that only God can do. And in both the Gospel of John *and the Synoptic Gospels*, Jesus is handed over to the Romans to be crucified because some Jewish authorities regarded his claims about himself as blasphemy.

With that said, there is one important point that Lewis's Liar, Lunatic, or Lord argument overlooks. Yes, Jesus acted as if he were God. Yes, Jesus spoke as if he were God. Jesus was even crucified for claiming to be divine. However, as we saw in chapter 10, Jesus did not go around shouting in the streets: "I am God!" Instead, when he taught about the mystery of his identity, he did so gradually, using parables, riddles, and questions. These teachings were designed to lead people to ask for themselves: Who is this man? In other words, Jesus did not shove his divinity down people's throats. He invited them into the mystery of who he was claiming to be.

I think that's very significant. I think it's important that Jesus taught about his divine identity in this way. For it shows that Jesus knew that what he was asking people to believe about him was something that, humanly speaking, couldn't be forced upon them. I think it shows that Jesus understood his identity as a *mystery* that needed to be *revealed*.

Should there be any doubt about this, let's take a look at one final example of how Jesus revealed the mystery of his divinity. It is, perhaps, the most famous example in all the Gospels. So I've saved it for last.

"Flesh and Blood Has Not Revealed This to You"

I am speaking of the revelation to Simon Peter at Caesarea Philippi (Matthew 16:13-16; Mark 8:27-30; Luke 9:18-21). Consider the account recorded in the Gospel of Matthew:

> Now when Jesus came into the district of Caesarea Philippi, he asked his disciples, "Who do men say that the Son of Man is?" And they said, "Some say John the Baptist, others say Elijah, and others Jeremiah or one of the prophets." He said to them, *"But who do you say that I am?"* Simon Peter replied, *"You are the Christ, the Son of the living God."* And Jesus answered him, "Blessed are you, Simon Bar-Jona! *For flesh and blood has not revealed this to you, but my Father who is in heaven.* And I tell you, you are Peter, and on this rock I will build my church, and the powers of death shall not prevail against it. I will give you the keys of the kingdom of heaven, and whatever you bind on earth shall be bound in heaven, and whatever you loose on earth shall be loosed in heaven." Then he strictly charged the disciples to tell no one that he was the Christ. (Matthew 16:13-20)

As with every other episode we've looked at in the book, there's lots that could be said here. In fact, this may be one of the most debated passages in the New Testament.[1] For our purposes, I'll make two main points.

First, when it comes to the question of the identity of "the Son of Man"—Jesus's typical way of referring to himself—there are many competing opinions on offer. Some people say Jesus is John the Baptist come back to life, others that he's Elijah returned, still others one of "the prophets" (a modern version of this last option is still popular). The striking thing about this list is that the suggested candidates are all dead. In other words, whoever Jesus is, he's no ordinary man. He has come (or come back) from some other realm. On the other hand, none of the suggestions gets to the heart of what is different and new about Jesus.[2] As a result, Jesus throws the question back on his disciples. Although they are his students, he doesn't just give them the answer. He wants *them* to answer the question: "Who do you say that I am?" (Matthew 16:15). They have to decide for themselves.

Second, when Simon Peter steps up and answers Jesus's question, he doesn't just affirm that Jesus is the Messiah, which is what "the Christ" (Greek *ho Christos*) means. Simon goes *beyond* messiahship when he confesses that Jesus is also "the Son of the living God" (Matthew 16:16). Here again the Old Testament background is important. The expression "son of God" in Jewish Scripture can be used to refer to an angel, the Davidic king, or the people of Israel. However, in context, Simon Peter's use of the expression clearly means something much more. It seems to be a confession that Jesus is the *unique Son of God*—that is, the divine Son of God—in a way that's fundamentally different from the sonship of Israel, or King David, or even the angels.

That, at least, is the only way to explain Jesus's otherwise baffling response: "Blessed are you, Simon. . . . *For flesh and blood has not revealed this to you*, but my Father who is in heaven" (Matthew 16:17). In other words, Peter's ability to recognize that Jesus is the "Son of the living God" is not, in the final analysis, the result of his human effort or intellectual abilities. He was, after all, an "uneducated" fisherman (see Acts 4:13). Peter doesn't come to believe in Jesus because he was so smart or because he had finally "figured it all out." Instead, Jesus's words show that his identity as "the Son" is revealed to Peter by the "Father in heaven" *because Peter is open to receiving the mystery.* In other words, Peter's insight into who Jesus really is is a result of divine revelation. It's something that God the Father has to "reveal" (Greek *apokalyptō*) to Simon for him to be able to grasp it (Matthew 16:17).

Should there be any doubt about this, compare Jesus's response to Peter at Caesarea Philippi with what Jesus says about himself in one of the most exalted claims he makes in all the Gospels (Matthew 11:25-27; Luke 10:21-22). Consider Matthew's version:

> At that time Jesus declared, "I thank you, Father, Lord of heaven and earth, *that you have hidden these things from the wise and understanding and revealed them to babes;* yes, Father, for such was your gracious will. All things have been delivered to me by my Father; and

no one knows the Son except the Father, and no one knows the Father
except the Son and any one to whom the Son chooses to reveal him."
(Matthew 11:25-27)[3]

With these words, we have yet another saying of Jesus that is often ignored by those who believe that Jesus never claimed to be divine.[4] For
in this passage, Jesus speaks of himself as the unique "Son" of God
"the Father" to whom "all things" (Greek *panta*) have been handed
over. Moreover, the mystery of God the Father, the Lord of heaven and
earth, and the mystery of his Son Jesus, is something "hidden." As a
result, it has to be "revealed" (Greek *apekalypsas*) by God the Father
himself (Matthew 11:25; Luke 10:21). And it *is* revealed to those who are
little, like children. Not to those who are proud because they are wise
and learned.

     In other words, Peter's ability to recognize and accept the unfath-
omable mystery of the God of the universe becoming a human being
in the person of Jesus of Nazareth is a gift of grace. Now, Peter's confession of faith in the divine sonship of Jesus is not contrary to his
human intellect. After all, Peter witnesses lots of events that point to
Jesus's unique identity, such as the walking on water, the stilling of
the storm, and the Transfiguration. In the end, however, according to
Jesus, Peter is only able to believe the incomprehensible mystery that
Jesus is really "the Son of the living God" because *God himself reveals
it to him*. As the apostle Paul would later put it: "No one can say 'Jesus is
Lord' except by the Holy Spirit" (1 Corinthians 12:3).

     The same thing, I would suggest, is true for us today. I can give you
all the historical arguments for how we got the Gospels, all the reasons
we should believe they go back to the apostles and their disciples. I can
give you all the historical evidence for concluding that Jesus of Nazareth claimed to be the long-awaited Jewish Messiah, the heavenly Son
of Man, and the divine Son of God. I can do all these things—and I've
tried to do them to the best of my ability. But there is one thing I can't
do. I can't answer the *ultimate* question—the question of whether
Jesus of Nazareth *was in fact God*. That is a question you have to answer for yourself.

At least, that's what Jesus seems to have thought. For today, as in the first century, there are lots of opinions about who the man from Nazareth really was. Apparently, it has always been that way, and it probably always will be. But the question Jesus poses to his disciples— the question of his identity—abides. It does not pass away. Despite the almost two thousand years that have transpired since the writing of the Gospels, Jesus's words to Simon Peter at Caesarea Philippi echo down through the centuries, inviting each and every one of us to encounter him as a real historical person and to answer the question he once asked a lowly fisherman from Galilee: "But who do *you* say that I am?"

About ten years ago I found myself at the Pittsburgh Airport waiting for a car to pick me up and take me to a biblical conference at which I was scheduled to speak. I was, soon enough, joined by two other scholars who were also presenters. Then this young man ambled toward our circle and shyly announced that he was heading to the conference as well. Since he looked as though he were about twenty years old, I presumed that he was a collegiate attendee and I asked him, "Where do you go to school?" To which he responded, "No, no, I already have my doctorate from Notre Dame. I'm a speaker, too!" That's how I met Dr. Brant Pitre—who now looks about twenty-five.

While in the car on the way to the conference, all four of us fell into a lively conversation about biblical interpretation, especially regarding the matter of the reliability of the Gospels. Dr. Pitre averred how annoyed he was by the oft-used comparison between the transmission of the story of Jesus and the "Telephone game." At which point I turned around (I was in the front seat and he in the back) and said, "Yes! Someone needs to write a book dedicated to refuting that stupid comparison." As I'm sure you know, Telephone is the parlor game in which one person whispers a message to another and then he to another through a long line until the final participant announces what she has heard. Invariably, to everyone's amusement, the original communication has been substantially distorted, even to the point of being unrecognizable.

What Dr. Pitre and I were bemoaning together was the use of this analogy by an army of biblical specialists endeavoring to demonstrate that what was ultimately written in the Gospels most likely bears little, if any, resemblance to the experiences of Jesus's first witnesses. After so many years of oral transmission, their argument goes, the original message was undoubtedly twisted out of shape, enhanced, mythologized, or lost altogether. And, therefore, what we have reveals far more about the attitudes, interests, and hang-ups of the various "communities" that surrounded the Gospel writers than it does about Jesus himself. Of course, to no one's surprise, the mythologized add-ons invariably had to do with supernatural elements: miracles, healings, the resurrection, and, above all, Jesus's divinity. The thoroughgoing use of this form-critical approach (to give its technical name) produced the portraits of the Lord that are on wide offer today: Jesus as ethical teacher, eschatological prophet, wandering philosopher, critic of the Roman system, zealot, etc.—anything but the Son of God, truly human and truly divine.

An observation I made to Dr. Pitre in the car that day was that the Telephone game "works" precisely because it is a trivial parlor game and absolutely no one involved cares one whit about the content of the message that he is communicating. As a counterexample, I would propose the manner in which news of the Kennedy assassination spread from person to person, to all corners of the world. To be sure, small distortions and exaggerations occurred along the way, but did anyone anywhere miss the message that the president of the United States, John Kennedy, was shot to death in Dallas on November 22, 1963? The reason that this information got through with remarkable accuracy to absolutely everyone is, first, that it was intrinsically important and, second, that all those involved in the chain of communication cared deeply about it. I would humbly suggest that the transmission of the good news concerning the life, teaching, death, and resurrection of Jesus had far more in common with the spreading of the message of JFK's assassination than with a game of Telephone.

Relying on the groundbreaking work of E. P. Sanders, N. T. Wright, Richard Bauckham, and others, Dr. Pitre has persuasively shown that the Gospels were written by either eyewitnesses (Matthew and John) or those in close association with eyewitnesses (Mark and Luke), that they properly fit into the genre of ancient biography (and not folklore), that they were composed far earlier than the standard scholarly consensus has it, and that they are the results of a disciplined process of communication that commenced even during the earthly life of Jesus. He has thereby mounted what I think is the most successful argument against the Telephone game nonsense and has given Christian evangelists renewed confidence in the message they are bearing to the world.

The second great contribution that Dr. Pitre has made to evangelization is his insistence upon the Jewishness of the Gospel. Though this might strike us as counterintuitive (wouldn't a de-Judaized Jesus be more relevant to our times?), it actually serves to shed light in every direction. It is a commonplace of many of the debunkers today that the divinity of Jesus is stressed only in the Gospel of John and that John's version of the life of Jesus is at the furthest remove from the historical figure of the Lord—and hence most susceptible to distortion and accretion. In point of fact, the Synoptic Gospel writers are just as insistent upon the divinity of the Lord as John, but their communication is offered in a distinctively Jewish idiom. To give just a few examples from Dr. Pitre's analysis, the Jesus who calms the storm at sea is acting in the person of the God of Israel, whom the Old Testament describes as the one who uniquely has lordship over the wind and the waves; the Jesus who dares to purify the Temple shows an authority that belongs exclusively to the one worshiped in the that holy place; the Jesus who blithely pronounces the forgiveness of the paralytic's sins is, as the bystanders themselves testify, doing something that only God can do. Say that they got it wrong, but please don't say that Matthew, Mark, and

Luke present only the human Jesus. Truth be told, their Christologies are just as high as John's, but we have to refamiliarize ourselves with the Jewish roots of the Gospels in order to see it.

I am incomparably grateful that Dr. Pitre has followed up so successfully on the suggestion I made ten years ago. This book will prove to be a most effective weapon in the arsenal of Christian evangelists in their struggle against the debunking and skeptical attitudes toward the Gospels that are so prevalent not only in academe but also on the street, among young people who, sadly, are leaving the churches in droves. Numerous studies have shown that what galvanizes young people is not when their religious teacher attempts to be relevant (that usually strikes them as pathetic), but rather when he demonstrates profound knowledge of his subject and passion for it. Any prospective teacher, catechist, or evangelist who wants to deepen his or her knowledge of and passion for the Lord Jesus should read this book— and use it.

ACKNOWLEDGMENTS

First, thanks must go to then Father—now Bishop—Robert Barron, who gave me the idea for this book several years ago when, in the midst of a very stimulating conversation, he suggested that someone needed to write something refuting the popular Telephone game analogy for the origins of the Gospels. I hope this book does the job. Next in line: my incredible editor, Gary Jansen, whose brilliant suggestions fundamentally transformed this book in ways that he alone knows but from which all of its readers will benefit. It is a pleasure and an honor to work with you. Every single time. Thanks also to Archbishop Gregory Aymond, Fr. James Wehner, and Notre Dame Seminary for graciously granting me a yearlong research and writing sabbatical in 2014–15. This book is among several fruits of that unforgettable year, for which I am profoundly grateful. I'd also like to thank friends and colleagues who read through drafts of the manuscript and helped enormously with their excellent feedback, especially Michael Barber, John Bergsma, Jeffrey Morrow, Brian Rohm, Todd Russell, Jimmy Seghers, and Andrew Swafford. You guys are the best. A much-belated word of gratitude is owed to my brother-in-law Chris Scott: thanks for over twenty years of great conversations, great friendship, and one blazing insight into Jesus's response to the rich young man (which you may not remember but I will never forget). To my children—Morgen, Aidan, Hannah, Marybeth, and Lillia—thank you for bringing joy and light into my life every day. I hope one day you'll read this book and come away knowing Jesus better. It's the least I can do in exchange for all that you have taught me about him. Morgen, this one is for you in a special way. Last, but certainly not least, to my lovely wife, Elizabeth, who moonlights as my "in-house" editor: how I wish I were as good a writer (and as beautiful a soul) as you. Thank you for sticking with me through the darker years when I was really searching, and for being there when the dawn finally broke.

NOTES

Chapter 1: The Quest for Jesus

1 See Amy-Jill Levine, *Short Stories by Jesus: The Enigmatic Parables of a Controversial Rabbi* (San Francisco: HarperOne, 2014); Amy-Jill Levine and Mark Zvi Brettler, *The Jewish Annotated New Testament* (Oxford: Oxford University Press, 2011); Amy-Jill Levine, *The Misunderstood Jew: The Church and the Scandal of the Jewish Jesus* (San Francisco: HarperOne, 2006).

2 See Bart Ehrman, *The New Testament: A Historical Introduction to the Early Christian Writings*, 5th ed. (New York: Oxford University Press, 2012), 72–74. In the late 1990s, we used the first edition of Ehrman's textbook. Despite criticisms of the analogy by other scholars (see next note), the "Telephone game" analogy is present in every subsequent edition.

3 See, e.g., Anthony Le Donne, *Historical Jesus: What Can We Know and How Can We Know It?* (Grand Rapids, MI: Eerdmans, 2011), 70–71.

4 C. S. Lewis, *Mere Christianity* (London: Collins, 1952), 54–56 (emphasis added).

5 Bart D. Ehrman, *Jesus, Interrupted: Revealing the Hidden Contradictions in the Bible (and Why We Don't Know about Them)* (San Francisco: HarperOne, 2009), 142.

6 See, for example, Ehrman, *The New Testament*, 183. See also the notes on John 8:56-58; 10:31 in Levine and Brettler, eds., *The Jewish Annotated New*

Testament, 177, 179: Jesus's words are "a violation of monotheism" and "perhaps a claim to preexistence." See also Craig S. Keener, *The Gospel of John: A Commentary,* 2 vols. (repr., Grand Rapids, MI: Baker Academic, 2010), 1.280–83.

7 Author's translation. Unless otherwise noted, all translations of Scripture found herein are from the Revised Standard Version, Catholic Edition (Toronto: Thomas Nelson & Sons, 1966), cited hereafter as RSVCE. All emphasis in quotations is the author's, and all archaic English ("thee," "thou," "thy," etc.) has been updated.

8 See, e.g., Bart D. Ehrman, *How Jesus Became God: The Exaltation of a Jewish Preacher from Galilee* (San Francisco: HarperOne, 2014), 125. See also Gerd Lüdemann, *Jesus After 2000 Years: What He Really Did and Said,* trans. John Bowden (Amherst, NY: Prometheus, 2001), 417: "Anyone who is in search of the historical Jesus will not find him in the Gospel of John. For the Fourth Gospel has already left far behind what Jesus really did and said. This verdict is a consensus among New Testament scholars." Such doubts about Jesus's claims to divinity in John's Gospel go back at least as far as the nineteenth-century work of David Friedrich Strauss, *The Life of Jesus Critically Examined,* ed. Peter C. Hodgson (London: SCM, 1973), 288–90. For a prominent critique of this skeptical view of John's Gospel, see Joseph Ratzinger (Pope Benedict XVI), *Jesus of Nazareth,* 3 vols. (New York: Doubleday, 2007; San Francisco: Ignatius, 2011; New York: Image, 2012), 1.218–37.

9 See Ratzinger, *Jesus of Nazareth,* 1.xii: "[T]he impression that we have very little certain knowledge of Jesus and that only at a later stage did faith in his divinity shape the image we have of him . . . has by now penetrated deeply into the minds of the Christian people at large. This is a dramatic situation for faith, because its point of reference is being placed in doubt: Intimate friendship with Jesus, on which everything depends, is in danger of clutching at thin air."

Chapter 2: Were the Gospels Anonymous?

1 Compare Alejandro Bermúdez, *Pope Francis: Our Brother, Our Friend: Personal Recollections about the Man Who Became Pope* (San Francisco: Ignatius, 2013). See also Georg Ratzinger, *My Brother, the Pope,* trans. Michael Hesemann (San Francisco: Ignatius, 2012).

2 See Martin Hengel, *Studies in the Gospel of Mark* (London: SCM, 1985), 65, 162n1. According to Hengel, the theory goes back primarily to two prominent late-nineteenth-century German scholars: Adolf von Harnack and Theodor Zahn, who (wrongly) came to this conclusion before the twentieth-century discoveries of the second-century papyri with the full titles. See Theodor Zahn, *Introduction to the New Testament,* trans. John Moore Trout et al., 3 vols. (repr., Minneapolis: Klock & Klock, 1977), 2.386–400.

3 Richard Bauckham, *Jesus and the Eyewitnesses: The Gospels as Eyewitness Testimony* (Grand Rapids, MI: Eerdmans, 2006), 300. Unfortunately, Bauckham does not adequately integrate the manuscript evidence for the originality of the Gospel titles into his overall theory of Gospel origins. Instead, he leans heavily on a questionable theory of implicit eyewitness inclusions within the Gospels as indicators of authorship. However, if Bauckham is right and the Gospels were not originally anonymous, the titles themselves would function as sufficient signals to the readers as to authorship, and the use of such subtle inclusions would seem redundant.

4 Ehrman, *How Jesus Became God*, 90.

5 Ehrman, *The New Testament*, 79.

6 Ehrman, *How Jesus Became God*, 90.

7 Ibid.

8 See Bart D. Ehrman, *Forgery and Counterforgery: The Use of Literary Deceit in Early Christian Polemics* (Oxford: Oxford University Press, 2013), 51–52, 6.

9 Ehrman, *How Jesus Became God*, 90.

10 In his earlier work, Bart Ehrman included a fifth argument, in which he claims that the form of the titles—"the Gospel according to X"—proves that the titles were added by "someone else" other than the author. See Bart D. Ehrman, *Jesus: Apocalyptic Prophet of the New Millennium* (Oxford: Oxford University Press, 1999), 42. At first glance, this may sound convincing to modern readers who are accustomed to authors referring to themselves exclusively in the first person. From a historical perspective, however, the argument fails on three points: (1) As we will see in chapter 6, the Gospels are a form of ancient Greco-Roman biography. As experts in ancient biography have pointed out, "authors of biographies . . . normally were named." Craig S. Keener, *The Gospel of Matthew: A Socio-Rhetorical Commentary* (Grand Rapids, MI: Eerdmans, 2009), 40. Moreover, one of the standard "opening features" of an ancient Greco-Roman biography was ordinarily some kind of "title." Richard Burridge, *What Are the Gospels?*, 156–57. These titles sometimes identify the author in the third person (see, e.g., Josephus, *Life of Josephus;* Tacitus's *Agricola;* Diogenes Laertius, *Lives of Eminent Philosophers*). This makes perfect sense, since when it comes to biography, the reader will want to know who is giving the account of the subject's life, and how they got their information. In fact, even authors of biographies who refer to themselves in the first person often do not ever give their names in the body of the book (e.g., Josephus, *Life* 1–2, 430; Lucian, *Demonax*, 1–2). But this does not transform their works into "anonymous" books. In short, the Gospels are no more "strictly anonymous" than are other ancient biographies in which there is no explicit information about authorship in the body of the book. Information about authorship of such works is often reserved for the title. (2) We have references to

ancient books whose titles are strikingly similar to the titles of the Gospels, such as "the memoirs according to Nehemiah" (Greek *tois hypomnēmatismois tois kata ton Neemian*) (2 Maccabees 2:13) or the "birth and life of Hippocrates according to Soranus" (Greek *Hippokratous genos kai bios kata Sōranon*) or "The histories according to Herodotus" (Greek *hē kat' hērodoton historia*). In one case, Josephus refers to the histories of Thucydides as "his history work" (Greek *tēn kat' auton historian*) (Josephus, *Against Apion*, 1.18). See Martin Hengel, *Studies in the Gospel of Mark* (London: SCM, 1985), 163n8. In light of such parallels, there is nothing implausible about the evangelists using the title "Good News according to [author]," especially if they saw themselves as proclaiming the good news about Jesus using the form of historical biographies (see chapter 6). Moreover, these examples also show that the claim sometimes made that "according to" (Greek *kata*) does not refer to authorship is erroneous. (3) Even if the title of the first written Gospel was added by a scribe who knew the identity of the author shortly after or concomitant with the publication of the book, this is still not the same thing as a "strictly anonymous" book. Moreover, once the first title was added to the first Gospel, it strains credulity to suggest that subsequent Gospel authors would imitate and copy from virtually everything in the book except the title. To the contrary, it is perfectly plausible to suggest that later Gospel writers would imitate the form of the title ("Good News according to . . .") but alter the author's name. If we know anything about the Gospel authors, it is that they had no compunctions whatsoever about copying material from one another! There is no reason this should not be true of the titles as well. On all this, cf. Michael F. Bird, *The Gospel of the Lord: How the Early Church Wrote the Story of Jesus* (Grand Rapids, MI: Eerdmans, 2014), 257–58.

11 See, for example, Reza Aslan, *Zealot: The Life and Times of Jesus of Nazareth* (New York: Random House, 2014). One of the first things Aslan does is insist that "none of the gospels we have were written by the person after whom they were named" (xxvi). This frees him up to construct a Jesus who is radically different from the one who is presented by the Gospels.

12 See Simon J. Gathercole, "The Titles of the Gospels in the Earliest New Testament Manuscripts," *Zeitschrift für die Neutestamentliche Wissenschaft* 104 (2013): 33–76.

13 For a discussion of the dates of the manuscripts, see Bruce M. Metzger and Bart D. Ehrman, *The Text of the New Testament: Its Transmission, Corruption, and Restoration* (Oxford: Oxford University Press, 2005), 52–94. See also D. C. Parker, *An Introduction to the New Testament Manuscripts and Their Texts* (Cambridge: Cambridge University Press, 2008).

14 See especially Martin Hengel, *The Four Gospels and the One Gospel of Jesus Christ,* trans. John Bowden (Harrisburg, PA: Trinity Press International, 2000), 48–56. See also Hengel, *Studies in the Gospel of Mark*, 64–84.

15 See Bird, *The Gospel of the Lord*, 259: "[T]here is an absolute uniformity in the authors attributed to the four Gospels. Matthew is always called 'Matthew,' and Luke is always called 'Luke,' and so forth."

16 Ehrman, *Jesus: Apocalyptic Prophet*, 248–49n1.

17 Gathercole, "The Titles of the Gospels in the Earliest New Testament Manuscripts," 71: "[T]he longer version appears to have been closer to a 'real' title, and the shorter version an abbreviation, rather as scholarly footnotes today first cite a title in full and thereafter abbreviate it." See also David E. Aune, "The Meaning of *Euangelion* in the *Inscriptiones* of the Canonical Gospels," in *Jesus, Gospel Traditions and Paul in the Context of Jewish and Greco-Roman Antiquity: Collected Essays*, Wissenschaftliche Untersuchungen zum Neuen Testament 303 (Tübingen: Mohr-Siebeck, 2013), 24.

18 See Bart D. Ehrman, *Misquoting Jesus: The Story Behind Who Changed the Bible and Why* (San Francisco: HarperOne, 2005), 130: "Probably the most important external criterion that scholars follow is this: for a reading to be considered 'original,' it normally should be found in the best manuscripts and the best groups of manuscripts." Indeed, not only are the titles of the Gospels found in the "best manuscripts" and the "best groups of manuscripts"; they are found in *all* the manuscripts—without a single exception. Hence, according to Ehrman's own text-critical criterion, the titles of the Gospels should be considered original.

19 Hengel, *The Four Gospels and the One Gospel of Jesus Christ*, 55.

20 See Bird, *The Gospel of the Lord*, 258–59.

21 Graham Stanton, *Jesus and Gospel* (Cambridge: Cambridge University Press, 2004), 79.

22 See Harold Attridge, *The Epistle to the Hebrews*, Hermeneia (Minneapolis: Fortress, 1989), 1–2, 410n87; see also Barbara and Kurt Aland et al., *Novum Testamentum Grace*, 27th ed. (Stuttgart: Deutsche Bibelgesellschaft, 1993), 587.

23 For the dates of the manuscripts, see Metzger and Ehrman, *The Text of the New Testament*, 52–94.

24 See Eusebius, *Church History*, 6.1–3, 20.3; 25.13–14; Jerome, *Lives of Illustrious Men*, 5.59.

25 Hengel, *The Four Gospels*, 54 (emphasis added).

26 Ehrman, *How Jesus Became God*, 90.

27 See, for example, Ehrman, *Forgery and Counterforgery*, 324–44. See also John P. Meier, *A Marginal Jew: Rethinking the Historical Jesus*, 4 vols., Anchor Yale Bible Reference Library (New Haven: Yale University Press, 1991, 1994, 2001, 2009), 1.112–66.

28 This point is consistently overlooked by scholars who claim that the false attribution to Mark and Luke is no problem. See, for example, Ehrman, in *Forgery and Counterforgery*, 51–52, where he fails to explain why scribes would not just attribute the Gospels to Peter and Paul themselves rather than disciples of Peter and Paul.

Chapter 3: The Titles of the Gospels

1 See Papyrus 4, Papyrus 62, Codex Washingtonianus, Codex Alexandrinus, Codex Ephraemi, Codex Bezai. The shorter form, "According to Matthew," is found in Codex Sinaiticus and Codex Vaticanus. Gathercole, "The Titles of the Gospels in the Earliest New Testament Manuscripts," 63–65.

2 On literacy at the time of Jesus, see Chris Keith, *Jesus' Literacy: Scribal Culture and the Teacher from Galilee* (London: T. & T. Clark, 2011), 71–123; Claudia Hezser, *Jewish Literacy in Roman Palestine*, Texts and Studies in Ancient Judaism 81 (Tübingen: Mohr Siebeck, 2001); Alan Millard, *Reading and Writing in the Time of Jesus* (Sheffield: Sheffield Academic Press, 2001).

3 Ehrman, *Misquoting Jesus*, 39 (emphasis added).

4 Ehrman, *How Jesus Became God*, 244.

5 See also Ehrman, *The New Testament*, 79, where he likewise appeals to the argument that it is unlikely for "the disciples" to have written the Gospels when they were "peasant fisherman." But this is to ignore that Matthew was not a fisherman but a tax collector—to say nothing of the fact that no one is claiming Mark and Luke were disciples anyway.

6 Ehrman, *Misquoting Jesus*, 38 (emphasis added).

7 See Michael W. Graves, "Languages of Palestine," in *Dictionary of Jesus and the Gospels*, ed. Joel B. Green, Jeannine K. Brown, and Nicholas Perrin (Downers Grove, IL: IVP Academic, 2013), 484–92 (here 486); Stanley E. Porter, "The Language(s) Jesus Spoke," in *Handbook for the Study of the Historical Jesus*, ed. Tom Holmén and Stanley E. Porter (Leiden: Brill, 2011), 3.2455–71.

8 Cf. Epictetus, *Discourses*, 1.1. On note-taking among ancient students, see Craig S. Keener, *The Historical Jesus of the Gospels* (Grand Rapids, MI: Eerdmans, 2009), 148–49.

9 Bauckham, *Jesus and the Eyewitnesses*, 288. See also Hezser, *Jewish Literacy in Roman Palestine*, 489–90: "It almost goes without saying that the Jews who collaborated with the Romans in the administrative realm had to be loyal supporters of the foreign government and knowledgeable of Greek, that is, they must have belonged to the most assimilated circles of the Jewish population."

10 R. T. France, *Matthew: Evangelist and Teacher* (repr., Eugene: Wipf & Stock, 2004), 68.

11 Ehrman, *The New Testament*, 80. See also Ulrich Luz, *Matthew 1–7*, trans. James E. Crouch, Hermeneia (Minneapolis: Fortress, 2007), 59: "If the author had been an apostle, as an eyewitness he would not have used the book of a non-eyewitness as his main source."

12 See Xenophon, *Memorabilia, Oeconomicus, Symposium, Apology*, trans. E. C. Marchant et al., Loeb Classical Library 168 (Cambridge, MA: Harvard University Press, 2013), 669–89.

13 See Xenophon, *Memorabilia*; Plato, *Phaedo*, 52b.

14 See Codex Washingtonianus, Codex Alexandrinus, Codex Ephraemi, Codex Bezae. Once again, the shorter form is present as a "running header" in Codex Sinaiticus and Codex Vaticanus. See Gathercole, "The Titles of the Gospels in the Earliest New Testament Manuscripts," 65–66.

15 See Adela Yarbro Collins, *Mark*, Hermeneia (Minneapolis: Fortress, 2007), 3–6; C. Clifton Black, *Mark: Images of an Apostolic Interpreter* (Minneapolis: Fortress, 2001).

16 Contemporary scholars are divided on whether 1 Peter was actually authored by the apostle Peter. For a discussion, see John H. Elliot, *1 Peter*, Anchor Yale Bible 37 (New Haven: Yale University Press, 2001), 118–30.

17 We know that he is not Peter's biological son, because Mark's mother, "Mary," is a resident of Jerusalem (Acts 12:12-14) and is never identified as Peter's wife.

18 See Papyrus 75, Codex Washingtoninaus, Codex Alexadrinus, Codex Bezae. The shorter form appears in Codex Sinaiticus and Codex Vaticanus. Gathercole, "The Titles of the Gospels in the Earliest New Testament Manuscripts," 66–67.

19 For an overview, see Joseph A. Fitzmyer, *The Gospel according to Luke*, 2 vols., Anchor Yale Bible (New Haven: Yale University Press, 1983, 1985), 1.35–52; and Joseph A. Fitzmyer, *The Acts of the Apostles*, Anchor Yale Bible (New Haven: Yale University Press, 1998), 49–51.

20 In the twentieth century, the Pauline authorship of both Colossians and Timothy was widely disputed. In recent years, however, major Pauline scholars have come out in favor of their Pauline authorship. On Colossians, see Douglas A. Campbell, *Framing Paul: An Epistolary Biography* (Grand Rapids, MI: Eerdmans, 2014), 276–304; N. T. Wright, *Paul and the Faithfulness of God* (Minneapolis: Fortress, 2013), 56–61. On 2 Timothy, see Luke Timothy Johnson, *The First and Second Letters to Timothy*, Anchor Yale Bible 35A (New York: Doubleday, 2001), 55–90. Even if one should be inclined to dispute the value of Colossians and

2 Timothy, the undisputed evidence from Philemon for Luke's association with Paul still stands.

21 For a full study, see Loveday Alexander, *The Preface to Luke's Gospel*, Society of New Testament Studies Monograph Series 78 (Cambridge: Cambridge University Press, 1993).

22 RSVCE, slightly adapted (in order to give as literal a translation as possible).

23 See especially Craig A. Keener, *Acts: An Exegetical Commentary*, 3 vols. (Grand Rapids, MI: Baker Academic, 2012, 2013, 2014), 1.402–15.

24 Bauckham, *Jesus and the Eyewitnesses*, 301 (emphasis added).

25 See Papyrus 66, Papyrus 75, Codex Washingtonianus, Codex Alexandrinus, Codex Bezae. Shorter form present in Codex Sinaiticus and Codex Vaticanus. See Gathercole, "The Titles of the Gospels in the Earliest New Testament Manuscripts," 68–69.

26 Although many scholars in the twentieth century speculated that the Gospel originally ended with John 20:30-31, there is no text-critical evidence to support this claim. For strong arguments that John 21 is original to the Gospel, see Richard Bauckham, *The Testimony of the Beloved Disciple: Narrative, History, and Theology in the Gospel of John* (Grand Rapids, MI: Baker Academic, 2007), 271–84; Keener, *The Gospel of John*, 1219–22.

27 For example, Ehrman, *Jesus: Apocalyptic Prophet*, 42.

28 Bauckham, *Jesus and the Eyewitnesses*, 362.

29 Ratzinger, *Jesus of Nazareth*, 1.222.

30 Augustine recognized this literary device centuries ago: "For that, indeed, is a mode of speech which the evangelists Matthew and John are in the habit of using in reference to themselves. Thus Matthew has adopted the phrase, 'He found a man sitting at the receipt of custom,' instead of 'He found me.' John, too, says, 'This is the disciple which testifieth of these things, and wrote these things, and we know that his testimony is true,' (John 21:24) instead of 'I am,' etc., or, 'My testimony is true.' Yea, our Lord Himself very frequently uses the words, 'The Son of man,' or, 'The Son of God,' (John 5:25) instead of saying, 'I' " (Augustine, *Harmony of the Gospels*, 1.12.25). Translation in *Nicene and Post-Nicene Fathers*, First Series, ed. Philip Schaff, 14 vols. (repr., Peabody, MA: Hendrickson, 1994), 6.116.

31 See Bauckham, *Jesus and the Eyewitnesses*, 379–80.

32 See Keener, *The Gospel of John*, 81–114.

33 For arguments for and against John the son of Zebedee, see Keener, *The Gospel of John*, 81–104.

37 See Anti-Marcionite Prologue to John 2; Jerome, *Lives of Illustrious Men* 9, cited in Orchard and Riley, *The Order of the Synoptic Gospels*, 204–5.

38 Irenaeus of Lyons, *Against Heresies*, 3.11.1–2, trans. ANF, 1.426–27. For more on Cerinthus, see also Irenaeus, *Against Heresies*, 1.26; 3.3, 11; Eusebius, *Church History*, 3.38.2; Epiphanius, *Against Heresies*, 28.

39 See John Chrysostom, *Homilies on the Gospel of Matthew*, 1.7; Augustine, *Harmony of the Gospels*, 1.4.7; Jerome, *Lives of Illustrious Men* 9.

40 Translated in Orchard and Riley, *The Order of the Synoptics*, 151.

41 Irenaeus, *Against Heresies*, 3.11.7, trans. ANF, 1.428.

42 It is not until the late fourth century AD that we find any evidence for doubts about apostolic authorship. According to Epiphanius (ca. AD 390), one early Christian group known as the Alogi denied the apostolic authorship of the Gospel of John and attributed it instead to an obscure Christian heretic named Cerinthus (see Epiphanius, *Panarion*, 51.1–3). Even skeptical scholars do not give any credit to the claim attributed to the Alogi, especially since Cerinthus seems to have denied the reality of the incarnation and the divinity of Jesus—something one can hardly accuse the Gospel of John of doing! (See Irenaeus, *Against Heresies*, 1.26; Epiphanius, *Panarion*, 28). Along similar lines, it is not until the late fourth century that we find the Manichean Faustus beginning to argue that the Gospels were not written by the apostles. See Augustine, *Against Faustus*, 32.2, 33.6, and the brief discussion in Ehrman, *Forgery and Counterforgery*, 74, 92, 140–41, 275.

43 Cited in Origen, *Contra Celsus*, 2.15, 16, trans. ANF, 4.437, 438. See also Celsus, *On the True Doctrine: A Discourse Against the Christians*, trans. R. Joseph Hoffman (New York: Oxford University Press, 1987).

44 See Henry Chadwick, *Contra Celsum* (repr., Cambridge: Cambridge University Press, 1980), 80.

45 Once again, the sole possible exception is the rejection of the apostolic authorship of the Gospel of John by the Alogi. But little is known about this group apart from Epiphanius's late-fourth-century description of them. See Epiphanius, *Panarion* 51.1–3.

Chapter 5: The Lost Gospels

1 For discussion of the apocryphal gospels, see Bird, *The Gospel of the Lord*, 281–98; Bart D. Ehrman and Zlatko Pleše, *The Apocryphal Gospels: Texts and Translations* (Oxford: Oxford University Press, 2011); Paul Foster, *The Apocryphal Gospels: A Very Short Introduction* (Oxford: Oxford University Press, 2009); Paul Foster, ed., *The Non-Canonical Gospels* (London: T. & T. Clark, 2008); Nicholas Perrin, *Thomas: The Other Gospel* (Louisville: Westminster John Knox, 2007);

34 Raymond E. Brown, *The Gospel according to John*, 2 vols., Anchor Bible; New York: Doubleday, 1966), 1.xcviii. In his later writing, Brown changed his mind on this point and no longer gave weight to the external evidence for John the son of Zebedee. See Raymond E. Brown, *An Introduction to the New Testament*, Anchor Bible Reference Library (New York: Doubleday, 1997), 370. See also the more recent comments of Joseph Ratzinger (Benedict XVI): "Since the time of Irenaeus of Lyon (d. ca. 202), Church tradition has unanimously regarded John, the son of Zebedee, as the beloved disciple and the author of the Gospel. This fits with the identification markers provided by the Gospel, which in any case point to the hand of an Apostle and companion of Jesus from the time of the Baptism in the Jordan to the Last Supper, Cross, and Resurrection." Ratzinger, *Jesus of Nazareth*, 1.224. Ratzinger also goes on to suggest that the Gospel may have been redacted by "John the Presbyter," a shadowy figure who may have been one of the apostle John's "closest followers" as well as the "sender and author" of 2 and 3 John. Nevertheless, Ratzinger concludes that "the contents of the Gospel go back to the disciple whom Jesus (especially) loved." See Ratzinger, *Jesus of Nazareth*, 1.226.

35 Ehrman, *Misquoting Jesus*, 39. See also Ehrman, *The New Testament*, 80.

36 Joel Marcus, *Mark 1–8*, Anchor Yale Bible 27 (New Haven: Yale University Press, 2000), 181.

37 Ratzinger, *Jesus of Nazareth*, 1.224.

38 See Keener, *Acts*, 2.1154.

39 See Luke Timothy Johnson, *Acts*, Sacra Pagina 3 (Collegeville, MN: Liturgical Press, 1991), 78.

40 Bauckham, *Jesus and the Eyewitnesses*, 362.

Chapter 4: The Early Church Fathers

1 See Mike Aquilina, *The Fathers of the Church: An Introduction to the First Christian Teachers*, 3rd ed. (Huntington, IN: Our Sunday Visitor, 2013); Hubertus R. Drobner, *The Fathers of the Church: A Comprehensive Introduction*, trans. Siegfried S. Schatzmann (Grand Rapids, MI: Baker Academic, 2007).

2 For example, in his various books on the Gospels, Bart Erhrman often simply ignores the evidence from the early church fathers that contradicts his claim that the Gospels were falsely attributed. See, e.g., Ehrman, *Forgery and Counterforgery*, 51–52.

3 For more patristic quotations, see Bird, *The Gospel of the Lord*, 214–20.

4 Cited in Eusebius, *Church History*, 3.39.16. Author's translation.

5 Justin Martyr, *Dialogue with Trypho*, 103.8. For the translation used here, see Justin Martyr, *Dialogue with Trypho*, trans. Thomas B. Falls (Washington, DC: Catholic University of America Press, 2003), 157.

6 Cited in Eusebius, *Church History*, 5.8.2. Unless otherwise noted, translations of Eusebius are from Eusebius, *Ecclesiastical History*, 2 vols., Loeb Classical Library (Cambridge, MA: Harvard University Press, 1926, 1932) (hereafter cited as LCL).

7 Cited in Eusebius, *Church History*, 3.24.5–6.

8 I will not take up the question about where the Gospels were written because we simply do not have enough information to know the answer with any degree of certitude. So John Chrysostom: "Now, where each one was abiding, when he wrote, it is not right for us to affirm very positively" (Chrysostom, *Homilies on Matthew*, 1.8). Translation in *Nicene and Post-Nicene Fathers*, First Series, ed. Philip Schaff, 14 vols. (repr., Peabody, MA: Hendrickson, 1994), 1.4.

9 See Eusebius, *Church History*, 3.39.16. Author's translation.

10 Translation in Bernard Orchard and Harold Riley, *The Order of the Synoptics: Why Three Synoptic Gospels?* (Macon, GA: Mercer University Press, 1987), 203.

11 Cited in Eusebius, *Church History*, 3.39.15, trans. Michael W. Holmes, in *The Apostolic Fathers: Greek Texts and English Translations* (Grand Rapids, MI: Baker Academic, 2007).

12 Cited in Eusebius, *Church History*, 5.8.3.

13 Cited in Eusebius, *Church History*, 2.15.1–2, trans. Michael W. Holmes; *The Apostolic Fathers*, 759.

14 Eusebius, *Church History*, 3.39.15, trans. Michael W. Holmes.

15 Ibid.

16 Irenaeus, *Against Heresies*, 3.1.

17 See Eusebius, *Church History*, 2.15.1–2, trans. Michael W. Holmes.

18 Cited in Eusebius, *Church History*, 5.8.3; compare Irenaeus, *Against Heresies*, 3.1.1.

19 Lines 2–8 translated by Bruce Metzger, *The Canon of the New Testament: Its Origin, Development, and Significance* (Oxford: Oxford University Press, 1987), 305–6.

20 Tertullian of Carthage, *Against Marcion* 4.2.5. Translation in *Ante-Nicene Fathers*, ed. Alexander Roberts and James Donaldson, 12 vols. (repr., Peabody, MA: Hendrickson, 1994), 3.347; hereafter abbreviated as ANF.

21 Cited in Eusebius, *Church History*, 6.25.4.

22 Irenaeus, *Against Heresies*, 3.1; Tertullian, *Against Marcion*, 4

23 See Eusebius, *Church History*, 6.25.4.

24 RSVCE, slightly adapted.

25 Translated in Orchard and Riley, *The Order of the Synoptics*, 2

26 Justin Martyr, *Dialogue with Trypho*, 103.8 (author's translatio some scholars claim that Justin did not know the Gospel of John, St *and Gospel*, 76, rightly points out that (1) Justin implies that there we pels and that at least two of these were written by "apostles" and (2) els tin clearly quotes the Gospel of John 3:3. See Justin Martyr, *1 Apolog Christ also said, 'Except ye be born again, ye shall not enter into the heaven.' "

27 Cited in Eusebius, *Church History*, 5.8; compare Irenaeus, *A esies*, 3.1.1.

28 Translated in Metzger, *The Canon of the New Testament*, 305–7.

29 Cited in Eusebius, *Church History*, 3.24.1–13.

30 Tertullian, *Against Marcion*, 4.2., trans. ANF, 3.347.

31 Irenaeus, *Against Heresies*, 1.9.2, trans. ANF, 1.329. Read in its fu this passage demolishes any attempt to make the evidence in Irenaeu anyone other than John the apostle, the son of Zebedee.

32 See Bauckham, *Jesus and the Eyewitnesses*, 438–68, following Mai gel, *The Johannine Question*, trans. John Bowden (London: SCM, 1990). Bauckham and Hengel's view is different from that of Pope Benedict, wl that "the 'presbyter' John" is "evidently not the same as the Apostle." Ra *Jesus of Nazareth*, 1.226.

33 See Eusebius, *Church History*, 3.39.1–8.

34 Bauckham's attempt to make Irenaeus's repeated references to the of the Gospel as John "the apostle" refer to someone other than the son o dee is unconvincing in large part because it fails to explain the presence Beloved Disciple with the twelve at the Last Supper. See Bauckham, *Jesus a Eyewitnesses*, 461–63.

35 See Joel Elowsky, *John*, 2 vols., Ancient Christian Commentary on ture, New Testament IVa–b (Downers Grove, IL: IVP, 2006–2007), 1.xxvii: "the consensual understanding among the ancient exegetes that John the a and disciple of Jesus was the author of the Gospel."

36 See Anti-Marcionite Prologue to John 2.

Hans-Josef Klauck, *Apocryphal Gospels: An Introduction* (London: T. &. T. Clark, 2004).

2 Translation in Wilhelm Schneemelcher, *New Testament Apocrypha*, vol. 1, *Gospels and Related Writings*, trans. R. McL. Wilson (Cambridge, UK: James Clark & Co., 1991), 444.

3 Greek Manuscript B, see Schneemelcher, *New Testament Apocrypha*, 1.441.

4 Trans. Schneemelcher, *New Testament Apocrypha*, 444.

5 Trans. Marvin Meyer, *The Gospel of Thomas: The Hidden Sayings of Jesus* (San Francisco: HarperCollins, 1992), 23, 65.

6 Ibid., 65.

7 For discussion, see Bart D. Ehrman, *The Lost Gospel of Judas Iscariot: A New Look at Betrayer and Betrayed* (Oxford: Oxford University Press, 2006).

8 Trans. Ehrman and Pleše, *The Apocryphal Gospels*, 395.

9 Ibid., 396–97.

10 See Ibid., 390; and April DeConick, *The Thirteenth Apostle: What the Gospel of Judas Really Says*, 2nd ed. (New York: Continuum, 2009).

11 Trans. Ehrman and Pleše, *The Apocryphal Gospels*, 387.

12 Trans. Schneemelcher, *New Testament Apocrypha*, 223–24 (following the enumeration of Ehrman and Pleše).

13 See Ehrman and Pleše, *The Apocryphal Gospels*, 372.

14 For an excellent study of Thomas's relationship to the earlier Gospels and its setting in early Christianity, see Mark Goodacre, *Thomas and the Gospels: The Case for Thomas's Familiarity with the Synoptics* (Grand Rapids, MI: Eerdmans, 2012), esp. 154–92.

15 Trans. ANF, 1.344–45.

16 See *Infancy Gospel of Thomas* 6.

17 Trans. ANF, 1.358.

18 Quoted in Eusebius, *Church History*, 6.12.4. Translation in *Nicene and Post-Nicene Fathers*, Second Series (14 volumes; ed. Philip Schaff and Henry Wace; repr. Peabody, MA: Hendrickson, 1994) 1.258 (hereafter cited as *NPNF 2*).

19 See Ehrman, *Forgery and Counterforgery*, 32.

20 Trans. LCL, slightly adapted.

21 Trans. *NPNF 2*, 7.27, slightly adapted.

Chapter 6: Are the Gospels Biographies?

1 Cf. Ehrman, *How Jesus Became God*, 92–93.

2 See Bird, *The Gospel of the Lord*, 251–52; Hengel, *The Four Gospels and the One Gospel*, 212n13.

3 Graham Stanton, *The Gospels and Jesus*, 2nd ed. (Oxford: Oxford University Press, 2002), 16–17.

4 See Bauckham, *Jesus and the Eyewitnesses*, 290–318.

5 Rudolf Bultmann, *History of the Synoptic Tradition*, trans. John Marsh, 2nd ed. (Oxford: Basil Blackwell, 1968), 371–72 (emphasis added).

6 Ibid., 6–7. For critique, see Keener, *The Historical Jesus of the Gospels*, 81–83.

7 Ehrman, *The New Testament*, 75.

8 Ibid.

9 Ibid., 75, 244–50. For recent criticisms of these criteria, see esp. Chris Keith and Anthony Le Donne, eds., *Jesus, Criteria, and the Demise of Authenticity* (London: T. & T. Clark, 2012); Dale C. Allison, "How to Marginalize the Traditional Criteria of Authenticity," in *The Handbook for the Study of the Historical Jesus*, ed. Tom Holmén and Stanley E. Porter, 4 vols. (Leiden: Brill, 2009), 1:3–30

10 Somewhat surprisingly, Bart Ehrman elsewhere accepts the scholarly conclusion that the Gospels are examples of ancient Greco-Roman biographies. See Ehrman, *The New Testament*, 84. Yet this conclusion has little impact on how he deals with the historicity of the Gospel claims. Instead, Ehrman insists that most ancient biographers were less intent on relaying what "actually happened" than on painting a picture of their subject's character and personality (Ehrman, *The New Testament*, 84). He bases this claim on Plutarch's preface to his life of Alexander the Great, in which Plutarch states that he is not going to relate "all" that Alexander did in "full detail" (Plutarch, *Life of Alexander*, 1). In doing so, Ehrman seriously misinterprets Plutarch. Plutarch is not saying he was not interested in what actually happened in the life of Alexander the Great; he is saying that he did not have the space to give "full detail" but rather must "abridge the story."

11 Richard Burridge, *What Are the Gospels? A Comparison with Graeco-Roman Biography*, 2nd ed. (Grand Rapids, MI: Eerdmans, 2004).

12 See Bird, *The Gospel of the Lord*, 221–98; Luke Timothy Johnson, *The Writings of the New Testament: An Interpretation* (Minneapolis: Fortress, 2010), 139; Craig S. Keener, *The Historical Jesus of the Gospels* (Grand Rapids, MI: Eerdmans, 2009), 73–108; Samuel Byrskog, *Story as History, History as Story: The Gospel Tradition in the Context of Ancient Oral History* (Leiden: Brill, 2002); Stanton, *The*

Gospels and Jesus, 14–18. These more recent studies are indebted to the earlier work of my teacher David E. Aune, *The New Testament in Its Literary Environment* (Philadelphia: Westminster John Knox, 1987), 17–76.

13 Richard Burridge, "About People, by People, for People: Gospel Genre and Audiences," in *The Gospels for All Christians: Rethinking the Gospel Audiences*, ed. Richard Bauckham (Grand Rapids, MI: Eerdmans, 1998), 122.

14 See Bird, *The Gospel of the Lord*, 236, citing Quintilian, *Institutes of Oratory* 3.7.15–16.

15 The Latin is *neque per tempora sed per species*. Translation in *Suetonius*, trans. John C. Rolfe, 2 vols., Loeb Classical Library 31 (Cambridge, MA: Harvard University Press, 1998, 1997), 1.161.

16 Cited in Eusebius, *Church History*, 3.39.15, trans. Michael W. Holmes.

17 Trans. in Plutarch, *Lives*, trans. Bernadotte Perkin; Loeb Classical Library 99 (Cambridge, MA: Harvard University Press, 1919), 225.

18 See Bauckham, *Jesus and the Eyewitnesses*, 220.

19 Trans. in Lucian, *Volume 1*, trans. A. M. Harmon, Loeb Classical Library 14 (Cambridge, MA: Harvard University Press, 1913), 173.

20 Foreword to Burridge, *What Are the Gospels?*, ix.

21 James D. G. Dunn, *Jesus Remembered: Christianity in the Making*, vol. 1, (Grand Rapids, MI: Eerdmans, 2003), 185

22 See Stanton, *Jesus and Gospel*, 13.

23 RSVCE, slightly adapted.

24 Trans. LCL.

25 Trans. Samuel Byrskog, *Story as History, History as Story*, 180.

26 RSVCE, slightly adapted.

27 Fitzmyer, *The Gospel According to Luke*, 1.288. Compare Josephus, *Against Apion*, 1.1–3.

28 Fitzmyer, *The Gospel According to Luke*, 1.292.

29 Ibid., 1.300.

30 Ehrman, *How Jesus Became God*, 93.

31 See the massive work of Keener, *The Gospel of John*, 3–52.

32 Trans. LCL, cited in Aune, *The New Testament in Its Literary Environment*, 92.

33 Meier, *A Marginal Jew*, 1.43 (emphasis added).

34 Ratzinger, *Jesus of Nazareth*, 1.229 (emphasis added; speaking specifically of the Gospel of John).

Chapter 7: The Dating of the Gospels

1 Ehrman, *How Jesus Became God*, 91.

2 Ibid., 92.

3 Ibid.

4 Ibid.

5 For an excellent overview, see Eric Eve, *Behind the Gospels: Understanding the Oral Tradition* (Minneapolis: Fortress, 2014). See also Bird, *The Gospel of the Lord*, 75–124; James D. G. Dunn, *The Oral Gospel Tradition* (Grand Rapids, MI: Eerdmans, 2013); Robert K. McIver, *Memory, Jesus, and the Synoptic Gospels* (Atlanta: Society of Biblical Literature, 2011); Robert B. Stewart and Gary R. Habermas, eds. *Memories of Jesus: A Critical Appraisal of James D. G. Dunn's "Jesus Remembered"* (Nashville: B&H Academic, 2010); Paul Rhodes Eddy and Gregory A. Boyd, *The Jesus Legend: A Case for the Historical Reliability of the Synoptic Jesus Tradition* (Grand Rapids, MI: Baker Academic, 2007), 237–308.

6 Jesus is called "teacher" (*didaskalos*) or "Rabbi" (*rabbi*) over fifty times in the Gospels. See Matthew 23:6-8; 26:25, 49; Mark 9:5; 10:51; 11:21; 14:45; John 1:38; 3:2; 4:31; 6:25; 9:1; 11:8; 20:16. For Jesus teaching his disciples to remember what he said, see Matthew 16:9; Mark 8:18; John 15:20; 16:4. For his command for the disciples to begin teaching while he was still alive, see Matthew 9:36–10:15; Mark 6:7-13, 30; Luke 9:1-6; 10:1-16. See Rainer Riesner, "Teacher," in *Dictionary of Jesus and the Gospels*, ed. J. B. Green, J. K. Brown, and N. Perrin, 2nd ed. (Downers Grove, IL: IVP Academic, 2013), 934–39.

7 For the disciples remembering Jesus's teaching, see John 2:22; 12:16; Acts 20:35. For them "teaching" others, see Mark 6:30; Acts 4:2, 19; 5:21, 25, 42; 11. On the skilled memory of disciples in the ancient world, see Keener, *The Historical Jesus of the Gospels*, 144–48.

8 See John 19:35; 21:24; Luke 1:1-4. For a similar reconstruction of the three stages, see esp. Pontifical Biblical Commission, Instruction Concerning the Historical Truth of the Gospels, *Sancta Mater Ecclesia* (April 21, 1964); Vatican II, Dogmatic Constitution on Divine Revelation, *Dei Verbum*, no. 19; *Catechism of the Catholic Church*, no. 126.

9 See Meier, *A Marginal Jew*, 3.53. See also M. J. Wilkins, "Disciples and Discipleship," in Green, Brown, and Perrin, eds., *Dictionary of Jesus and the Gospels*, 202–12; D. O. Wenthe, "The Social Configuration of the Rabbi-Disciple

Relationship: Evidence and Implications for First Century Palestine," in *Studies in the Hebrew Bible, Qumran, and the Septuagint: Presented to Eugene Ulrich,* ed. P. W. Flint, E. Tov, and J. C. VanderKam, Vetus Testamentum Supplements 101 (Leiden: E. J. Brill, 2006), 143–74; Meier, *A Marginal Jew,* 3.40–82.

10 Meier, *A Marginal Jew,* 3.53.

11 See the comments of Tom Thatcher, "Why John Wrote a Gospel: Memory and History in an Early Christian Community," in *Memory, Tradition, and Text: Uses of the Past in Early Christianity,* ed. Alan Kirk and Tom Thatcher (Atlanta: SBL, 2005), 95.

12 Dale C. Allison, Jr., *Constructing Jesus: Memory, Imagination, and History* (Grand Rapids, MI: Baker Academic, 2010), 25–26.

13 Bauckham, *Jesus and the Eyewitnesses,* 334, cf. 323, 346.

14 See Brant Pitre, *Jesus and the Jewish Roots of the Eucharist: Unlocking the Secrets of the Last Supper* (New York: Image, 2011).

15 Regarding Polycarp, Irenaeus wrote: "I remember the events of that time more clearly than those of recent years. For what boys learn, growing with their mind, becomes joined with it; so that I am able to describe the very place in which the blessed Polycarp sat as he discoursed, and his goings out and his comings in, and the manner of his life, and his physical appearance, and his discourses to the people, and the accounts which he gave of his intercourse with John and with the others who had seen the Lord" (Irenaeus of Lyons, Letter to Florinus). Cited in Eusebius, *Church History,* 5.20.5–6, trans. *NPNF 2,* 1.238–39.

16 Elie Wiesel, *All Rivers Run to the Sea: Memoirs* (New York: Knopf, 1995); *And the Sea Is Never Full: Memoirs, 1969–* (New York: Schocken, 2000).

17 Bart D. Ehrman, *Did Jesus Exist? The Historical Argument for Jesus of Nazareth* (San Francisco: HarperOne, 2012), 75, actually calls the claim that Mark's Gospel was written some forty years after Jesus's death a "brute fact."

18 Ehrman, *The New Testament,* 70. His claim that almost all scholars agree on these dates is misleading and ignores the wide variety of dates given by scholarship in the last two hundred years. See the survey of wildly different dates just for the Gospel of Matthew in W. D. Davies and Dale C. Allison Jr., *The Gospel According to Saint Matthew,* 3 vols., International Critical Commentary (London: T. & T. Clark, 1988, 1991, 1998), 1:127.

19 See Irenaeus, *Against Heresies,* 3.1.1; Muratorian Canon of Rome, nos. 9–16; Eusebius, *Church History,* 3.24.1–13; 5.8; Jerome, *Lives of Illustrious Men,* 9. The sole exception I am aware of is Tertullian, *Against Marcion,* 4.5.

20 See Ehrman, *The New Testament,* 102, whose primary "arguments" for the dating of Mark to ca. AD 70 include the assertion that Mark 13 reflects current

events and an appeal to the many scholars who think the Gospel was written be-tween AD 66 and AD 70. See also Marcus, *Mark 1–8*, 35.

21 See Luz, *Matthew*, 1:58 ("the *terminus a quo* is . . . the destruction of Je-rusalem"); François Bovon, *Luke: A Commentary*, trans. C. M. Thomas and J. E. Crouch, 3 vols., Hermeneia (Minneapolis: Fortress, 2002, 2012, 2013), 1.9 ("defi-nitely after the fall of Jerusalem"); Davies and Allison, *Saint Matthew*, 1.131–32 ("the events of 70 lie near to hand").

22 As admitted by Werner Georg Kümmel when he writes that while "Mk 13 shows traces of the threatening nearness of the Jewish war," "no overwhelming argument for the years before or after 70 can be adduced." As a result, "we must content ourselves with saying that Mk was written ca. 70." Werner Georg Kümmel, *Introduction to the New Testament*, trans. H. C. Kee (Nashville: Abingdon, 1975), 98. In other words, the AD 70 date is based almost entirely on the *ex eventu* reading of Mark 13.

23 C. H. Dodd, "The Fall of Jerusalem and the 'Abomination of Desolation,'" *Journal of Roman Studies* 37 (1947): 52, cited in John A. T. Robinson, *Redating the New Testament* (London: SCM, 1976), 27.

24 Trans. LCL. See Josephus, *The Jewish War*, books 5–7, trans. H. St. J. Thack-eray, Loeb Classical Library 210 (Cambridge, MA: Harvard University Press, 1997), 265–67.

25 See Brant Pitre, *Jesus, the Tribulation, and the End of the Exile: Restoration Eschatology and the Origin of the Atonement*, Wissenschaftliche Untersuchungen zum Neuen Testament 2.204 (Tübingen: Mohr Siebeck; Grand Rapids: Baker Ac-ademic, 2005), 219–380. Unfortunately, Marcus's recent commentary on Mark 13 mentions my book but never responds to any of its arguments against an *ex eventu* reading of the chapter and for the authenticity of the discourse with Jesus. Com-pare Marcus, *Mark*, 2.896, 1003.

26 See Mishnah, *Taanith* 4:6: "On the 9th of Ab . . . the Temple was de-stroyed the first and the second time, and Beth-Tor was captured and the City was ploughed up." See Herbert Danby, *The Mishnah* (Oxford: Oxford University Press, 1933), 200.

27 Davies and Allison, *Saint Matthew*, 3.349.

28 E. P. Sanders and Margaret Davies, *Studying the Synoptic Gospels* (London: SCM, Trinity Press International, 1989), 117.

29 James G. Crossley, *The Date of Mark's Gospel: Insight from the Law in Ear-liest Christianity*, Journal for the Study of the New Testament Supplement Series 266 (London: T. & T. Clark, 2004), 206.

30 For an excellent recent defense of the Two-Source Theory, see Bird, *The Gospel of the Lord*, 125–213.

31 See Ehrman, *The New Testament,* 70. See also Ehrman, *Did Jesus Exist?*, 74–76.

32 See especially David Laird Dungan, *A History of the Synoptic Problem: The Canon, the Text, the Composition, and the Interpretation of the Gospels,* Anchor Yale Bible Reference Library (New Haven: Yale University Press, 1999), 11–112.

33 See John Wenham, *Redating Matthew, Mark, and Luke: A Fresh Assault on the Synoptic Problem* (Downers Grove, IL: Intervarsity, 1992). The theory was popular in early-twentieth-century British Catholic biblical scholarship. See B. C. Butler, OSB, *The Originality of St. Matthew: A Critique of the Two-Document Hypothesis* (Cambridge: Cambridge University Press, 1951); and John Chapman, OSB, *Matthew, Mark, and Luke: A Study in the Order and Interrelation of the Synoptic Gospels* (London: Longmans, Green, & Co., 1937).

34 See David Alan Black, *Why Four Gospels? The Historical Origins of the Gospels* (Gonzalez, FL: Energion, 2010); Bernard Orchard and Harold Riley, *The Order of the Synoptics/Why Three Synoptic Gospels* (Macon, GA: Mercer University Press, 1987), 3–108; Bernard Orchard, OSB, *Matthew, Luke, and Mark* (Greater Manchester: Koinonia, 1976); William R. Farmer, *The Synoptic Problem: A Critical Analysis,* 2nd ed. (Macon, GA: Mercer University Press, 1976).

35 See John C. Poirier and Jeffery Peterson, eds., *Marcan Priority without Q: Explorations in the Farrer Hypothesis,* Library of New Testament Studies (London: Bloomsbury, 2015); Francis Watson, *Gospel Writing: A Canonical Perspective* (Grand Rapids, MI: Eerdmans, 2013), 117–216; Marc S. Goodacre and Nicholas Perrin, *Questioning Q: A Multidimensional Critique* (Downers Grove, IL: IVP Academic, 2004). For the original formulation, see Austine Farrer, "On Dispensing with Q," in *Studies in the Gospels: Essays in Memory of R. H. Lightfoot,* ed. D. E. Nineham (Oxford: Basil Blackwell, 1955), 55–88.

36 "As I see the matter, we cannot hope for a definitive and certain solution to it, since the data for its solution are scarcely adequate or available to us." Joseph Fitzmyer, "The Priority of Mark and the 'Q' Source in Luke," in *Jesus and Man's Hope,* ed. David A. Buttrick (Pittsburgh: Pittsburgh Theological Seminary, 1970), 132.

37 See Mark Goodacre, *The Case Against Q* (Harrisburg, PA: Trinity Press International, 2002). Watson, *Gospel Reading,* 119nn3–4, regards Goodacre's work as a turning point in contemporary discussion of the Synoptic Problem.

38 Sanders and Davies, *Studying the Synoptic Gospels,* 117 (emphasis added).

39 RSVCE adapted.

40 E.g., Ehrman, *The New Testament,* 159.

41 Wenham, *Redating Matthew, Mark, and Luke,* 228.

42 See Ehrman, *The New Testament,* 160–61; Robert Tannehill, *The Narrative Unity of Luke-Acts: A Literary Interpretation,* 2 vols. (Minneapolis: Fortress, 1989, 1991).

43 Notice here that Ehrman, *The New Testament,* 160–61, gets this half right. He rightly claims that Luke draws parallels between Jesus and the apostles, but he wrongly states that Luke tells us how they "suffer similar fates" or "experience similar fates." But Luke tells us nothing of the ultimate fate of Peter or Paul.

44 Adolf von Harnack, *The Date of the Acts and of the Synoptic Gospels* (trans. J. R. Wilkinson; repr. Eugene, OR: Wipf & Stock, 2004 [original 1911]), 99 (emphasis altered).

45 See Alexander Mittelstaedt, *Lukas als Historiker: Zur Datierung des lukanischen Doppelwerkes* (Tübingen: A. Francke Verlag, 2005), 219–21. See also Colin J. Hemer, *The Book of Acts in the Setting of Hellenistic History* (Winona Lake, IN: Eisenbrauns, 1990), 365–410. Cf. Keener, *Acts,* 385–88.

Chapter 8: Jesus and the Jewish Messiah

1 See Adela Yarbro Collins and John J. Collins, *King and Messiah as Son of God: Divine, Human, and Angelic Messianic Figures in Biblical and Related Literature* (Grand Rapids, MI: Eerdmans, 2008); Joseph A. Fitzmyer, SJ, *The One Who Is to Come* (Grand Rapids, MI: Eerdmans, 2007); Stanley E. Porter, ed., *The Messiah in the Old and New Testaments* (Grand Rapids, MI: Eerdmans, 2007); James H. Charlesworth, ed., *The Messiah: Developments in Earliest Judaism and Christianity* (Minneapolis: Fortress, 1992).

2 So Dunn, *Jesus Remembered,* 383; Meier, *A Marginal Jew,* 2:237. See also Ratzinger, *Jesus of Nazareth,* 1.47.

3 See Meier, *A Marginal Jew,* 2:238.

4 See Craig A. Evans, "Daniel in the New Testament: Visions of God's Kingdom," in *The Book of Daniel: Composition and Reception,* ed. John J. Collins and Peter Flint, vol. 2 (Leiden: Brill, 2002), 490–527.

5 See, e.g., Josephus, *Antiquities,* 10.209, in which he identifies the third "king" as being "from the west"—that is, the Greek Empire of Alexander the Great. It is worth noting here that in modern times, some scholars have proposed an alternative interpretation of Daniel's sequence: (1) Babylon; (2) Media; (3) Persia; (4) Greece; (5) kingdom of God. The major problem with this proposal is that the book of Daniel makes clear that the Medes and Persians united to form one empire, not two. Indeed, the text of Daniel explicitly states that the kingdom is given to "the Medes and Persians" (Daniel 5:28; cf. 6:8, 12, 15; 8:20). For this reason, the stone "not cut out by human hand" with the kingdom of God (Daniel 2:44-45) cannot be

identified as coming during the time of the Greek Empire. Instead, it comes during the fourth kingdom, which historically was interpreted by ancient Jews as the Roman Empire, for Rome followed Greece in reigning over the Jewish people. For a brief history of interpretation, see John J. Collins, *Daniel*, Hermeneia (Minneapolis: Fortres, 1993), 166–70.

6 E. P. Sanders, *Judaism: Practice and Belief 63 BCE–70 CE* (Harrisburg, PA: Trinity Press International, 1992), 289: "Even the present-day reader of Daniel can see that the stone that breaks all other kingdoms is the Kingdom of God, Israel."

7 N. T. Wright, *Jesus and the Victory of God*, Christian Origins and the Question of God 2 (Minneapolis: Fortress, 1996), 500.

8 Josephus tells us elsewhere that "an ambiguous oracle" from the Jewish Scriptures "more than all else incited [the Jews] to the war" with Rome, since it proclaimed that "one from their country would become ruler of the world" (Josephus, *War*, 6.312–15). See N. T. Wright, *The New Testament and the People of God*, Christian Origins and the Question of God 1 (Minneapolis: Fortress, 1992), 304.

9 See, e.g., Matthew 8:20; 9:6; Mark 8:38; 9:9; 10:45; Luke 6:22; 12:8-10; 17:24; John 3:13-14; 6:53, 62. For a discussion, see Russell Morton, "Son of Man," in *The Routledge Encyclopedia of the Historical Jesus*, ed. Craig A. Evans (London: Routledge, 2010), 593–98; Allison, *Constructing Jesus*, 293–303; Michael F. Bird, *Are You the One Who Is to Come? The Historical Jesus and the Messianic Question* (Grand Rapids, MI: Baker Academic, 2009), 63–116; Ratzinger, *Jesus of Nazareth*, 1.321–35; Keener, *The Historical Jesus of the Gospels*, 200–202.

10 Keener, *The Historical Jesus of the Gospels*, 202; Allison, *Constructing Jesus*, 294–95; Wright, *Jesus and the Victory of God*, 514. See also Raymond E. Brown, *The Death of the Messiah*, 2 vols., Anchor Bible Reference Library (New York: Doubleday, 1994), 1.509–14; Benjamin E. Reynolds, *The Apocalyptic Son of Man in the Gospel of John*, Wissenshaftliche Untersuchungen zum Neuen Testament 2.249 (Tübingen: Morh Siebeck, 2008).

11 Collins, *Daniel*, 312: "The beasts are not simply collective symbols but can be also understood to represent the rulers." For example, the first beast has the "mind of man" given to it, just as King Nebuchadnezzar of Babylon loses his mind and acts like an animal until God gives him back the mind of a man (Daniel 4:16).

12 See Pitre, *Jesus, the Tribulation, and the End of the Exile*, 54–55, 340.

13 See Timo Eskola, *Messiah and the Throne: Jewish Merkabah Mysticism and Early Christian Exaltation Discourse*, Wissenschaftliche Untersuchungen zum Neuen Testament 2.142 (Tübingen: Mohr Siebeck, 2001), 43–120.

14 See John Collins, *Daniel*, 306–7: "The earliest interpretations and adaptations of the 'one like a human being,' Jewish and Christian alike, assume that the

phrase refers to an individual and is not a symbol for a collective entity." See also Marcus, *Mark*, 1.529: "the beasts to whom the figure [of the son of man] is contrasted all stand for kings (7:17), so it might be logical to see the 'one like a son of man' as a king too." Not only "might" it be logical; it *was* the logical reading of every ancient Jewish interpreter we possess, which is the evidence on which historians interested in how Jesus interpreted Daniel should be focused.

15 See Brant Pitre, "Apocalypticism and Apocalyptic Teaching," in *Dictionary of Jesus and the Gospels*, ed. J. B. Green, J. K. Brown, and N. Perrin, 2nd ed. (Downers Grove, IL: IVP Academic, 2013), 23–33.

16 See Pitre, *Jesus, the Tribulation, and the End of the Exile*, 436. For a full discussion, see Scot McKnight, *Jesus and His Death: Historiography, the Historical Jesus, and Atonement Theory* (Waco, TX: Baylor University Press, 2005), 226–43.

17 RSVCE, slightly adapted.

18 See Pitre, *Jesus, the Tribulation, and the End of the Exile*, 56–57.

19 See Collins, *Daniel*, 356.

20 See Pitre, *Jesus, the Tribulation, and the End of the Exile*, 393–99.

21 For the identification of Artaxerxes in Ezra 7:1-28 as Artaxerxes I (who ruled from 464–424 BC), see Edwin M. Yamauchi, *Persia and the Bible* (Grand Rapids, MI: Baker Academic, 1997), 241–78. For the interpretation of "the word to restore and build Jerusalem" (Daniel 9:25) as the decree under Artaxerxes I (Ezra 7:1-28), see Jacque Doukhan, "The Seventy Weeks of Daniel 9: An Exegetical Study," *Andrews University Seminary Studies* 17 (1979): 15; cited in Collins, *Daniel*, 354 n. 64.

22 For a discussion, see Roger T. Beckwith, *Calendar and Chronology, Jewish and Christian: Biblical, Intertestamental, and Patristic Studies* (Leiden: Brill, 1996), 260–75; Harold Hoehner, "Daniel's Seventy Weeks and New Testament Chronology," in *Vital Old Testament Issues*, ed. R. B. Zuck (Grand Rapids, IL: Kregel, 1996), 171–86; Roger T. Beckwith, "Daniel 9 and the Date of Messiah's Coming in Essene, Hellenistic, Pharisaic, Zealot, and Early Christian Computation," *Révue de Qumrân* 40 (1981): 521–42.

23 Trans. LCL, slightly adapted. See Josephus, *Jewish Antiquities*, books 9–11, trans. R. Marcus, Loeb Classical Library 326 (Cambridge, MA: Harvard University Press, 1937), 305–6.

24 See Eusebius, *The Proof of the Gospel*, trans. W. J. Ferrar (repr., Eugen: Wipf & Stock, 2001), 124–25. Eusebius is quoting Julius Africanus's explanation in the fifth book of his *Chronography*, which is no longer extant.

25 See Blaise Pascal, *Pensées*, trans. W. F. Trotter (repr., Mineola, NY: Dover, 2003), 201 (see also 214, 223).

Chapter 9: Did Jesus Think He Was God?

1 Ehrman, *How Jesus Became God*, 125, cf. 269–70, as well as Ehrman, *Jesus Interrupted*, 76–82.

2 Ehrman, *The New Testament*, 190.

3 See Ehrman, *How Jesus Became God*, 211–46.

4 For a start, see especially Sigurd Grindheim, *God's Equal: What Can We Know about Jesus' Self-Understanding in the Synoptic Gospels?*, Library of New Testament Studies 446 (London: T. &. T. Clark, 2011).

5 Contra Ehrman, *How Jesus Became God*, 125.

6 See Ratzinger, *Jesus of Nazareth*, 1.229; Meier, *A Marginal Jew*, 1.43. See also Allison, *Constructing Jesus*, 10–20, on the preservation of the "gist" of Jesus's teachings.

7 Out of respect for both ancient Jewish and Christian traditions, I will not vocalize the proper Hebrew name of God herein. Instead, I will follow the custom of avoiding using the tetragrammaton wherever possible and replacing it with "LORD" (cf. Hebrew *'Adonai*; Greek *Kyrios*). Whenever scholars who are quoted herein have chosen to vocalize the tetragrammaton, I have adapted their quotations and simply written the four unvocalized consonants YHWH. In this, I am also following the Congregation for Divine Worship and the Discipline of the Sacraments, "Letter to the Bishops Conferences on 'The Name of God'" (June 29, 2008), which contains a directive to avoid pronunciation and use of the tetragrammaton, as well as the *Catechism of the Catholic Church*, which does not vocalize the divine name and only uses the Hebrew consonants YHWH when necessary for explanation (See CCC nos. 206, 209, 210, 446, and 2666).

8 Some elements are unique to particular Gospel accounts. For example, only Matthew's account contains Jesus's question "Why are you afraid, O men of little faith?" (Matthew 8:26), and only Mark's account contains Jesus's command to the sea: "Peace! Be still" (Mark 4:39) and his question to the disciples "Why are you afraid?" (Mark 4:40). Other elements are differently phrased or formulated. For example, in Mark's account the disciples ask a question: "Teacher, do you not care if we perish?" (Mark 4:38), whereas in Matthew and Luke, they simply cry out, "We are perishing!" (Matthew 8:25; Luke 8:24). See Kurt Aland, ed., *Synopsis of the Four Gospels*, English Edition (New York: United Bible Society, 1982), 77–78. For a summary of the basic content, see Meier, *A Marginal Jew*, 2.925–28.

9 See Levine and Brettler, *The Jewish Annotated New Testament*, 69: Jesus's act evokes the ancient theme of "the god who conquers the sea (e.g., Ps 65.7; 89.9; 107.29)."

10 Fitzmyer, *The Gospel According to Luke*, 2.728 (tetragrammaton adapted).

11 Meier, *A Marginal Jew*, 2.932 (tetragrammaton adapted).

12 Bovon, *Luke*, 1.321 (emphasis added; omitting Greek term).

13 Grindheim, *God's Equal*, 41–42. See also Eric Eve, *The Jewish Context of Jesus' Miracles*, Journal for the Study of the New Testament Supplements 231 (Sheffield, UK: Sheffield Academic Press, 2002), 386.

14 Marcus, *Mark*, 1.340 (emphasis added).

15 RSVCE, slightly adapted.

16 Most of the differences are details that are unique to individual accounts. For example, only Mark says that Jesus "meant to pass them by" (Mark 6:48), and only Matthew goes on to relate the famous story of Peter (temporarily) walking on the water (Matthew 14:28-31). In terms of differences between the Synoptics and John, only Matthew and Mark state that it was the "fourth watch of the night" (Matthew 14:25; Mark 6:48), and only John states they had rowed "about three or four miles" out before they encountered Jesus (John 6:19). See Aland, *Synopsis of the Four Gospels*, 138. For a summary of the common elements, see Meier, *A Marginal Jew*, 2.912–14.

17 See Marcus, *Mark*, 1.427, citing also Mark 13:6.

18 See Meier, *A Marginal Jew*, 909–10, who sees a "double meaning" in both Mark and John. See also Ratzinger, *Jesus of Nazareth*, 1.351–52.

19 See David Noel Freedman, "Yhwh," in *Theological Dictionary of the Old Testament*, ed. G. J. Botterweck et al., 15 vols. (Grand Rapids, MI: Eerdmans, 1974–2006), 5:501–511; Brevard S. Childs, *The Book of Exodus: A Critical, Theological Commentary*, Old Testament Library (Philadelphia: Westminster, 1974), 61–70.

20 Meier, *A Marginal Jew*, 2.918.

21 Marcus, *Mark*, 1.427.

22 See Keener, *The Gospel of John*, 1.673: "Already in Mark, Jesus' self-revelation on the waters appears as a theophany"; Ratzinger, *Jesus of Nazareth*, 1.352: "There is no doubt that the whole event [of the walking on water] is a theophany, an encounter with the mystery of Jesus' divinity."

23 See Meier, *A Marginal Jew*, 2.917; Marcus, *Mark*, 1.423, who considers the phrase "to pass by" to be "almost a technical term for a divine epiphany."

24 Adela Yarbro Collins, *Mark: A Commentary*, Hermeneia (Minneapolis: Fortress, 2007), 335 (emphasis added). She goes on to qualify this by saying that "Jesus is being portrayed here as divine in a functional, not necessarily in a metaphysical sense." I find this qualification puzzling, especially since the LORD's declaration "I AM" in Exodus 3:14 is arguably the most metaphysical statement in the entire

34 Ratzinger, *Jesus of Nazareth*, 1.310 (emphasis added).

35 M. David Litwa, *Jesus Deus: The Early Christian Depiction of Jesus as a Mediterranean God* (Minneapolis: Fortress, 2014), 114 (emphasis added). See also Crispin Fletcher-Louis, "The Revelation of the Sacral Son of Man: The Genre, History of Religions Context, and Meaning of the Transfiguration," in *Auferstehung-Resurrection*, ed. Friedrich Avemarie and Hermann Lichtenberger, Wissenschaftliche Untersuchungen zum Neuen Testament 135 (Tübingen: Mohr Siebeck, 2001), 253–54. Among older works, Litwa cites Bultmann's description of the Transfiguration as a "theophany." See Bultmann, *The History of the Synoptic Tradition*, 259–61.

36 See Grindheim, *God's Equal*, throughout. Despite the fact that Grindheim's book is the most thorough and recent treatment of the divine identity of Jesus in the Synoptic Gospels and was published in a prestigious academic series several years before *How Jesus Became God*, Ehrman never even mentions Grindheim's book or engages any of his arguments.

37 Ehrman, *How Jesus Became God*, 206–7.

Chapter 10: The Secret of Jesus's Divinity

1 See Neil Elliot, "Messianic Secret," in *The Routledge Encyclopedia of the Historical Jesus*, ed. C. A. Evans (New York: Routledge, 2010), 404–6. The phrase goes back to the work of William Wrede, *The Messianic Secret*, trans. J. C. G. Greig (1901; repr., London: James Clark, 1971).

2 Keener, *The Historical Jesus of the Gospels*, 263–64.

3 Ehrman, *How Jesus Became God*, 125.

4 See Keener, *The Historical Jesus of the Gospels*, 262, 537n50; D. Moody Smith, *John* (Nashville: Abingdon, 1999), 210.

5 Keener, *The Gospel of John*, 76–77, even speaks of "a form of the Messianic Secret" in the Fourth Gospel.

6 See the fascinating study by Tom Thatcher, *Jesus the Riddler: The Power of Ambiguity in the Gospels* (Louisville: Westminster John Knox, 2006). For the idea that Jesus taught in riddles in order not to give his enemies something to accuse him of, see Augustine, *On the Gospel of John*, 113.3.

7 Ratzinger, *Jesus of Nazareth*, 1.303.

8 There are a few interesting differences in detail. For example, in Matthew and Mark, Jesus refers to the paralytic as "my son" (Matthew 9:2; Mark 2:5). More significantly, Matthew's account lacks the explicit question "Who can forgive sins but God alone?" (Mark 2:7; cf. Luke 5:21). Though much of the body of the story is

229 *Notes*

Hebrew Bible. In any case, the difference between a functional and a metaphysical divinity is a later distinction not made by the biblical text itself.

25 Larry Hurtado, *How on Earth Did Jesus Become a God? Historical Questions about Earliest Devotion to Jesus* (Grand Rapids, MI: Eerdmans, 2005), 147; Davies and Allison, *Saint Matthew*, 1:237. See also Keener, *The Gospel of Matthew*, 406, "Commentators also often recognize Jesus' deity in his 'It is I' in 14:27, which literally declares, 'I am' "; Davies and Allison, *Saint Matthew*, 2.510: "[Jesus] has performed actions which the OT associates with YHWH alone"; and R. T. France, *The Gospel of Matthew* (Grand Rapids, MI: Eerdmans, 2007), 571, who speaks of the disciples' "instinctive recognition of Jesus' more-than-human nature."

26 Davies and Allison, *Saint Matthew*, 2.510 (emphasis added; tetragrammaton adapted).

27 See Levine and Brettler, eds., *The Jewish Annotated New Testament*, 28 (see their note on Matthew 14:31; emphasis added).

28 Keener, *The Gospel of Matthew*, 408: "One may doubt, however, that the disciples had yet grasped the full implications of Jesus' claim (such as 'I am' in 14:27)."

29 Contra Ehrman, *The New Testament*, 190.

30 In terms of differences between the accounts, the most noteworthy are these. Matthew and Mark say that Jesus took the disciples up the mountain "after six days" (Matthew 17:1; Mark 9:2), while Luke tell us that Jesus took them up the mountain "about eight days" after he had finished "these sayings" (Luke 9:28). Second, the Gospels also use different adjectives to describe the whiteness of Jesus's clothing (Matthew 17:2; Mark 9:3; Luke 9:29). Third, in two of the three accounts, God says, "This is my beloved Son" (Matthew 17:5; Mark 9:7), whereas in Luke's account, he says, "This is my Son, my Chosen" (Luke 9:35)—an excellent example of how the Gospels are not verbatim transcripts but can differ on sayings that were conceivably uttered only once without doing violence to the basic meaning (Latin *sensus*) of the words. Finally, Luke's account is unique in telling us about the topic of conversation between Jesus, Moses, and Elijah: they spoke of Jesus's "departure" or "exodus" (Greek *exodos*), "which he was to accomplish in Jerusalem" (Luke 9:30)—a reference to Jesus's passion, death, resurrection, and ascension. See Aland, *Synopsis of the Four Gospels*, 153–54.

31 See Davies and Allison, *Saint Matthew*, 2.697–99. Yarbro Collins, *Mark*, 422, traces this traditional interpretation back at least as far as Tertullian, *Against Marcion*, 4.22.

32 So Marcus, *Mark*, 2.632; Davies and Allison, *Saint Matthew*, 2.697.

33 RSVCE (with archaic English adapted).

substantially the same, the reactions of the crowds are described differently: in Matthew, they "glorified God," who had "given such authority to men" (Matthew 9:8); whereas in Mark they say, "We never saw anything like this!" (Mark 2:12), and in Luke "We have seen strange things today" (Luke 5:26). See Aland, *Synopsis of the Four Gospels*, 40–41.

9 See Adela Yarbro Collins, "Blasphemy," in *The Eerdmans Dictionary of Early Judaism*, ed. John J. Collins and Daniel C. Harlow (Grand Rapids, MI: Eerdmans, 2010), 445.

10 Author's translation.

11 See Josephus, *Antiquities*, 4.212–13. Mishnah, *Tamid* 5:1; *Berakoth* 2:2. For a cautious discussion of the Shema in first-century Judaism, see Meier, *A Marginal Jew*, 4. 586n29; and Joel Marcus, "Authority to Forgive Sins upon the Earth: The Shema in the Gospel of Mark," in *The Gospels and the Scriptures of Israel*, Journal for the Study of the New Testament Supplement Series 104, ed. C. A. Evans and W. R. Stegner (Sheffield, UK: Sheffield Academic Press, 1994), 196–211.

12 Yarbro Collins, *Mark*, 185. See also Ratzinger, *Jesus of Nazareth*, 1.311: "Forgiveness of sins is the prerogative of God alone, as the scribes rightly object." Compare Sanders, *Jesus and Judaism*, 273–74, who argues that Jesus was "presumably speaking for God (note the passive) not claiming to be God"; that he is only "announcing forgiveness on God's behalf"; and that "it goes too far, however, to say that Jesus, in claiming to speak for God, was guilty of blasphemy." According to Sanders "the saying attributed to him . . . does not mean that he forgives sins" (p. 273). All these evasive maneuvers completely ignore the fact that Jesus explicitly states, "The Son of man has authority on earth to forgive sins (Greek *aphienai hamartias*)." He nowhere claims to simply "speak for God."

13 See Markus Zehnder, "Why the Danielic 'Son of Man' Is a Divine Being," *Bulletin of Biblical Research* 24.3 (2014): 331–47; Peter Stuhlmacher, "The Messianic Son of Man: Jesus' Claim to Deity," in *The Historical Jesus in Recent Research*, ed. Scot McKnight and James D. G. Dunn (Grand Rapids, MI: Eisenbrauns, 2005), 325–46.

14 Allison, *Constructing Jesus*, 296: "Riding the clouds and assembling the quick and the dead for judgment are beyond human ability." See also Seyoon Kim, *The Son of Man as the Son of God*, Wissenschaftliche Untersuchungen zum Neuen Testament 30 (Tübingen: Mohr Siebeck, 1983), 14. It may also be worth noting that the Septuagint, the most ancient Greek translation of Daniel we possess, does not interpret the Aramaic as saying the son of man comes "to" (Greek *heōs*) the Ancient of Days. Instead, it says that the Son of Man comes "as" (Greek *hōs*) the Ancient of Days" (Daniel 7:13 LXX). In other words, the son of man "looks" like the LORD himself. For the parallels between the son of man and the Ancient of Days, see Benjamin E. Reynolds, "The 'One Like a Son of Man' According to the Old Greek of Daniel 7, 13-14," *Biblica* 89 (2008): 70–80 (esp. 77).

15 Daniel Boyarin, *The Jewish Gospels: The Story of the Jewish Christ* (New York: The New Press, 2012), 32–33.

16 Ibid., 34.

17 Yarbro Collins, *Mark*, 186, 187 (emphasis added; Greek omitted).

18 Here the differences are so minor as to be negligible. In Matthew's Gospels, Jesus is speaking to "the Pharisees" (Matthew 22:41), while in Mark he attributes the description of the Messiah as David's son to "the scribes" (Mark 12:35). Also, while Mark emphasizes that the crowd enjoyed the riddle (Mark 12:37), Matthew stresses that no one dared to "ask him any more questions" after this stumper (Matthew 22:46). See Aland, *Synopsis of the Four Gospels*, 249–50.

19 See Keener, *The Historical Jesus of the Gospels*, 270; Craig Evans, *Mark 8:27–16:20*, Word Biblical Commentary 34b (Nashville: Thomas Nelson, 2011), 275; Wright, *Jesus and the Victory of God*, 509.

20 Evans, *Mark 8:27–16:20*, 276: "Jesus regarded the epithet 'son of David' as insufficient as a reference to the Messiah. Evidently Jesus held a higher view of the Messiah."

21 Author's translation.

22 Marcus, *Mark*, 2.850–51. See also Keener, *The Historical Jesus of the Gospels*, 270; Martin Hengel, *Studies in Early Christology* (London: T. & T. Clark, 1995), 175–79.

23 Although Psalm 110:3 is difficult to translate, and the medieval Masoretic Text (MT) reads *yalduteyka* ("your youth"), the ancient Greek Septuagint interprets the unpointed Hebrew text as "I have begotten you" (seemingly vocalizing the text as *yelidtiyka*). Thus, in the Septuagint, God says quite clearly to the king: "From the womb, before the morning-star, I have begotten you" (Greek *ek gastros pro heōsphorou exegennēsa se*) (Psalm 109:3, LXX; author's translation). See Albert Pietersma and Benjamin G. Wright, eds., *A New English Translation of the Septuagint* (New York: Oxford University Press, 2007), 603: "From the womb, before the Morning-star, I brought you forth." Regarding the Hebrew, see John Goldingay, *Psalms*, 3 vols. (Grand Rapids, MI: Baker Academic, 2008), 295. On the pre-existence of the Messiah in the Septuagint version of Psalm 110, see Joachim Schaper, *Eschatology in the Greek Psalter*, Wissenschaftliche Untersuchungen zum Neuen Testament 2.81 (Tübingen: Mohr Siebeck, 1995), 104.

24 See Gathercole, *The Preexistent Son*, 236–37: "Ps. 110:3 . . . would have been taken to imply the pre-existence of the Messiah." Davies and Allison, *Saint Matthew*, 3:250: "The text assumes Jesus' status as Messiah and Lord, perhaps even his pre-existence." Compare Bultmann, *History of the Synoptic Tradition*, 137; he rejects the idea that Jesus could have quoted Psalm 110 because we would then "have to ascribe to Jesus some consciousness of pre-existence." One can of course

flip the coin and see Jesus's question about Psalm 110 as *evidence* from the Synoptic Gospels that he taught about his pre-existence. See also *1 Enoch* 48:3 for an early Jewish affirmation of the pre-existent Messiah.

25 Cf. Augustine, *Harmony of the Gospels*, 2.63.123.

26 See Ambrose, *Exposition of the Christian Faith*, 2.1.15–16.

27 Adolf von Harnack, *Das Wesen des Christentums* (Leipzig: J. C. Hinrichs, 1902), 91, 80. Translation in Hilarin Felder, *Christ and the Critics: A Defence of the Divinity of Jesus against the Attacks of Modern Sceptical Criticism*, 2 vols.; trans. John Stoddard (repr. Eugene: Wipf & Stock, 2006 [orig. 1924]), 1.245. See Adolf von Harnack, *What Is Christianity?*, trans. Thomas Bailey Saunders (New York: Harper, 1957). See also Strauss, *The Life of Jesus Critically Examined*, 289: "Here Jesus so tenaciously maintains the distinction between himself and God, that he renounces the predicate of (perfect) goodness, and insists on its appropriation to God alone."

28 Dunn, *Jesus Remembered*, 544n5: "Jesus is recalled as assuming both the Shema and God's unique goodness as givens (Mark 12.29; 10.18)."

29 Marcus, *Mark*, 2.728.

30 Simon Gathercole, *The Preexistent Son: Recovering the Christologies of Matthew, Mark, and Luke* (Grand Rapids, MI: Eerdmans, 2006), 74.

31 Grindheim, *God's Equal*, 187 (emphasis added). See also John M. McDermott, "Didn't Jesus Know He Was God? (Mark 10:17-22)," *Irish Theological Quarterly* 73 (2008): 319–20.

32 Wright, *Jesus and the Victory of God*, 302.

33 Gathercole, *The Pre-existent Son*, 74.

34 See Thomas C. Oden and Christopher A. Hall, *Mark*, Ancient Christian Commentary on Scripture New Testament 2 (Downers Grove, IL: InterVarsity, 1998), 28.

35 See Ibid., 28.

36 Trans. (with archaic language updated) in *Nicene and Post-Nicene Fathers, Series 1* (14 vols.; ed. Philip Schaff; repr.; Peabody: Hendrickson, 1994), 6.397–98 (hereafter cited as *NPNF 1*).

37 For the idea that Jesus revealed the mystery of his divine identity gradually, see John Chrysostom, *Homilies on the Gospel of John*, 3.4: "Christ himself . . . used this reserve. For he did not at once reveal to us his divinity, but was at first held to be a prophet and a good man; but afterwards his real nature was shown by his works and words," trans. *NPNF 1*, 14.13.

38 Trans. *NPNF* 2, 10.226.

39 See Manlio Simonetti, *Matthew*, 2 vols., Ancient Christian Commentary on Scripture New Testament Ia–b (Downers Grove, IL: InterVarsity, 2001, 2002), 1.98.

Chapter 11: The Crucifixion

1 For a closer look at the crucifixion of Jesus, see David W. Chapman, *Ancient Jewish and Christian Perceptions of Crucifixion*, Wissenschaftliche Untersuchungen zum Neuen Testament 2.244 (Tübingen: Mohr Siebeck, 2008); Michael O. Wise, "Crucifixion," in *The Eerdmans Dictionary of Early Judaism*, ed. John J. Collins and Daniel C. Harlow (Grand Rapids, MI: Eerdmans, 2010), 500–501. For a popular level overview, see Brant Pitre, *Jesus the Bridegroom: The Greatest Love Story Ever Told* (New York: Image, 2014), 95–101.

2 See Meier, *A Marginal Jew*, 1.177.

3 Ehrman, *The New Testament*, 275–76.

4 Meier, *A Marginal Jew*, 1.177.

5 Ehrman, *The New Testament*, 277–79. In his extremely influential study, E. P. Sanders, *Jesus and Judaism* (Philadelphia: Fortress, 1985), 334, describes Jesus's action in the Temple as "the crucial act which led to his execution."

6 For an extensive recent defense of the historical plausibility of Jesus's exchange with Caiaphas and the Sanhedrin and the charge of blasphemy, see esp. Darrell L. Bock, "Trial of Jesus," in *The Routledge Encyclopedia of the Historical Jesus*, 656–62. Bock rightly notes that Joseph of Arimathea and Nicodemus, both of whom were members of the Sanhedrin, could have acted as sources of the exchange. I would also add that the Gospels strongly suggest that Peter himself was in proximity to the examination and following what happens (cf. John 18:12-27). For example, he goes "right into the courtyard of the high priest" (Mark 14:54) and remains there while Jesus is examined (Mark 14:55-66). In Matthew's account, Peter not only goes "inside," but he sits with the guards "to see the end" (Matthew 26:58). Finally, in Luke, Jesus is apparently at one point able to "turn and look at Peter" (Luke 22:61), although exactly when this occurs with reference to the examination is unclear. See also L. H. Cohick, "The Trial of Jesus," in *Dictionary of Jesus and the Gospels* ed. Joel B. Green, Jeanine K. Brown, and Nicholas Perrin, 2nd ed. (Downers Grove, IL: IVP Academic, 2013), 972–79; Adela Yarbro Collins, "The Charge of Blasphemy in Mark 14.6," *Journal for the Study of the New Testament* 26 (2004): 379–401; Ratzinger, *Jesus of Nazareth*, 3.167–201; Raymond E. Brown, *The Death of the Messiah*, 2 vols., Anchor Bible Reference Library (New York: Doubleday, 1994), 1.315–562.

7 Ratzinger, *Jesus of Nazareth,* 2.178–79: "With regard to the precise formulations, Matthew, Mark, and Luke differ in detail . . . [H]ere an exact reconstruction of Caiaphas' question and Jesus' answer is not possible. The essential content of the exchange nevertheless emerges quite unequivocally from the three different accounts."

8 See Levine and Brettler, eds., *The Jewish Annotated New Testament,* 92: "The titles Messiah and Son of the Blessed One are not blasphemy, since a Jewish king could be both."

9 Yarbro Collins, *Mark,* 704; Ratzinger, *Jesus of Nazareth,* 2.180.

10 Davies and Allison, *Saint Matthew,* 3:528; Fitzmyer, *The Gospel According to Luke,* 2:1468.

11 Gerhard Lohfink, *Jesus of Nazareth: What He Wanted, Who He Was,* trans. Linda M. Maloney (Collegeville, MN: Liturgical Press, 2012), 275.

12 See Fitzmyer, *The Gospel of Luke,* 2:1461: "No reference is made to Jesus having spoken of the destruction of the Temple. . . . The entire questioning is addressed to Jesus himself. . . . The questioning concerns his messiahship and divine sonship alone."

13 Author's translation.

14 See Allison, *Constructing Jesus,* 296; Kim, *The Son of Man as the Son of God,* 14: "The accompaniment of the clouds in his appearance . . . indicates that he is a divine figure. For in the Old Testament clouds regularly accompany theophany. So, the figure Daniel sees is a deity in human form or likeness."

15 Yarbro Collins, *Mark,* 706. For the same point, see Michael F. Bird, "Did Jesus Think He Was God?," in *How God Became Jesus: The Real Origins of Belief in Jesus' Divine Nature* (Grand Rapids, MI: Zondervan, 2014), 65–67.

16 Marcus, *Mark,* 2:1008: "[T]he high priest's ensuing charge of blasphemy probably picks up on Jesus' implicit affirmation of his divine sonship. . . . Jesus, then, seems to be affirming, in a way understood by his interlocutor, that he is not only the Son of God but also the Son of Man." See also Ratzinger, *Jesus of Nazareth,* 2.180–81: "Jesus was claiming to be close to the 'Power', to participate in God's own nature, and this would have been understood as blasphemy"; E. Earl Ellis, "Deity-Christology in Mark 14:58," in *Jesus of Nazareth: Lord and Christ: Essays on the Historical Jesus and New Testament Christology,* ed. Joel B. Green and Max Turner (Grand Rapids, MI: Eerdmans, 1994), 192–203.

17 See Yarbro Collins, "Blasphemy," 445.

18 Davies and Allison, *Saint Matthew,* 3.534.

19 See also Philo, *Embassy to Gaius,* 45.367–68.

20 Cited in Yarbro Collins, "Blasphemy," 445.

21 For example, Ehrman, *How Jesus Became God*, does not discuss the charges of blasphemy in Mark 2:6-7 and John 10:30-33.

22 In his discussion of the charge of blasphemy against Jesus, Ehrman, *The New Testament*, 100, admits that it wasn't blasphemy to claim to be the Messiah. However, instead of recognizing that Jesus is claiming to be divine when he responds to Caiaphas's question about his identity, Ehrman postulates the implausible interpretation that Jesus was not actually referring to himself when he spoke about the Son of Man being seated on the throne next to God (*The New Testament*, 100). The problem with this is that *Caiaphas's question is specifically about the identity of Jesus himself*, not about someone else. One gets the feeling that Ehrman is grasping at straws in order to make the Synoptic evidence in which Jesus claims that he is divine effectively disappear.

23 On the charge of blasphemy in John's Gospel, see Keener, *The Gospel of John*, 826–27; John A. T. Robinson, *The Priority of John* (London: SCM, 1985), 262–64.

24 Brown, *The Death of the Messiah*, 1.829.

25 Ratzinger, *Jesus of Nazareth*, 1.303.

26 In this case, Matthew and Mark's accounts are extremely close, although Matthew gives the words of the psalm in a form closer to the original Hebrew. See Aland, *Synopsis of the Four Gospels*, 320–21.

27 Rudolf Bultmann, "The Primitive Christian Kerygma and the Historical Jesus," in *The Historical Jesus and the Kerygmatic Christ: Essays on the New Quest for the Historical Jesus*, ed. Carl E. Braaten and Roy A. Harrisville (Nashville: Abingdon, 1964), 28–29. See likewise Albert Schweitzer, *The Quest of the Historical Jesus: A Critical Study of Its Progress from Reimarus to Wrede*, trans. William Montgomery, rev. ed. (1906; repr., New York: Macmillan, 1968), 371.

28 I have adapted the archaic pronouns ("thee" and "thou") of the RSVCE.

29 See P. J. Williams, "The Linguistic Background to Jesus' Dereliction Cry (Matthew 27:46; Mark 15:34)," in *The New Testament in Its First Century Setting: Essays on Context and Background in Honour of B. W. Winter on His 65th Birthday*, ed. P. J. Williams et al. (Grand Rapids, MI: Eerdmans, 2004), 1–12. See Mishnah, *Taanith*, 2.3, which cites the first lines of Psalms 120, 121, 130, and 102 with the implication that the entire psalms are invoked, "each of them with its proper ending."

30 See Judith H. Newman, "Psalms," in *The Eerdmans Dictionary of Early Judaism*, ed. J. J. Collins and D. C. Harlow (Grand Rapids, MI: Eerdmans, 2010), 1105–7. See also David C. Mitchell, *The Message of the Psalter: An Eschatological*

Programme in the Book of Psalms, Journal for the Study of the Old Testament Supplement Series 252 (Sheffield, UK: Sheffield Academic Press, 1997).

31 Pietersma and Wright, *A New English Translation of the Septuagint*, 557. The Greek reads *ōryxan cheiras mou kai podas* (Psalm 21:17 LXX).

32 Newman, "Psalms," 1107.

33 Keener, *The Historical Jesus of the Gospels*, 576: "Jesus had to know that Psalm 22 went on to declare the psalmist's vindication."

34 For what follows, see Brant Pitre, "Jesus, the New Temple, and the New Priesthood," *Letter & Spirit* 4 (2008): 47–83. See also Nicholas Perrin, *Jesus the Temple* (Grand Rapids, MI: Baker Academic, 2010).

35 See Ratzinger, *Jesus of Nazareth*, 224–26; Brown, *The Death of the Messiah*, 2.1176–88.

36 On Passover, see Daniel K. Falk, "Festivals and Holy Days," in *The Eerdmans Dictionary of Early Judaism*, ed. John J. Collins and Daniel C. Harlow (Grand Rapids, MI: Eerdmans, 2010), 636–45; James C. VanderKam, "Passover," in *Encyclopedia of the Dead Sea Scrolls*, ed. Lawrence H. Schiffman and James C. VanderKam, 2 vols. (Oxford: Oxford University Press, 2000), 2.637–38; Sanders, *Judaism: Practice and Belief*, 132–38.

37 See Sanders, *Judaism: Practice and Belief*, 47–54.

38 Trans. William H. Whiston, *Josephus: Complete Works* (repr., Peabody, MA: Hendrickson, 1994), 749.

39 Trans. Herbert Danby, *The Mishnah* (Oxford: Oxford University Press, 1933), 594.

40 Sanders, *Judaism: Practice and Belief*, 70–71.

41 See Keener, *The Gospel of Matthew*, 356: "Jesus' self-claim is veiled enough to prevent accusations of blasphemy—especially since his opponents would not expect him to claim what he is claiming—but obvious enough to enrage them."

Chapter 12: The Resurrection

1 For full-length studies, see Michael Licona, *The Resurrection of Jesus: A Historiographical Approach* (Downers Grove, IL: InterVarsity Press, 2010); Dale C. Allison, Jr., *Resurrecting Jesus* (London: T. & T. Clark, 2005), 198–376; N. T. Wright, *The Resurrection of the Son of God*, Christian Origins and the Question of God 3 (Minneapolis: Fortress, 2003).

2 Ratzinger, *Jesus of Nazareth*, 243.

3 See Wright, *The Resurrection of the Son of God*, 7, 276, 342.

4 This is particularly clear in the case of Lazarus, who, as a result of his being raised, was the subject of a plot by the chief priest "to put Lazarus also to death" (John 12:10)!

5 Cf. Luke Timothy Johnson, *The Real Jesus: The Misguided Quest for the Historical Jesus and the Truth of the Traditional Gospels* (San Francisco: HarperCollins, 1995), 134–36, who downplays the importance of the empty tomb and claims instead that "resurrection" meant that "after his crucifixion . . . Jesus entered into the powerful life of God" or "the passage of the human Jesus into the power of God." For a critique, see Wright, *The Resurrection of the Son of God*, 204. See also Marcus Borg's affirmation that Jesus is somehow "alive" in a way that does not involve an empty tomb. Marcus Borg and N. T. Wright, *The Meaning of Jesus: Two Visions* (San Francisco: HarperCollins, 1999), 129–44.

6 See George W. E. Nickelsburg, *Resurrection, Immortality, and Eternal Life in Intertestamental Judaism and Early Christianity*, 2nd ed. (Cambridge, MA: Harvard University Press, 2006), for the range of views.

7 See Acts 1:21-22; 2:31; 4:33; 17:18; Romans 1:4; 1 Corinthians 15:35-45; Philippians 3:20-21; 1 Peter 1:3; 3:21. Wright, *The Resurrection of the Son of God*, 31, puts it well: "Here there is no difference between pagans, Jews, and Christians. They all understood the Greek word *anastasis* and its cognates . . . to mean . . . new life after a period of being dead. . . . All of them were speaking of a new life after 'life after death' in the popular sense, a fresh living embodiment following a period of death as a state."

8 Allison, *Resurrecting Jesus*, 625, notes that there is no evidence for early Christian belief in a "non-physical resurrection."

9 Compare Rudolf Bultmann, *History of the Synoptic Tradition*, 290: "Originally there was no difference between the Resurrection of Jesus and his Ascension; this distinction first arose as a consequence of the Easter legends."

10 For a fuller discussion of the ascension, see Keener, *Acts*, 1.711–31; Ratzinger, *Jesus of Nazareth*, 2.278–93. See also Douglas Farrow, *Ascension Theology* (London: Bloomsbury T. & T. Clark, 2011); Gerritt Dawson, *Jesus Ascended: The Meaning of Christ's Continuing Incarnation* (London: Bloomsbury T. & T. Clark, 2004).

11 See Ratzinger, *Jesus of Nazareth*, 2.244.

12 See Ratzinger, *Jesus of Nazareth*, 2.268; Wright, *The Resurrection of the Son of God*, 657–58.

13 See Wright, *The Resurrection of the Son of God*, 655–56.

14 Keener, *The Gospel of John*, 2:1211: "In this case, as in the prologue, the

confession of Jesus' deity is unmistakable. It cannot simply represent an accla-
mation to the Father, since John explicitly claims that the words are addressed to
Jesus (*autō*)."

15 Ratzinger, *Jesus of Nazareth*, 2.274–77.

16 See Meier, *A Marginal Jew*, 2:520, on the "academic sneer factor" and the
widespread assumption, "especially in religion departments," that "Modern
man cannot believe in miracles"—a view which he associates above all with Rudolf Bultmann's famous claim that "It is impossible to use electric light and the
wireless and to avail ourselves of modern medical and surgical discoveries, and
at the same time to believe in the New Testament world of . . . miracles." See
Rudolf Bultmann, "The New Testament and Mythology," in *New Testament and
Mythology and Other Basic Writings*, ed. Schubert Ogden (Philadelphia: Fortress,
1984), 5. On miracles in modern and ancient minds see Meier, *A Marginal Jew*,
2.509–616. The definitive work for some time to come on the subject of ancient
and modern views of miracles is the massive study by Craig S. Keener, *Miracles:
The Credibility of the New Testament Accounts*, 2 vols. (Grand Rapids, MI: Baker
Academic, 2011).

17 Cf. N. T. Wright, *Surprised by Scripture* (San Francisco: HarperOne, 2014),
41–63.

18 Licona, *The Resurrection of Jesus*, 333–34, 461–63, 629–32.

19 Ehrman, *Jesus: Apocalyptic Prophet*, 228. Unfortunately, in his more recent
work, Ehrman does not follow his own criterion of multiple attestation when it
comes to the burial of Jesus by Joseph of Arimathea or the discovery of the empty
tomb. Instead, he makes the claim—for which he can produce no positive historical evidence—that Jesus's body was not buried by Joseph. Instead, Ehrman asserts that Jesus's body was either left to decompose on the cross, eaten by dogs
and birds, or thrown into a common grave for criminals. See Ehrman, *How Jesus
Became God*, 151–67. In keeping with his tendency to ignore widely known recent
works by major scholars who disagree with him (e.g., R. Bauckham, R. Burridge,
M. Hengel), Ehrman never engages the extensive arguments for Jesus's burial by
Joseph of Arimathea by Dale Allison in Allison, *Resurrecting Jesus*, 352–63. More
important, Ehrman ignores the evidence from Josephus that Jews were noted for
their concern for burying the victims of crucifixion: "They [the Idumeans] actually went so far in their impiety as to cast out the corpses without burial, although
the Jews are so careful about funeral rites that even malefactors who have been
sentenced to crucifixion are taken down and buried before sunset" (Josephus,
War, 4.317). Trans. H. St. J. Thackeray, *Josephus: The Jewish War*, books 3–4, Loeb
Classical Library 487 (Cambridge, MA: Harvard University Press, 1927), 249. Ehrman's argument that Pilate did not bow to Jewish custom and that "it was not
Jews who killed Jesus, so they had no say about when he would be taken down
from the cross" (*How Jesus Became God*, 157) also ignores two other facts: (1) Jesus
was crucified during Passover, when hundreds of thousands of Jews would have

been in the city of Jerusalem (see Josephus, *War*, 6.423–37) and there would have been the serious threat of a riot (see Mark 14:2). (2) On occasion Pilate did "bow to Jewish demands" when there was enough Jewish crowd pressure (see Josephus, *Antiquities*, 18.3.1). Therefore, it does not strain credulity to imagine Pilate giving the body of Jesus to a Jewish leader like Joseph of Arimathea in order to avoid the violence that may have ensued when several hundred thousand Jews discovered that their "land" had been "defiled" by an explicit violation of the Torah during the most solemn festival of the liturgical year (see Deuteronomy 21:22-23; 11QTemple 64:6-13). See David W. Chapman, *Ancient Jewish and Christian Perceptions of Crucifixion* (Grand Rapids, MI: Baker Academic, 2008), 117–47.

20 Allison, *Resurrecting Jesus*, 332.

21 See Josephus, *Antiquities*, 4.219: "Put not trust in a single witness, but let there be three or at the least two, whose evidence shall be accredited by their past lives. From women let no evidence be accepted, because of the levity and temerity of their sex." See Licona, *The Resurrection of Jesus*, 349–58; Byrskog, *Story as History*, 73–82; Richard Bauckham, *Gospel Women: Studies of the Named Women in the Gospels* (Grand Rapids, MI: Eerdmans, 2002), 259; Claudia Setzer, "Excellent Women: Female Witnesses to the Resurrection," *Journal of Biblical Literature* 116 (1997): 259–72. Bart Ehrman admits the "force" of the argument that no one in an ancient Jewish context would invent the discovery of the tomb by women if they wanted their story to be believed. He nevertheless goes to great lengths to imagine various literary and other reasons it would have been invented, none of which is very convincing. The problem with such a response is that any scholar can use their imagination to come up with all kinds of *possible* scenarios. But historical investigation is supposed to rely on actual *evidence*. In this case, Ehrman can produce no evidence that the multiply attested stories of the women discovering the tomb were invented and therefore should be discarded. See Ehrman, *How Jesus Became God*, 166–68. For a serious critique of Ehrman's attempt to make the empty tomb disappear, see Craig A. Evans, "Getting the Burial Traditions and Evidences Right," in Michael F. Bird et al., *How God Became Jesus: The Real Origins of Belief in Jesus' Divine Nature: A Response to Bart D. Ehrman* (Grand Rapids, MI: Zondervan, 2014), 71–93 (though Evans misidentifies the Idumeans as Romans on p. 79).

22 Ratzinger, *Jesus of Nazareth*, 2.254: "The empty tomb is no proof of the Resurrection, that much is undeniable."

23 The historical truth of this penalty for soldiers is corroborated by literally dozens of ancient Roman sources. Luke is not making it up. See Keener, *Acts*, 2:1954–56.

24 For full discussions with an eye for the historical issues involved, see Keener, *The Historical Jesus of the Gospels*, 342–44; Licona, *The Resurrection of Jesus*, 318–71; Wright, *The Resurrection of the Son of God*, 585–682.

25 Cf. Ehrman, *Jesus: Apocalyptic Prophet*, 229.

26 Ibid., 228–29.

27 See especially Licona, *The Resurrection of Jesus*, 343–49, 595–600.

28 See Licona, *The Resurrection*, 597–98, who also gives the ancient example of the burning of the city of Rome in the mid-first century AD. Just because ancient Roman historians disagree about whether Nero himself openly set the city on fire (Suetonius) or had it done secretly (Dio Cassius) or was not at all to blame (Tacitus), it doesn't mean that Rome didn't go up in flames.

29 For example, despite their massive size, the fulfillment of Scripture as a motive of credibility receives virtually no discussion in Licona, *The Resurrection of Jesus*; Allison, *Resurrecting Jesus*; Wright, *Jesus and the Victory of God*. It is also not discussed in Ratzinger, *Jesus of Nazareth*, 2.241–77. Ehrman, *How Jesus Became God*, 141, mentions the argument from Jonah 2 and Hosea 6 in passing as one of the grounds for why early Christians came to think Jesus was raised from the dead, but does not return to the point.

30 See A. J. M. Wedderburn, *Beyond Resurrection* (Peabody, MA: Hendrickson, 1999), 50–51: "Curiously nowhere is this text [Hosea 6:1-2] expressly quoted in the New Testament as fulfilled in Jesus' resurrection. The text that is expressly quoted in this connection is Jonah 2.1."

31 See Davies and Allison, *Saint Matthew*, 2.355–58.

32 See Robert Chisholm, *Handbook on the Prophets* (Grand Rapids, MI: Baker Academic, 2002), 411: "In ancient Near Eastern literature, the trip to the underworld land of the dead was viewed as a three-day journey." See also George M. Landes, "The 'Three Days and Three Nights' Motif in Jonah 2:1," *Journal of Biblical Literature* 86 (1967): 246–50.

33 See Luz, *Matthew*, 2:217: "Jonah's rescue from the fish is a rescue from death."

34 See Luz, *Matthew*, 2:17–18.

35 See Davies and Allison, *Saint Matthew*, 2:356, in support of the historicity of the saying.

36 See Arthur A. Just, SJ, *Luke*, Ancient Christian Commentary on Scripture New Testament III (Downers Grove, IL: InterVarsity, 2003), 196.

37 See Eusebius, *The Proof of the Gospel*, trans. W. J. Farrer (repr., Eugene, OR: Wipf and Stock, 2001), 37–39.

Chapter 13: At Caesarea Philippi

1 See Ratzinger, *Jesus of Nazareth*, 1.287–304; Luz, *Matthew*, 2.353–79; Davies and Allison, *Saint Matthew*, 2.602–47.

2 Ratzinger, *Jesus of Nazareth*, 1.292.

3 RSVCE (with archaic English adapted).

4 Although this saying may be one of Jesus's most explicit affirmations of his divinity in all the Gospels, Bart Ehrman never discusses Matthew 11:25-27 or Luke 10:21-22 in his book *How Jesus Became God*—even though he would (presumably) regard it as early "Q" material. For arguments in support of the substantial historicity of the saying, see Fitzmyer, *The Gospel According to Luke*, 2.870. For exposition, see Ratzinger, *Jesus of Nazareth*, 1.339